DATE			

® THE BAKER & TAYLOR CO.

RURAL LIFE IN ENGLAND
IN THE FIRST WORLD WAR

Other books by Pamela Horn:

Joseph Arch (1971)
The Victorian Country Child (1974)
Agricultural Trade Unionism in Oxfordshire 1872-81
    (Vol. XLVIII, Oxfordshire Record Society, 1974)
The Rise and Fall of the Victorian Servant (1975)
Labouring Life in the Victorian Countryside (1976)
Education in Rural England 1800-1914 (1978)
Village Education in Nineteenth-Century Oxfordshire
    (Vol. LI, Oxfordshire Record Society, 1979)
The Rural World 1780-1850 (1980)
The Changing Countryside in Victorian England and Wales
    (1984)

Pamela Horn

Rural Life in England
in
The First World War

GILL AND MACMILLAN

ST. MARTIN'S PRESS, NEW YORK

Published in Ireland by
Gill and Macmillan Ltd
Goldenbridge
Dublin 8
with associated companies in
Auckland, Dallas, Delhi, Hong Kong,
Johannesburg, Lagos, London, Manzini,
Melbourne, Nairobi, New York, Singapore,
Tokyo, Washington
© Pamela Horn, 1984
7171 1268 3

First published in the United States of America in 1984.

All rights reserved. For information, write:
St. Martin's Press, Inc., 175 Fifth Avenue, New York 10010

ISBN 0-312-69604-3

Library of Congress Cataloging in Publication Data

Horn, Pamela.
    Rural life in England in the First World War and after.

    Bibliography: p. 288
    Includes index.
    1. Agriculture—Economic aspects—England—History—20th century.
2. Agriculture—Economic aspects—Wales—History—20th century.
3. England—Rural conditions.   4. Wales—Rural conditions.   I. Title.
HD1930.E5H67   1984   307.7'2'0942   84-17885
ISBN 0-312-69604-3

Print origination in Ireland by
Keywrite, Dublin
Printed in Great Britain by
Biddles Ltd, Guildford and King's Lynn

Contents

As the team's head-brass flashed out on the turn
The lovers disappeared into the wood.
I sat among the boughs of the fallen elm
That strewed the angle of the fallow, and
Watched the plough narrowing a yellow square
Of charlock. Every time the horses turned
Instead of treading me down, the ploughman leaned
Upon the handles to say or ask a word,
About the weather, next about the war.
Scraping the share he faced towards the wood,
And screwed along the furrow till the brass flashed
Once more. . . .
. . .'Have many gone
From here?' 'Yes.' 'Many lost?' 'Yes, a good few.
Only two teams work on the farm this year.
One of my mates is dead. The second day
In France they killed him. It was back in March,
The very night of the blizzard, too. Now if
He had stayed here we should have moved the tree'. . . .

From *As the Team's Head-Brass* by Edward Thomas (1878-1917)

List of Illustrations

11. A member of the Leicester Women's Volunteer Reserve assisting a farmer with the harvest *c.* 1916. (British Library)

12. A school boy helping on the land. (Imperial War Museum)

Between pages 214 and 215

13. Boy scouts acting as despatch riders as part of the 'war effort'. (Imperial War Museum)

14. German prisoners of war bagging potatoes in 1918. (Museum of English Rural Life, Reading)

15. German prisoners of war in the YMCA games room at Dorchester Camp, Dorset. Some of the men from this camp went out to work on local farms. (Imperial War Museum)

16. The labour shortage in blacksmiths' shops meant that women lent a hand here, too. A wife assisting her husband. (Imperial War Museum)

Acknowledgments

I should like to thank all who have helped in the preparation of this book, either by providing material or in other ways. Clive Hughes of the Imperial War Museum has generously supplied information from his own researches into conditions in North Wales during the First World War, and Mrs May G. Morris of Oxford, Miss D.B. Dew of Lower Heyford, Oxon., and Mr W.J. Shepherd of Sandleigh, Oxon., have given their personal reminiscences of the period. I am likewise indebted to Mr Bertram J. Saunders of Eastbourne for permission to quote from his father's letters and to Mr Donald T. Cox of London for allowing me to use the reminiscences of his father, William Cox of Settle, Yorkshire; both of these collections are held at the Imperial War Museum.

I am grateful to the Marquess of Tavistock and the Trustees of the Bedford Estates for permission to quote from material in the Bedford Estate Office, London, and the Bedfordshire County Record Office, and to the Imperial War Museum for permission to use copyright material they hold. As always, my thanks are due to the staff in the many Libraries and Record Offices in which I have worked for their ready co-operation and help. These include the Bodleian Library, Oxford; the Public Record Office; the British Library; the British Library Newspaper Library, Colindale; the National Library of Wales; the Institute of Agricultural History and Museum of English Rural Life, Reading; and the University Libraries at Reading and the University College of North Wales, Bangor. County Record Offices visited include those for Bedfordshire, Buckinghamshire, Derbyshire, Essex, Hampshire, Northamptonshire, Oxfordshire, and Pembrokeshire.

The National Federation of Women's Institutes, too, readily made their records available to me. Their help was much appreciated.

Finally, I owe a debt of gratitude to my family for their help and support and, in particular, to my husband for his advice and encouragement. Without them neither this nor any of my books would have been written.

Pamela Horn, April 1984

Chapter 1

Introduction: Rural Life before 1914

'... a few years before 1914 agriculture had turned the corner economically. By any test that might be applied this amelioration could be seen. The prices of almost everything the farmer produced had tended upwards from about 1906, the acreage under cereal crops reached its minimum in 1908... and land itself was enhanced in value'. J.A. Venn, *The Foundations of Agricultural Economics*, Cambridge 1933, 473.

'The special peculiarity of the present "rural exodus" is that the normal movement to the towns and to industrial life — which has perhaps rather diminished than increased — is supplemented to so large an extent by a movement to the oversea Dominions.... The low wages in the rural districts are mentioned as a cause of discontent, but it may be doubted whether this in itself is so powerful a factor as the lack of opportunity.... Better education, and, as is remarked by some, a kind of education which gives a distaste for country life is referred to; while the desire for shorter hours of work, for free Sundays, and for more holidays is also mentioned;... The lack of housing accommodation is frequently mentioned as influencing men to leave the villages.... In this connection, the competition of the townsmen has aggravated the situation, and allusion is made to the turning of cottages into "villas" and to the increasing tendency, fostered by bicycles, of urban workers to live in the rural districts'. Evidence of R.H. Rew to the *Royal Commission on the Dominions*, Parliamentary Papers, 1914, Vol. XVIII, Qu. 2.

If the final quarter of the nineteenth century is often labelled as a period of agricultural depression — a time when prices fell and British farmers came under increasing pressure from foreign competitors on their own home market — then the decade before the First World War is equally marked out as one of comparative prosperity. There was a steady revival in the value of agricultural output from the low point reached in the mid and late 1890s (see Appendix 2), with livestock and livestock products leading the way. Their relative importance was confirmed by the first Census of Agricultural Output in Great Britain, undertaken in 1908:[1]

1

Table 1: Total output of agricultural land in England and
Wales in 1908: relating to plots of 1 acre or more

	£m.
Farm crops	40.2
Fruit, flowers and timber	4.7
Animals	50.8
Wool	2.1
Dairy produce	25.5
Poultry	4.35
Total	127.65

N.B. These figures ignore crops consumed on the farm where
they were grown as animal fodder.

Although the pace of revival, like the incidence of the
depression itself, proved variable, the Wiltshire agriculturist,
A.G. Street, was certainly not alone in regarding this as a time of
'Farmer's Glory', when men were able to thrust aside the penny-
pinching habits of their late Victorian predecessors. As Street
nostalgically recalled

> one didn't consider whether the crop one was sowing would
> pay a profit over the cost of production or not. That never
> entered anyone's head. In good seasons farmers did pretty
> well, and in bad ones, presumably not quite so well. Granted,
> there were occasional instances of farmers going bankrupt,
> but these rare cases could always be traced definitely to drink,
> gambling, or some other vice or extravagance causing neglect
> of the farm by the master. If one attended to one's business
> decently, one got along all right. Some did better than others,
> but all got along all right.
>   The fact was that the four-course system allied to a
> Hampshire Down flock paid pretty well in those days, and
> was the accepted practice of the district. Farms were laid out
> for it, and let on the understanding that the customary
> rotation would be followed. And once you were fairly into
> that system, it swept you with it, round and round, year after
> year, like a cog in a machine, whether you liked it or not.[2]

It was a sign of the growing confidence of farmers, as well as of their determination to protect their own interests, that in 1908 the National Farmers' Union came into existence, under the leadership of a Lincolnshire-based Scotsman, Colin Campbell. Membership was confined to 'farmers in actual practice', thereby excluding landowners and their agents, and its object was to publicise the grievances of the farming community and to press for rectification. These included a reduction in the allegedly over-high rates charged by railway companies for carrying farm produce, the promotion of a uniform national system of weights and measures, the improvement of a tenant farmer's security of tenure in his holding, and the transfer of the cost of maintaining such services as the police, main roads, and education from local to national taxation. Although party politics were eschewed, from an early stage consideration was given to recruiting NFU candidates to stand for election to Parliament, where they could represent the tenant farmer's point of view.[3] It was during the First World War that the NFU came into its own as a political force with which the Government could negotiate, but even before 1914 it had established branches in most parts of England and Wales.

Landowners, too, enjoyed an Indian summer as rent receipts revived. This was the era of weekend country-house parties, arranged during the London Season and in the winter months for shooting or for attending hunt balls. Entertainments were organised on a lavish scale, and the comfort of those attending was carefully ministered to by a large staff of domestic workers. In the households of some of the wealthier landowners, servant numbers were huge, with the Duke of Portland employing around 320 at Welbeck Abbey, including fourteen housemaids and thirty-eight male and female servants in the kitchens and allied departments. The reminiscences of Frederick John Gorst, who worked as a young footman at Welbeck, reveal that the estate was 'more like a principality than anything else; there were scores of people working beside me whom I did not know. . . . Within the borders of Welbeck Abbey, His Grace the Duke of Portland, wielded an almost feudal indisputable power.'[4] Gorst, like, all the footmen employed by the Duke, was required to wear livery. Elsewhere Lady Cynthia Asquith remembered the lengthy dinners, with their seven or eight courses, and the intricate household arrangements which accompanied them. 'When large houses were fully open,' she wrote, 'each room... was kept for its own particular purpose. The dining-room was for eating only, and no meal except possibly tea was ever served in the drawing-room. In many houses one room would be called The Breakfast Room, another The Tea Room. The mistress of the house had her "boudoir," the master his "library" and often his "office".'[5]

Admittedly, during the years before 1914 some landowners, disillusioned with the poor returns derived from their estates, began to divest themselves of outlying farms in order to free capital resources for entry into more lucrative channels, perhaps by investing in industrial or mining enterprises in this country, or in railways, mining, and government stock overseas. Many were reinforced in their decision by the fact that ownership of agricultural land no longer carried with it the prestige and political power it had enjoyed in the middle of the nineteenth century. Although, within their own rural communities, the nobility and gentry still exercised an undisputed social leadership and were expected, in return, to contribute to the material equipment of the villages in which they had an interest, this scarcely compensated for the loss of a broader political influence. In addition, the operation of the various Agricultural Holdings Acts passed between 1906 and 1914, which increased the tenant's freedom to cultivate his farm as he thought fit, and the imposition of new death duties in the Budget of 1894, shook confidence in the security of land as a long term investment. By 1914, as Orwin and Whetham point out, the State had

> so far altered the balance of economic advantage between landowners and tenants that occupiers could farm in any way they pleased; and they could claim compensation at the end of their tenancy for the unexhausted value of any improvement made, and for the costs of disturbance. Landowners still had the right to choose their tenants, to agree with them the rent properly payable and... to terminate any tenancy on a year's notice or at the end of a dated lease, subject only to the payment of such costs.[6]

Land sales increased particularly sharply in the last five years before the First World War, with perhaps 800,000 acres changing hands.[7] This was partly a reaction to the political attacks made upon the landowning class by the Liberal

Government and its threats to increase the tax burden upon agricultural estates still further. There were also proposals to set up a system of land courts, along lines pioneered for small farms in Scotland, which would have power to fix 'fair rents' and to increase the tenant-farmer's security of tenure. As the Report of the Liberal Party's Land Enquiry Committee firmly declared in 1913: 'the present legal power of the landowner to raise the rent upon a tenant's own improvements, where it is exercised, is harmful to agriculture and can only be kept in check by a judicial body which can fix rent.'[8] Although the scheme never came into operation, it undoubtedly aroused concern about possible State intervention among some landowners. In Lincolnshire, indeed, as early as 1907 a small group of estate owners had banded together to form the Central Landowners Association, in order to combat the threats of higher taxation from the Liberal Government. This later became the Country Landowners Association.

However, more to the point in accounting for the increased land sales of 1909-14 was the memory of the long years of depression in the late nineteenth century, when rent yields had slumped and property sales had been impossible to arrange. Some followed the example of the Duke of Bedford, who sold his Thorney and some of his Tavistock property to the sitting tenants on terms favourable to them. Significantly, in May 1896 the Duke had declared gloomily of his estates: 'rent had disappeared... and ... the possession of these properties, even after excluding all expenditure on the Abbey, park, and farm, at Woburn, now involved upon their owner a heavy annual loss'.[9] Many found buyers from within the rising class of business-men, South African mining millionaires, and property speculators, who welcomed the status which ownership of land could still bestow. Others again managed to avoid both alternatives either by letting their mansions and moving to a smaller house elsewhere on the estate or, more positively, by going into the City and taking company directorships to supplement their agricultural incomes. Already by 1896 there were 167 noblemen, or more than a quarter of the peerage, holding directorships, many of them in more than one company. They included men like the third Earl of Verulam, who by 1913 was a director of thirteen companies, many of them based on foreign mining enterprises. At this date directors' fees and dividends were supplying more than one-third of his total income. From the proceeds he was able to return to the family seat at Gorhambury, which had been abandoned in less prosperous times, and to install a new domestic hot-water system of his own devising.[10] By 1914 the editors of Burke's *Landed Gentry* had to admit ruefully that land had often become 'a luxury to be maintained from extraneous sources', despite the improvements secured in the financial returns from estates since 1900.

Nevertheless, most landowners, whether they sought outside sources of revenue in this businesslike fashion or not, undoubtedly derived much pleasure and some profit from the running of their properties. They particularly relished the field sports which formed an integral part of this, notably hunting, fishing and the shooting of game. Neville Lytton in *The English Country Gentleman* enthusiastically described fox-hunting as providing a training 'not only for the body, but for the brain and character and everything else.' As such it occupied 'the entire time and attention of thousands of Englishmen'. Other estate owners concentrated on game preservation, and in parts of the south and east of England this was carried on to such an extent that it interfered with farming efficiency. By 1911 there were more than twice as many gamekeepers in rural districts as there were policemen (viz. 15,657 to 7,041), and the size of the 'bag' secured by a shooting party became a subject of pride and comment. In December 1913 a party of seven 'guns', including the King, George V, shooting on an estate at Beaconsfield in Buckinghamshire, accounted for no less than 3,937 pheasants, three partridges, four rabbits and one 'various' in a single day.[11] Those tenants who protested at the ravages wrought upon their crops by birds, rabbits and hares were given short shrift by most owners. As an exasperated Lincolnshire farmer declared in 1913: 'it is very trying after ploughing and sowing to have crops ruined, and while we have a legal claim, it is as good as asking for a discharge, in many cases, to make a claim against the landlord. . . . I have a field of 15 acres with one end adjoining a big wood. Mr. X has the shooting rights and it swarms with rabbits: they come and destroy my crops during the night and go back in the wood, and if I complain he says they are my rabbits while in my field'.[12] Every care had to be taken not to disturb the birds during the nesting season. On the Woburn estate, the Duke of Bedford personally issued instructions that between mid-April and 1 July each year the estate rabbiter was not to hunt the hedgerows with his dogs, 'neither must he use the dogs in the Covers, or in any ground where there is a Game keeper employed.'[13] During this period the rabbits were presumably multiplying at will, while the pheasants nested.

Normally, however, if damage were done, the landlord would at least offer compensation to his tenant for the losses suffered, thereby eliminating a major source of friction. It was also common for owners to invite the more substantial tenants to join their shooting parties from time to time. But, as the records of the Duke of Bedford's estates show, agreement as to the precise level of compensation to be offered could lead to prolonged correspondence between farmer and owner, or the latter's agent, while the precise amount of cash was assessed.[14] At Woburn an added problem for some tenants was the damage caused by marauding deer.

But these were relatively minor causes of discontent. Only for the agricultural labourer and some rural craft workers was the position in 1914 clearly less satisfactory than it had been in 1900. Although the number of jobs on the land had increased from the low point reached during the Boer War, as farmers turned to more labour intensive activities like market gardening, or were able to afford to increase their staff as their incomes rose (see Appendix 1), during the pre-war upsurge in prices, agricultural workers' earnings failed to keep pace with inflation. In the period 1900 to 1910, whilst the cost of living advanced by around 10 per cent, the average wage of ordinary labourers in England and Wales rose by only 3 per cent.[15] An increase in earnings between 1911 and 1914 did not make good that deficit. Indeed, an investigation carried out by B. Seebohm Rowntree and May Kendall on the eve of the First World War suggested that with the exception of the five counties of Northumberland, Durham, Westmorland, Lancashire, and Derbyshire, the average earnings of ordinary labourers were below the poverty line in every part of England and Wales. Of course, individual rates of pay varied with the age, skill, and physical strength of the worker concerned, and with the intensity of demand for labour in his particular area. Piecework earnings and perquisites, such as free housing, milk, potatoes, kindling for the fire, or the free haulage of coal, could also help those fortunate enough to receive them. But, as regards the former, the decline in the arable acreage reduced the scale of many piecework tasks, and only in counties like Kent, where hops and fruit were grown, each with their own particular harvests, did they continue to play a major role.[16] As for perquisites, the growing tendency was to pay wages solely in cash. Only in the North of England and parts of Wales were payments in kind still significant by 1914. Indeed, of forty-two families investigated by Rowntree and Kendall, a mere eleven received perquisites (mostly milk and potatoes). Of those, nine lived in Yorkshire. So even when these additional factors have been taken into account, there is little doubt of the severity of rural poverty in many areas, especially in those families where there was a large number of young children.

Another difficulty was that in many parishes, employers laid men off during wet or frosty weather, thereby reducing their cash incomes still further. This was a subject taken up by the Liberal Party's Land Enquiry Committee in 1912-13, and they discovered that out of 1,922 parishes investigated, 47 per cent admitted a reduction of basic wages on account of bad weather. In the south midland and eastern counties (where 520 parishes were surveyed), $67\frac{1}{2}$ per cent suffered those reductions. As a Sussex farmer declared, the custom of reducing the labourers' basic wages by 3d. per day, as happened on some of the larger farms in his area during the winter months, coupled with the 'loss of time altogether on days when it is too wet or frosty' created great hardship for many families: 'if it was not for the tradesmen giving them credit until after the harvests, many families would not have enough to eat.'[17] Only in the north of England and in better paid counties elsewhere, where labour was in relatively short supply, could the general worker count on regular employment. Stockmen, who were hired on annual or half-yearly contracts, were of course better placed in this regard, and by 1911 they made up about a third of the male farm labour force. (See Appendix 1). Less satisfactory was the fact that many of them lived in tied cottages, so that they might be close at hand to care for the livestock. This meant that if they lost their employment they also lost their home. As an Essex labourer bitterly observed, tied housing meant 'work for my standard of wages and have nothing to do with any agitation for higher wages or better social conditions'. He claimed to know of cases where men with children and a wife dependent upon them had been dismissed by the farmer and had then been given seven days' notice to leave their cottage.[18]

A modern writer has said of the rural labourer in southern England and parts of Wales in the period before 1914 that there was 'no major occupational group more worthy of compassion'.[19] Contemporaries were equally aware of the situation, as the flurry of surveys and books which appeared in the decade or so before 1914 bears witness. They ranged from classic studies like the Hammonds' *Village Labourer* (first published in 1911) or Rowntree's *How the Labourer Lives* (published in 1913) to governmental analyses of wages and conditions of employment produced under the aegis of the Labour Department of the Bord of Trade. The Liberal Party's own Land Enquiry Committee Report devoted two-fifths of its text to the position of the labourer, and in the spring of 1914 David Lloyd George, one of that Party's most dynamic leaders, boldly promised: 'the Government of which I am a member is firmly resolved that the strong arm of the State shall be used to obtain for the labourer a living wage, a decent house, and the right to cultivate, in independence and security, the soil of his native land'.[20]

But whilst these promises were no doubt welcome, for many farm workers, family income was only brought above the poverty line by the financial assistance of other members of the household, and the contribution made by produce grown in cottage gardens and allotments.[21] In some villages, like Corsley in Wiltshire, it was possible for cottagers to supplement their earnings by selling surplus fruit and vegetables in nearby towns. Certain of the Corsley women walked to Frome with baskets of produce which they hawked from door to door, while others disposed of their wares to larger suppliers in the neighbourhood.[22] There were opportunities, too, for a few women in most villages to supplement the family income by taking in washing from wealthier members of local society, or charring, or doing some sewing, while they and their children might earn a little by helping on the land at the busy seasons of the year. At Corsley, a number of wives also earned a shilling or two sewing gloves for two factories at Westbury and Westbury Leigh. In this village, significantly, only about one family in eight was classed as in a state of primary poverty, with earnings insufficient to maintain bare physical efficiency.

But not all cottagers possessed these opportunities to earn extra cash, or were prepared to rely upon them for their basic subsistence. An added grievance among many was the poor standard of housing in rural areas, which was itself made worse by the fact that tenants could not afford to pay rents sufficiently high to encourage landlords to undertake much-needed repairs. In 1913, the Liberal Party estimated that at least 120,000 new houses were needed in country districts, and claimed that large numbers of dwellings unfit for human habitation were not closed by the authorities, owing to the lack of alternative accommodation. For the same reason, despite the existence of public health and housing legislation, 'necessary repairs cannot be demanded by the local authority or the tenant, lest the land-lord should close the cottage rather than incur the expense of repairing it.' Only a major building programme by local authorities could meet this situation. Unfortunately, little was done to achieve that before the outbreak of War.[23]

A further cause of discontent was the limited prospects associated with work on the land. As a government report admitted in 1906, a quick-witted worker could probably master the skills he needed by the time he was twenty-one. But once he had risen to the post of horse-keeper, or shepherd, or perhaps foreman, there was 'little further outlook and a small hope of increased wages'.[24] From the 1890s, complaints were increasingly heard from agriculturists about labour shortages, especially of the more energetic and intelligent men. These preferred to seek employment outside farming, or to emigrate, particularly to Canada, whose agents were especially active during the early 1900s.

For those searching for new outlets in this country, the widespread sale of cheap bicycles helped, for these gave men freedom to work in a nearby factory or town workshop without leaving their home village. It was a trend which was to intensify in the inter-war years, but already by the turn of the century it had led to claims that, for example, the brickworks around Peterborough were denuding neighbouring parishes of their best workers.[25] Elsewhere, as in the north of England and South Wales, the rapid expansion of the coal industry drew in workers from a wide catchment area. In some parts of Wales critics sourly observed that young men only stayed on the farms long enough to earn their train fares to Glamorgan. And in that county itself, the farm labouring population was described as overwhelmingly English, having been recruited from migrants who had moved in when the Welsh went to the coal fields. 'Welshmen', it was said at one meeting of labourers, 'are not such fools as to work on the farms when they can obtain higher wages for fewer hours in the works and collieries'.[26] In other cases formerly rural parishes were themselves changed into industrial centres by the growth of mining and quarrying, or the construction of factories. Around St Austell in Cornwall it was the china clay works which destroyed the agricultural character of village life, while in the central vale of Bedfordshire the establishment of the new Fletton brick-making industry began its process of transforming the landscape in that area.

It was an indication of the labourers' discontent with their conditions that in 1906 a new agricultural trade union was formed in Norfolk. It was led by George Edwards, a quiet but determined man who had been associated with earlier attempts at unionism in the late nineteenth century, and it enjoyed support from local Liberal politicians. According to Edwards, after the general election of 1906, which brought the Conservative party the greatest defeat it had ever experienced, victimisation of workers suspected of voting Liberal became severe.[27] Men appealed to him to help form another union to oppose the dismissals and evictions and also to press for a general improvement in their circumstances. The Liberals proved ready allies in this cause, for they hoped thereby to mobilise the votes of rural workers to 'dish' the Conservatives once and for all in their rural strongholds. Progress was initially slow, for there was little money for propaganda, and by 1908 membership was still under four thousand, mainly in Norfolk. But over the next few years the union's sphere of operations was extended, and between 1912 and 1914, as prices continued to rise, there were countless strikes, mostly on a small scale, upon the farms of England. The most successful took place in south-west Lancashire during the early summer of 1913, and ultimately involved about two thousand men. As a result of this, the workers obtained a Saturday half-holiday, the payment of 6d an hour for overtime work, and some increase in wages. Significantly in their struggle with their employers they had been able to secure the support of railway and dock workers in the area, and they were also assisted by the fact that much of the local produce — vegetables and milk — was highly perishable. Employers thus had every incentive to settle the dispute rapidly, and this they did.[28] Nevertheless, even in 1914, membership of the National Agricultural Labourers' and Rural Workers' Union was only about 15,000 and there were a mere 360 branches in England and Wales.[29] A number of other men, mainly in East Anglia, the Cotswolds, Yorkshire and Shropshire, joined the farm workers' section of the Workers' Union, which was basically concerned with unskilled labourers in urban industry.[30] Its leaders adopted a policy of decentralisation, with members in each area left to formulate their own demands, with the assistance of union organisers, according to local conditions and needs. Yet overall that union had only about 150 agricultural branches in fourteen counties by the beginning of 1914, and the two groups together had clearly recruited but a tiny minority of the farm labour force. Lack of funds, the difficulty of organising men who were employed in a large number of small work units, and the opposition of employers were, as always, major reasons for their lack of success. Their influence on the working conditions of most men on the land obviously remained slight and as late as 1913, some expert observers of the agricultural scene could apparently be ignorant of their existence.[31]

Of more significance in improving workers' long-term prospects was the passage of the Old Age Pensions Act in 1908, which provided a modest payment of 5s. a week for old people aged seventy and above, who had no other significant source of income. It helped to ensure that they ended their days at home instead of in the workhouse. The National Insurance Act of 1911 similarly laid down that medical care and sickness benefit were to be available to land workers, as to other manual labourers, when they were ill. Although the contributory aspects of the scheme were a small additional drain on scanty earnings, it undoubtedly provided a degree of security which the numerous friendly societies of earlier years had been unable to bestow. Charitable efforts led to an expansion of the cottage hospital movement in country districts and the setting up of voluntary district nursing associations to improve care of the sick. They supplemented the work of the old-fashioned village nurse, often the wife of a local labourer or tradesman, whose only qualification for her post was that she had herself brought up a large

family. An attempt to reduce the level of infant mortality was
made with an Act of 1902 which provided for the training of
midwives and the exclusion of those who were untrained.

Efforts were likewise made to give labourers a stake in the soil
by extending the legislation relating to allotments and small
holdings. This culminated in an Act of 1907 which required
county councils to prepare schemes for consideration by the
Board of Agriculture of the number, nature, and size of small
holdings to be supplied, and the land to be acquired for that
purpose. Special commissioners were appointed to help the
councils in their work, and the President of the Board of Agriculture, Lord Carrington, rejoiced at the early progress made.
'The Small Holdings are going like wildfire', he wrote to his wife
in February 1908, '4,700 official applications for 87,000 acres,
i.e. 136 square miles of land in 6 weeks... not bad for a
beginning'.[32] Eventually some 200,000 acres were acquired and
over 14,000 holdings supplied between 1908 and 1914. The
Norfolk County Council, for example, proved so effective that by
1914 it owned 1,375 small holdings and was one of the major
landowners in the country. Elsewhere, the response was less
enthusiastic. In Oxfordshire, although 679 applicants were
'provisionally approved' as suitable by the County Council
during this period, by the beginning of 1914 a mere 200 or so
holdings had actually been created.[33] Clearly the movement
satisfied a need among certain labouring people, even if it had
little to offer the majority of agricultural workers and village
tradesmen. Sometimes, too, on account of the type of soil, a lack of
capital to purchase necessary equipment, or problems with
marketing, the ventures were not successful. As Marion Springall
wrote of the smallholders of Norfolk: 'Each... worked much
longer hours than the average labourer, and had the additional
worry of buying his own supplies and marketing his own produce.
Getting a living absorbed the whole of a man's vitality'.[34]
Furthermore, even where labourers benefited by such
opportunities, they scarcely compensated for the decline in
purchasing power which was taking place at this time among the
majority of land workers.

Rural craftsmen, by contrast, found their main problems
arising from the growing competition offered by mass-produced
goods from urban industry, at a time when local markets in
many areas were declining as a result of rural depopulation. The

bootmaker had to accept the diminished role of a repairer only, while the tailor saw his business undercut by the expansion of cheap ready-made clothing. And villages which in their mid-Victorian hey-day had been large enough to support three or four shoemakers and carpenters, and two or three blacksmiths and wheelwrights were now too small to provide a livelihood for more than one or two of each. The decline in the arable acreage inevitably reduced the demand for the services of blacksmiths and wheelwrights as makers and repairers of agricultural implements and farm waggons. They were also unable to compete with the major specialist producers of agricultural machinery, like the Ransomes of Ipswich or the Hunts of Earls Colne in Essex, who kept large stocks of implements ready to hand and had agencies throughout the country.

Fashion changes, too, played a part, as with the decline of the cottage lace industry in the south Midlands and Devon, although pressure was also experienced here from machine-made lace. Similar factors led to the decline of the glove knitting trade around Ringwood in Hampshire, the glove sewing trade of rural Worcestershire and Herefordshire, and stocking production in the villages of Leicestershire.[35] All of these were developments which affected the employment of women. Some rural industries disappeared because their raw materials were exhausted in the particular area in which they were located; others suffered because their exploitation was made uneconomic by the discovery of new and more easily worked sources of supply. The decline of the Cornish tin and copper mines provides an example of this.[36] Similarly, the greater use of slates and tiles for roofing, and of dutch barns on the farm, undermined the position of the thatcher, while galvanised buckets and other utensils made much of the work of the country cooper redundant. Inadequate costing and poorly kept accounts further contributed to the village tradesman's general problems at a time when factory-based industries were able to reap the benefits of large-scale production. As the Farnham wheelwright, George Sturt, later wrote: 'Well on into the present century these matters, in my trade, were settled by guesswork, not by calculation. We knew nothing, thought nothing, of how much we ought to have.'[37] Even when crafts were introduced or reintroduced into villages by enthusiastic middle-class philanthropists anxious to provide additional employment — as at

Woolhampton in Berkshire, where attempts were made to establish a local art-pottery industry — they rarely prospered. High unit costs and the difficulty of finding a reliable market proved the downfall of most.[38] So it was that the late Victorian and Edwardian countryside became a place 'where little save agriculture was carried on: the countryside found itself more and more denuded of its flow of non-agricultural incomes, and it was not a pleasing experience for the remaining inhabitants.'[39]

Even in farming itself, despite the improvement in prices and profitability in the early twentieth century, foreign suppliers still provided around three-quarters of the wheat, half the meat, three-quarters of the cheese, and seven-eighths of the butter consumed in this country. The main difference was that by 1900 the rate at which they were making their inroads had slackened and home producers had learned to come to terms with the changed circumstances. On a world basis, the level of expansion in the supply of foodstuffs had ceased to outstrip demand in the way it had done in the late Victorian years, and there were also general inflationary influences at work within the commercial and industrial world which pushed up price levels.

Meanwhile, among the adjustments made within domestic agriculture during the late nineteenth century was a reduction in rentals over much of England, and the widespread granting of rent rebates. Although in the more prosperous conditions after 1900 rents began to rise once more, the increase was not sufficient to rob farmers of their newly found profits. On the Savernake and Wilton estates in Wiltshire, there was an increase of 10 per cent between 1900 and 1914, and a similar rise was recorded on Lord Sidmouth's Devon estate, where by 1914 the rents were reported to be back to their 1882 level, but still 12 per cent below the 1876 peak.[40] But often there was a reluctance to raise the rents of sitting tenants, 'and the returning confidence in arable farming was not reflected in any return to the old structure of landlordism'. The main gain to the landowner was that it was no longer necessary to give rebates, and arrears had ceased to accumulate. It also became easier to find tenants for vacant farms, and owners did not have to incur the heavy expenditure of taking land in hand because no occupier could be found.

Farmers themselves altered their production methods, too, paying greater attention to the changing tastes of urban consumers. On more advanced holdings, progress was made in improving management methods and account-keeping. Although on the latter point, even in 1912 an agricultural correspondent of *The Times* could complain of the way that on many big farms, management depended on 'one man's instinct and memory; . . . very often he keeps no books beyond a cash record, sometimes he lets his bank pass-book serve even for that, while his dealings are jotted down on the backs of envelopes and the like'.[41] Any modern researcher who has investigated early twentieth century farm records will agree with most of these strictures.

More importantly, within the overall pattern of cultivation there was a move away from traditional arable cultivation in favour of dairying, meat production, poultry keeping, and the growing of fruit and vegetables, to satisfy the rising living standards of town dwellers and their demand for a more varied diet. During this period, the overall arable acreage continued to shrink, especially in the traditional pastoral areas of the north and west, even though the fall in the cereal area had been arrested. Some men turned to the production of potatoes, brussel sprouts, peas, and other vegetables. Potato growing became a money-making crop on the silt and warp soils of Lincolnshire and Yorkshire, and on the light soils of West Lancashire and Cheshire, while in parts of Cornwall it was possible to follow the earliest potato crops with a second crop of autumn and winter broccoli.[42] In Norfolk, although many of the larger farmers scorned these lesser crops, the smaller producers adopted them, despite the county's remoteness from major industrial centres. In the Fens, gooseberries, strawberries, celery and potatoes were raised, while on some holdings tomatoes and cucumbers were alternated with bulbs and chrysanthemums to supply markets in the north of England. The Great Eastern Railway promoted milk and vegetable production around Thetford by offering special transport facilities to London.[43] Again, from the Vale of Evesham in Worcestershire special vegetable trains were despatched on both the Great Western and the Midland Railway all the year round. Produce which left Evesham at 12.30 mid-day could reach Edinburgh or Glasgow by 6 a.m. the following morning. By the early twentieth century some forty different kinds of vegetables, fruit, and flowers were being sent from the area to places as far distant as the Channel

Islands, Scotland, and South Wales, this latter being regarded as 'the salvation of Evesham'.[44] Fruit and vegetables also became established on a major scale around Wisbech in Cambridgeshire and Sandy in Bedfordshire, while the newly-formed Spalding bulb industry consolidated its position during these years. From other farms, following more traditional rotations, oats, hay, and straw were sold to town stables, and, in return, dung was despatched by cart and railway to fertilise the market gardens. Around Heathfield in Sussex, agricultural prosperity was found in fattening chickens to send to the London market. The birds were purchased from neighbouring farmers by specialist higglers, and were then sold to 'crammers' who fed them ready for the table.[45]

Still more significant was the growing sale of liquid milk, which helped to compensate for the problems faced by the farm-based butter and cheese sectors of the dairy industry, as well as for the difficulties of mixed farmers. Thirteen counties, excluding Middlesex, showed by the age structure of their herds that milk selling was the dominant cattle enterprise in 1910, while in the midland grazing counties, Norfolk, and the valleys of Northumberland, meat production remained the major concern.[46] Already, however, milk was being carried to London from as far as 130 miles away by the Great Western Railway, although most came from stations in Berkshire, Hampshire, and Wiltshire. The Great Northern ran special trains to London from Egginton near Burton-on-Trent to meet the requirements of the Egginton Dairy Company, which also sent milk away via the North Staffordshire Railway. Under the terms of its agreements, farmers had to deliver their milk each day during the summer months before 7.30 a.m. and 6 p.m., although one delivery only was required during the winter, provided the milk kept satisfactorily. Minimum supply targets were laid down and the price paid per gallon varied according to the season. One surviving agreement shows a Derbyshire farmer receiving 6d. a gallon during May and June, 1914, when milk was plentiful, as compared to a maximum price of 9½d. per gallon paid during the 'scarce' period from the preceding October to March.[47] Alongside these major contractors, who supplied the large industrial areas as well as London, there were countless producer retailers, many of them operating from their own farms on the suburban fringes. Their milk floats appeared twice a day on the streets of outer London and the smaller towns, proudly advertising the sale of 'farm milk' as opposed to 'railway milk'.[48]

Elsewhere, improvements were attributable to a closer attention to points of detail. Traditional livestock breeds were replaced in many districts by varieties more suitable to contemporary needs, the Leicester sheep being displaced in its native county by Shropshire Downs and crossbreds, and low-yielding mongrel cows by pedigree animals, including, in some cases, Friesians.[49] Increasing attention was given to improving the quality of the heavy Shire and Suffolk horses, which were the principal draught animals in town and country alike. Stallion hiring societies were set up in a number of areas, to enable groups of farmers to obtain the services of a high grade animal which would raise the standard of their own bloodstock and would enable them to sell their young horses more profitably to the larger urban contractors. Elsewhere landowners purchased or reared prize stallions which they allowed tenants to use for a small fee.

Machinery, too, was introduced, as for the potato crop in south-west Lancashire, where potato diggers were reported to be 'greatly on the increase' in the Ormskirk district by 1913.[50] Among cereal producers, the double-furrow plough and the self-binder harvester came into widespread use after 1900, although there were still many farms where the latter displaced the old self-delivery reaper only during World War I.

It would be idle to pretend that all farmers conformed to these efficient ideals. As late as 1919, Alfred Mansell told an audience at the Farmers' Club of the large number of 'badly bred indifferent animals (more specially cattle)' which were entering markets and which he regarded as a 'national disgrace'.[51] Many agriculturists, too, continued to use in 1914 the same tools as those which had served earlier generations of their family. On the small moorland farms of north-east Yorkshire a plough, a cart, a waggon, a set of harrows, a grass cutter, and a reaper borrowed as occasion demanded, were considered quite adequate, while in the expanding dairying sector there was little use of advanced machinery before the inter-war years.[52] Especially on the smaller properties — and in 1914, 67 per cent of all holdings in England and Wales were under 50 acres[53] — there was a slowness to experiment with new crops or new ideas.

In north-east Yorkshire, men frankly admitted that they did not expect to make money: 'If you had one more calf than the year before you were satisfied'.

In a number of cases, the smaller farmers had secondary occupations to absorb a share of their time and attention, too. In Corsley, where there were thirty-four men and women calling themselves farmers in 1905-6, at least twelve had a second occupation or source of income. They included a 47-acre dairy farmer, who was also a coal and timber haulier, and a man cultivating 77 acres who acted as a publican. Haulage work was particularly popular among these smaller men because it enabled them to put their horses to profitable use during the slack periods of the farming year when there was little for them to do on the land.

In 1912, A.D. Hall, agricultural correspondent of *The Times* and director of the Rothamsted Experimental Station, pinpointed the weaknesses when he commented on the way that in Anglesey local farmers were missing the opportunity to supply milk and cream to summer visitors to the area, and were neglecting to provide vegetables and fruit to nearby seaside resorts. In writing of North Wales as a whole, he noted that there was 'not a single field of cabbages, cauliflowers, marrows or peas' to be seen, while even potatoes were imported. 'It is not merely a question of supplying the summer visitor for a two months' season; the light, easily worked soils, the absence of frosts, and the mild growing climate . . . might make Carnarvon and Anglesey the market garden of the thickly-populated slate-mining areas close at hand, and also of Lancashire, the Potteries, and the Black Country, with which there is direct and easy communication. . . . But we were informed that the Welsh farmer would scorn to grow a cabbage lest he should derogate from his social status as a farmer.'[54] He preferred instead to sell wool, store cattle, and sheep, or to make butter, as he and his forefathers had always done. In Hall's view, one of the major weaknesses of the average farmer was an inadequate education: 'by this we mean not so much additional knowledge of a technical sort, but the more flexible habit of mind that comes with reading, the susceptibility to ideas that is acquired from acquaintance with a different atmosphere than the one in which he ordinarily lives'. He then added harshly: 'the bad farming one sees so often in England alongside the best is not due to any lack of knowledge, but to the low mental calibre of many of the men occupying the land.'

The conservative attitudes thus adopted were reinforced by the strong community and kinship ties which characterised much of the agriculture of England and Wales on the eve of the First World War. Smaller farmers, for example in Wales or the dairying areas of the north-west and south-west of England, were used to working together at the busy seasons of the year. Indeed, in many parts of Wales farmers had begun their working life as farm servants, while in the west of the principality it was common for the women and girls to be expected to take charge of a holding's cattle. This included cleaning out the cow houses, milking, and feeding calves and pigs. Butter and cheesemaking, too, where carried out, fell within their purview.[55] (See also chapter 6).

Mr F.W. Brocklehurst, whose family occupied a small farm at Sheldon, Derbyshire, where stock rearing and sheep farming were the main occupations, along with the production of milk, cheese, and eggs, recalled that his family used to work in cooperation with his uncle. 'Our land for haymaking was close to Uncle John's land, and it was not much trouble to go from one field to another. Our father did the mowing and hacked the wallsides, pitching the hay in, stacking, etc., while we ... raked the backswath for the mower, tedded round the walls, did most of the swath-turning ... and loading. Uncle John's fields were very small. 16 acres in 13 fields, so there was quite a lot of wall sides and corners for so small an acreage.' Later, when he was aged about seventeen, his father's holding was increased to 150 acres: 'It may look as if farming were very prosperous, but we had no wages at all, only a bit of pocket money and our food and clothes. ... We now had two work horses. One did the milk running and odd jobs, and the other I took ploughing, manure carting, etc. ... Farming did not alter much for many years prior to the first World War.'[56] By carefully husbanding their resources, the family were able to achieve a modest prosperity, but it was hardly the dynamic response to agricultural opportunity which writers like A.D. Hall had in mind.

Finally, alongside this vision of a traditional, organic rural community it is important to emphasise the many new influences at work, which already foreshadowed the very different kind of village which was to emerge in the mid-twentieth century. One of these — the spread of manufacturing and mining industries — has already been discussed. Another, of equal significance, was the transformation of parishes on the edge of the larger towns into suburbs, and for those farther away to become dormitories for the new generation of railway commuters. Among the counties thus affected were several in the vicinity of London. They included Hertfordshire, which became increasingly industrial and residential as the metropolitan influence of the capital extended outwards, and Buckinghamshire, where by 1914 there were already complaints in the Chilterns of housing shortages. These were attributed to the fact that Londoners were acquiring cottages as week-end homes. Kent, Sussex, Surrey, and Hampshire were other residential counties increasingly linked with London. In the case of rural Sussex, the total population increased by 7.6 per cent between 1901 and 1911, while in Surrey the rise was 10.9 per cent, and Hampshire, 8.9 per cent.[57]

Inevitably many of the 'incomers' brought with them an idealised view of rural life, seeing it as a picturesque and peaceful backwater divorced from the hurly-burly of the urban world — what one writer has called 'the village of the mind'.[58] They also imported their own interests and values, which were often entirely different from those of the original inhabitants. It was a trend which the Surrey wheelwright, George Sturt, deplored when his small village was 'discovered' as a residential centre by people from the the neighbouring town of Farnham. Soon new villas sprang up and once quiet lanes became noisy with the motor cars of the richer residents: 'The valley is passing out of the hands of its former inhabitants' he bitterly declared. 'They are being crowded into corners, and are becoming as aliens in their own home'.[59] In their dealings with their propertied neighbours many of the 'natives' displayed a mixture of caution and distrust, a sense of being unprotected against the newcomers' greater power and privileges. 'It would be an exaggeration to say that they feel like outlaws; but they are vaguely aware of constraint imposed upon them by laws and prejudices which are none too friendly to people of their kind. One divines it in their treatment of the village policeman. There is probably no lonelier man in the parish than the constable. Of course he meets with civility, but his company is avoided.... The cottagers feel that they themselves are the people whom he is stationed in the valley to watch'.[60]

Although only a minority of villages had been thus affected by 1914, in the years which lay ahead that was to alter. They were merely the precursors of a fundamental change in the nature of the rural community, which only became clearly apparent after 1918.

So it was in this uncertain atmosphere of adherence to traditional values on the one hand, and a growing awareness of impending change on the other, that rumours of war began to circulate during the summer of 1914. They were given particular impetus by what must have seemed to many a distant event in an unknown land — the assassination of the Austrian Archduke Francis Ferdinand at Sarajevo on 28 June. By the end of July, the *Norfolk News* was already reporting that the demand for insurance against war risks had exceeded 'anything ever before experienced in this country'.[61] And in Warwickshire, the Ashby family, like many others, were watching the course of events with mounting concern. As Kathleen Ashby recalled, during the last week of July and the first days of August, she and her mother harnessed a pony cart every evening and drove five miles from their home in Tysoe to Kineton Post Office to read in its windows the most recent telegrams on the news from Serbia, Austria, Germany, Russia, and France. 'Each evening all the wide valley was bathed in golden serene sunset light', she wrote, 'but on the third of August the weather changed. The sunset was more gorgeous than ever; but the valley was filled with mist of raucous purple. When my mother recited the messages we had brought home there was a long stillness that Joseph broke with the only possible words: "Few things will ever be the same again." '[62]

Thus came knowledge of the imminence of war to one family in rural England. In another community, Rudston in the East Riding of Yorkshire, Winifred Holtby, also a farmer's daughter, remembered the little knots of people standing in the half-light around the open doorways of shops that would normally have closed hours before, as the news came through. The customary routine of daily life was temporarily forgotten, as the turn of events was anxiously discussed:

In a far-away farm-house, a dog barked persistently. Above the counter of the small crowded newspaper shop, large moths flopped clumsily round the swinging paraffin lamp. An old drunken woman wearing a man's cap planted herself in a chair beneath it.

'War's bloody hell,' she remarked in mild conversational tones. 'Ah'm tellin' you God's truth. Two o' my lads went i' South Africa. Bloody hell. That's wha' 'tis.'[63]

During those first hours of stunned awareness, few would have accepted the truth of her words. They had to guide them only their recollections of the Boer War, which had been fought many miles away against colonial guerillas, and, more distantly, folk memories of grandparents' stories of the Battle of Waterloo. They had yet to experience the horror of a twentieth century global conflict. That was knowledge they were to acquire slowly and painfully during the next four years.

Chapter 2

The Coming of War

'As German guns battered down the gates of Western civilisation there was a quickening of fellowship amongst all classes in rural England.... The farmer's boy, so long despised, was appealed to by patriotic songs sung by fine ladies to defend them and all English women; and the rich man's motor car swiftly sped these lads to the nearest recruiting station.... The squire who sat on the Bench looked for the moment with a tolerant eye upon the well-known poacher who might make a useful sniper in the ranks of the British Army.' F.E. Green, *A History of the English Agricultural Labourer*, London 1920, 233.

The outbreak of war on 4 August 1914, was greeted in rural communities, as elsewhere in English society, with a mixture of relief that the long weeks of rumour were at an end, and nervous apprehension as to what lay ahead. At the small Sussex village of Fletching — typical of many such places — the headmaster of the local school described the prevailing mood eleven days after the declaration of hostilities: 'Another week of excitement, everyone restless and ready to discuss war news on the slightest provocation.... Every night there is a rush for the evening papers which arrive at 9 p.m., then [the] doctor and his wife come in to compare notes and discuss the war generally'.[1]

This sense of whole-hearted involvement was nowhere stronger than among the landed classes themselves. Not only did they enjoy traditional links with the county yeomanry regiments, but the officers of the regular army were normally recruited from among their ranks. They included men like Julian Grenfell, eldest son of Lord and Lady Desborough and already in 1914 an army officer. He regarded the break with peacetime life which the war represented as a welcome change from a predictable social round, and as a means of fulfilling the destiny for which his education and training had fitted him. 'It must be wonderful to be in England now', he wrote, shortly before returning home with his regiment from South Africa. 'I suppose the excitement is beyond all words.... It reinforces

24

one's failing belief in the Old Flag and the Mother Country and the Heavy Brigade and the Thin Red Line and the Imperial Idea which gets rather shadowy in peace time, don't you think?'[2] Many others shared the sense of urgency of Sir Oswald Mosley, the son of a Staffordshire landed family, that they must join up quickly so as not to miss any of the action. 'Our one great fear', Mosley wrote of his generation, 'was that the war would be over before we got there'.[3] Events were to show how needless that particular anxiety was, and Mosley himself was ultimately to be invalided out with a badly injured leg before he was twenty, after service in the air and the trenches.

Even those, like Neville Lytton, who did not share Grenfell's and Mosley's enthusiasm for the cause, considered it their duty to enlist when their friends were doing likewise. Lytton decided to volunteer when his friend, Edward Horner, arrived at a nearby camp with members of the Somerset Yeomanry. Horner was the owner of an estate in Somerset and, according to his friend, prior to the outbreak of war had 'led a life of pure idleness'.[4] Now that was all changed and the greater sense of purpose he displayed caused Lytton's own doubts and misgivings to vanish.

The first to be mobilised were the reservists and the members of the territorial army, who marched or rode away from home and friends to the stirring accompaniment of bands and the cheers of admiring onlookers. One of many hundreds of such incidents occurred at Downham Market in Norfolk, where the men mustered in the market square before riding off towards Kings Lynn, to the strains of Hilgay Brass Band playing the National Anthem and other patriotic music.[5] While at Little Waltham in Essex a labourer remembered how several of his fellow workers who were members of the reserve were called up out of the harvest field. 'This was the last I saw of some of them, as they did not return.' He himself stayed behind to complete the harvest and then on 3 September decided to respond to Lord Kitchener's appeal of 7 August for 100,000 new recruits. He joined the Royal Artillery and was sent to Woolwich on the initial stages of his training — his first visit to London.[6]

Inevitably the sudden disappearance of labourers at harvest time created difficulties for the farmers who had been employing them. From the Driffield district of Yorkshire came complaints that as a result of the pre-war formation of a Waggoners'

Reserve of the Army Service Corps, comprising about a thousand men, the labour problem had become acute. Some farms had lost five or more workers apiece. The men had received £1 per annum to be registered as waggoners, and when war came they had been called up at once.[7] Similarly, in Wiltshire, where short-term labour shortages were also reported, Devizes Urban District Council offered to lend men and horses in their employ at cost price to any farmer who was unable to carry on because of lack of labour.[8] But most agriculturists managed to get by, with the help of casual workers and with their remaining men putting in longer hours.

Among the rest of the village population, meanwhile, there was also a quickening of activity. Some of the younger tradesmen, like their agricultural counterparts, felt it their duty to enlist. At Farnham, George Sturt recorded in his diary on 12 August how one of the assistants in his wheelwright's shop named Harry Goatcher had arrived at his door at 7.15 a.m. to announce that the previous night he had taken the first steps 'towards enlistment "for one year or as long as the war lasts", etc. etc. Poor boy — he was in a subdued gasp of excitement: had probably this morning (to say nothing of previous times) had to encounter opposition from his mother.... There is a strange subdued excitement about. Swain (of Swain and Jones) has enlisted on the same terms as Harry... and I hear of perhaps half a dozen others, all gone or ready to go.'[9]

Elsewhere meetings were held among the female members of the population to establish branches of the Red Cross to provide rudimentary training in first-aid, or to set up sewing and knitting parties to make 'comforts' for the troops. One woman, the daughter of an agricultural engineer from Ardleigh in Essex, recalled that her mother and a number of the other village women volunteered to sew hospital shirts. These were delivered cut out and were later collected complete.[10] Even the girl guides were recruited, learning to roll bandages, make swabs, receive telephone messages, and similar tasks, while the boy scouts were mobilised to act as messengers, or as guards against the possible sabotage of public utilities like gas works and reservoirs. For rumours were soon rife in many quiet communities that the enemy planned to pollute the water supply, and stories were told of attempts to introduce cholera germs into the water at Plymouth, Portsmouth, and Aldershot. Although the rumours proved groundless, it was felt that precautions must be taken. At Bridport in Dorset, for example, arrangements were made for parties of volunteers, including boy scouts, to keep the local waterworks under observation night and day.[11] Reports in provincial newspapers make clear that they were not alone in taking this action. Indeed, at Calne in Wiltshire, to quote one of many examples, there was an account of two 'suspicious individuals' seen loitering 'in the vicinity' of the Calstone reservoir. Prompt action was taken by the water company to safeguard local supplies as a consequence.

Impromptu home-guard units were also recruited in some market towns and larger villages. At Sedbergh on the Westmorland border, it was decided that all men over the age of eighteen should be invited to join, 'the conditions being that all who joined must put in three drills a week as well as miniature range practice and open range practice if possible'.[12] Within a fortnight about a hundred had volunteered and had begun regular training. A number of landowners even constructed their own rifle ranges so that men could learn how to shoot before they joined up, and the village poacher, hitherto regarded as a threat to pheasant coverts, now became valued as a possible recruit to the armed forces. Nor were these the only developments. As the *Mark Lane Express* commented, there was 'something almost mediaeval about the idea of drilling the youths of the village on the green ... but ... this is happening, with old soldiers acting as instructors'.[13] At one Cumbrian village, according to the *Westmorland Mercury* of 28 August, this included the recruitment of 80-year-old ex-soldiers to teach the youngsters how to shoot!

In the general upsurge of patriotic enthusiasm, numerous country houses were offered for use as hospitals and convalescent homes, to cater for the inevitable casualties. Already by 21 August, the *Hexham Weekly News* was reporting that the authorities had been 'literally inundated' with offers of properties, and the principal difficulty was to make the best choice of accommodation. The Earl of Sefton had lent Croxteth Hall near Liverpool for the purpose, while Earl Spencer was fitting up Dallington House in Northamptonshire, and Lord Desborough had offered his property at Taplow.[14] At Woburn Abbey, the riding-school and indoor tennis court were converted into a 100-bed hospital, and although trained nurses were employed, such duties as those of orderly and stretcher bearer were undertaken by household servants, gardeners, chauffeurs, and grooms on the estate who were unfit for military service.[15]

However, the landed classes took a lead not merely by offering their homes and their sons for war purposes, but by their zeal in promoting recruitment among those whom they employed. G.L. Courthope, MP for the Rye Division of Sussex, was one who not only joined up himself but took fifteen of his estate workers with him. 'While Mr Courthope's employees are on service', reported the *Sussex Express*, 'their families will not be worried about rent or food'.[16] In a similar spirit, Colonel Borton of Cheveney in Kent, although too old to serve himself, took his cowman, footman and 43-year-old butler to enlist at Maidstone within three weeks of the outbreak of war. On the Bedford estate those employees who volunteered were promised that half their weekly wages would be paid to their dependants at home while they were away. And on the Marquis of Lincolnshire's properties, instructions were given that where any adult member of cottager families had joined the colours or had volunteered for public service, those whom they left behind were to be allowed to live rent free for the duration of the war.[17] At that time, few envisaged that the struggle would last for more than four years, but it seems that the promises were kept. Certainly the families of some Bedford estate employees were still receiving their payments in 1918.[18]

In other cases, personal contacts were made with individual labourers. In Wiltshire, Lady Glenconner, sister-in-law of the Prime Minister and member of a land-owning family in the county, took on the role of an informal recruiting agent by visiting farms near her property in the Amesbury area. The aim was to persuade carters and agricultural workers to volunteer, and once she had succeeded in securing a few likely candidates she speedily took them by motor car to Salisbury, where they were handed over to an official recruiting officer.[19] Another Wiltshire landowner, the MP, Walter Long, preferred to use the forum of a public meeting to appeal to men at West Ashton, where he resided. His own two sons had been early recruits and he exhorted the villagers to join up without delay. 'Better far to die shouldering your rifle in any fight for the liberties and rights of your country', he vehemently proclaimed, 'than live at home in ease, a craven at heart, knowing full well that the rest of your life would be spent in the miserable reflection that your country lost her position amongst the nations of the world because her young men preferred to live at home in a temporary ease. . . . Here in this village and in other villages where I have influence I mean to have a great placard headed the roll of honour. On that will be inscribed the names of any man who joins the Colours; a copy of it will be sent to every house or cottage in which he has dwelt, and where his family are, and a permanent copy will be given to his family to keep as a lasting record of the fact that he did his duty'.[20]

Already before the end of August, women in Folkestone were handing out white feathers to young men who were allegedly 'shirking' in civilian clothes, and that practice soon spread even to small villages.[21] A paranoid suspicion took root in some quarters that a number of men were dodging the appeal to volunteer. Advertisements in the press played their part, too, ranging from direct statements of the 'Your country needs you' variety, to emotional calls to defend home and women 'from the German Huns'. The *Hexham Weekly News* of 25 December 1914, for example, showed a row of men crouching in the trenches. Alongside was the caption: 'BRITONS!! when your country is in danger The Post of Honour is in the Firing Line. Enlist to-day, and become fit to fight for England, Home and Duty'. Even employers of labour were not exempt from these demands. Early in 1915, five questions were posed to those keeping male servants, in the columns of *Country Life*:

1. Have you a Butler, Groom, Chauffeur, Gardener, or Gamekeeper serving *you* who, at this moment should be serving your King and Country?
2. Have you a man serving at your table who should be serving a gun?
3. Have you a man digging your garden who should be digging trenches?
4. Have you a man driving your car who should be driving a transport wagon?
5. Have you a man preserving your game who should be helping to preserve your Country?

A great responsibility rests on you. Will you sacrifice your personal convenience for your Country's need? Ask your men to enlist *TO-DAY*.[22]

In this, scant attention was paid to the wishes of the servants themselves. They were regarded almost as pawns on a chess board who could be moved around at their employer's will.

Occasionally extra financial inducements were offered to encourage enlistment. The Earl of Ancaster, for example, sent a circular letter to employees on his Lincolnshire and Rutland estates, encouraging them to join up by promising to keep a situation open for them when they returned, guaranteeing an income for the wives and families of the married men while they were away, and allowing the families of volunteers to live in their cottages rent free. In addition, any man prepared to enlist was to be given a bonus of £5. The offer seems to have proved effective, for within a week twenty-two men from the villages of Empingham and Normanton on the Ancaster estate had volunteered and had been taken in motor cars lent for the occasion to have a medical examination at Stamford. Fourteen were successful and within days were on their way to Lincoln barracks amidst the applause of fellow villagers. As a parting gift, the Countess of Ancaster and the local clergyman provided each with tobacco and a pipe.[23] A good deal less attractive was the approach adopted by the Earl of Lonsdale for staff on his extensive Cumberland and Westmorland properties. Here single men were advised to volunteer and, if they did so, were promised that a place would be kept open for them when they came back and their families cared for. But if they failed to act, they might be given notice instead and, in this case, would lose all allowances.[24] Not surprisingly, it was noted that a number of men had already enlisted 'owing to this statement'.[25] A similar policy was followed at Lord Rothschild's Tring Park estate in Hertfordshire, and within a few days of its promulgation about twenty men from the garden, timber yard, home farm, and other departments were on their way to Aylesbury recruiting office.[26] Only a few of the leaders of rural society were prepared to follow the example of Rowland Prothero, agent-in-chief to the Duke of Bedford, who resolutely refused to give 'personal advice to individuals' about the need to join up. He also refused to hold recruiting meetings at Oakley, where he lived, 'because I was coward enough to shrink from trying to influence my friends and neighbours'. As he frankly declared, he was not prepared to ask young men 'to do something which I was not doing and could not do myself'. Such sensitivity was rare.

In any case in these early days large numbers of men required no prompting. Three-quarters of a million Britons volunteered during August and September alone, and this had risen to 1.186 million by the end of the year. They included a substantial number of young country men. In East Anglia, the leaders of the Workers' Union complained that they had lost nearly all their active and energetic members by the end of the year: 'practically in every village the great bulk of the young men have joined the Army'. Similarly, the National Union saw a fall of about 13 per cent in its membership within the first months of hostilities.[27] Ironically, the scale and enthusiasm of recruiting were such that the resources of the military authorities could scarcely cope. Camps were hastily opened the length and breadth of the land, and in cases where no billets could be secured, men had to sleep under canvas or in farm outbuildings. On the south downs, Richard Hillyer recalled how a bare patch of chalky hillside near his home was commandeered for an encampment and each Sunday afternoon during that first autumn of the War he and his family, along with their neighbours, walked out to see what was happening. The turf was worn away by the passage of vehicles, men, and animals coming and going, while the troops lived in tents in the midst of a scene of general confusion. There was a chewed up parade ground in the middle and a tall fir tree, roughly barked, which served as a flagstaff. During the raw wet weeks which followed some of the men, unused to living out, succumbed to pneumonia and eventually billets had to be arranged. 'There must have been many people up north', where the men originated, wrote Hillyer, 'that wondered what had gone wrong; when the men whom they had cheered, and waved away to fight the Germans, got no further than a muddy death on a bleak hillside in the South of England'.[28]

However, at the beginning this, like many other dark aspects of the War, still lay in the future. Most of the new recruits in the late summer of 1914 responded to the discomforts of shortages, mismanagement, and stringent military discipline with determined goodwill. There was no possibility of uniforms for many of them, so they drilled for hours enthusiastically in tweed caps and flannel trousers, using broom handles as rifles.[29] An Essex farm worker, Mr A. Green, who served in the Royal Artillery, recalled how his uniform came in instalments. 'One of the first things I was issued with was a pair of spurs. I finally got a blue uniform complete with forage cap'. Prior to this, those men who had already received a uniform engaged in a profitable sideline by hiring it out for the weekend to anyone going on leave, who wished to impress his family.[30]

Much the same carefree atmosphere during these initial weeks is conveyed by Siegfried Sassoon's autobiographical novel, *The Complete Memoirs of George Sherston*. Sherston, like Sassoon, had enlisted as a trooper with a yeomanry regiment on 1 August, and had been despatched to an impromptu camp on a Kentish farm. Here he slept with eleven other troopers in a bivouac rigged up out of a rick-cloth and some posts. The whole affair seemed rather like a holiday:

> The flavour and significance of life were around me in the homely smells of the thriving farm where we were quartered; my own abounding health responded zestfully to the outdoor world, to the apple-scented orchards, and all those fertilities which the harassed farmer was gathering in while stupendous events were developing across the Channel. . . . I can remember the first time that I was "warned for guard", and how I polished up my boots and buttons for that event. And when, in the middle of the night, I had been roused up to take my turn as sentry, I did not doubt that it was essential that someone in a khaki uniform should stand somewhere on the outskirts of the byres and barns of Batt's Farm. My King and Country expected it of me. There was, I remember, a low mist lying on the fields, and I was posted by a gate under a walnut tree. In the autumn-smelling silence the village church clanged one o'clock. Shortly afterwards I heard someone moving in my direction across the field which I was facing. The significance of those approaching feet was intensified by my sentrified nerves. Holding my rifle defensively (and a loaded rifle, too) I remarked in an unemphatic voice: "Halt, who goes there?" There was no reply. Out of the mist and the weeds through which it was wading emerged the Kentish cow which I had challenged.[31]

In hard-pressed Sussex, where a multiplicity of camps was established in every suitable spot, the headmaster of Fletching school described the disorder created: 'there [has] been such a strain thrown suddenly on the authorities that things have gone wrong and the men have suffered a good deal of hardship.... The majority... simply had the clothes they stood up in when they marched off and for weeks the authorities have not been able to supply them. At Lewes... the people collected clothes, shirts, vests, pants, socks, etc. so as to enable the men to change.... Now they are putting up wooden huts and doing the work by contracts, the contractors being under a penalty of completing the work by November 1.'[32] But by February 1915, the county's difficulties had intensified: 'Every town you visit is a garrison town swarming with soldiers in the making.... Then there is a constant stream of trains to and from the ports on the S. coast taking troops, guns, stores etc. bringing back wounded and men on leave... the local papers are full of the tales told in every village by soldiers on leave'.[33]

Where permanent army camps grew up in this fashion, the impact on village life was enormous, with the normal routine disrupted by the noise and bustle of military activity. One of the areas early affected was the Chilterns in Buckinghamshire, where gunnery ranges were hastily rigged up on the downs. By mid-September 1914 around one thousand six hundred men had been billeted in the small market town of Tring, plus another thousand or so in nearby villages. Later the headmaster of neighbouring Ivinghoe school noted that many of the children were playing truant in order to witness the firing of cannon from a nearby hill. And on 9 and 10 February 1915, he added: 'large numbers of Lord Kitchener's Army have been passing through the village, drums beating, & the men singing disturbs, somewhat, the work, & excites the children, but they can see the true meaning of discipline'.[34]

The new developments also had their commercial side. Apart from the stimulus given to trade in the local shops, many men and boys were able to obtain highly paid employment in helping to construct the camps, while the women earned extra cash by carrying out laundry work for the military. There was an opportunity, too, to let rooms to the wives and families of officers and soldiers, who came to visit their menfolk from time to time. The rector of Aston Clinton, one Chilterns village, considered that these and similar changes attributable to the War had made the community more prosperous than it had ever been. Prior to 1914, people had been much dependent upon the charitable assistance of the Rothschilds, who were the principal landowners, but now they were able to be self-reliant. Morally, too, the presence of large bodies of soldiers had not had the bad effect he had once feared. 'The number of women who have morally suffered could be reckoned on the fingers of one's two hands. . . . Indeed, I should say that the presence of the Troops has had a good . . . effect on our villagers . . .; it has made them go out of themselves towards others, receive them into their houses, made them more selfless & broader in outlook'.[35]

Inevitably the constant convoys of men and materials which passed through the countryside of southern and eastern England added to the disruption of daily life. Christopher Holdenby described the incessant rumbling of distant trains which disturbed the stillness of the early autumn nights in his village and the unwonted cavalcades of men marching along the main road, often to the chorus of a music hall ditty.

> For some weeks we watched the pageant pass by in mere wonderment. . . . I remember one warm Sunday I was digging in my garden when 5,000 men came marching down the road. A halt was called; they rested on our green hedges and refreshed themselves before going on again. As far as the eye could see was one yellow line of orange and banana skins, dotted with silver paper. . . . Again and again they passed, some, men of uncouth ways, who jumped the hedge and broke open our faggots for walking sticks, and jeered at us who still worked by the roadside; others, perhaps reminded of home, treated the valley more tenderly.[36]

These military preparations were given particular impetus in the coastal areas by fears of German air attacks or even of a full-scale invasion. Special constables were sworn in, whose duty it was to patrol the roads at night, watching for undesirable strangers with motor-cars, cycles, or on foot, and to report any lights which might be shown as signals. They were also to record the course of foreign air-ships, and the 'number and nature of any falling bombs'.[37] An Essex woman recalled that each evening as she returned from hospital work as a V.A.D. she would be stopped with the challenge 'who goes there — friend or foe', and when she answered 'friend', the reply came, 'Pass friend, all's well', after she had been inspected closely.[38] In Kent, too, as early as October 1914, Lord Milner noted the 'considerable state of tension' which existed 'owing to the German occupation of Ostende & the probable extension of their line to Dunkirk & Calais', which brought with them fears of invasion of this country.[39]

The authorities clearly considered the threat must be taken seriously, and early plans were drawn up under Home Office direction for the evacuation of the civilian population from coastal districts. In many respects they bore an uncanny resemblance to those framed a century earlier to deal with a possible attack from the French during the Napoleonic Wars. Emergency Committees were to be established to supervise operations in each petty sessional division, and in February 1915, one of them — the Brentwood District Emergency Committee in Essex — in a typical leaflet warned the civilian population to be prepared to travel at short notice by cart or waggon, taking with them money, jewellery, sufficient food to last for forty-eight hours, and a blanket apiece. The railways and motor vehicles were, of course, reserved for military use only. Farmers were to collect their livestock together and to brand them in readiness for driving them away from the enemy, with special routes laid down which they were to follow. Any animals which could not be taken were to be shot in the fields and allowed to lie there so that their flesh would putrefy rapidly and be of no use to the enemy. Owners of pick-axes, spades, shovels, felling-axes, saws and other tools were to bring them to a pre-selected rendezvous, in order that they might be placed at the disposal of the military authorities. Watch was to be kept 'most carefully' upon the movements of aliens and 'in cases of emergency' they were to be put under arrest.[40] The signal of invasion was to be the continuous ringing of church or other alarm bells, and should orders for evacuation be given, the population must be ready to move off without delay. The people of Essex were to travel to previously designated centres in Oxfordshire, and en route were to be provided with billeting in workhouses, churches, and other public buildings. 'Every Town or Village should be prepared to billet, in cases of extreme pressure, up to a number equal to double the population.'[41] Warnings were given of the slow pace of the exodus: 'it is not safe to reckon on more than 1,000 refugees per mile of road space, nor to rely on a greater speed than 2 miles per hour. It is considered that wheeled traffic may accomplish 20 miles per

day, but that women and children on foot will only do a
maximum of 10 miles per day'.[42]

Similar arrangements were drawn up for other coastal
counties in southern England. In Dorset, they included the
gathering together of huge piles of wood and barrels of tar for use
as warning beacons. These were destined to remain in position,
untouched, throughout the War.[43] The rumours of invasion,
meanwhile, continued to circulate, and as late as January 1916
an inter-service committee agreed that a raid by up to 170,000
Germans was still a possibility.[44]

From the beginning of 1915, additional urgency was given to
these preparations by aerial attacks from Zeppelins, the first
raid on 19 January over Yarmouth and Sheringham killing four
people. Further raids followed, with increasing intensity, and
with both Zeppelins and aeroplanes taking part. Indeed, after
one attack near the small Essex village of Stondon Massey not
only were some of the inhabitants so alarmed that they were
afraid to go to bed for several subsequent nights, but the
animals, too, were affected. One old man described graphically
'the strange blending of sounds from frightened beasts & birds
which followed the explosions. "I never heard", said he, "such a
harmony:— bullocks, cows, calves. lambs, sheep, horses, dogs,
fowls, rooks, & pheasants: all might be heard calling in the
night: all terrified, & wondering what was the cause of the
sudden crash into the silence." '[45] Twelve days earlier a similar
attack had taken place a little farther away, and the Stondon
Massey Rector had commented on the strange experience of
hearing the corncrake 'rattling forth in the quiet night, and the
rooks and other birds disturbed in their slumbers calling out in
protest'.[46] Even the sound of an aeroplane was a frightening
experience initially to some creatures, and there were reports
from remote Cumbria of grouse, plovers, and other moorland
birds deserting their usual haunts at the approach of a machine.
'Their distressful cries filled the air, and grouse — the wildest of
birds — were found to have taken shelter in cowsheds and other
outbuildings, too terrified to remain longer in the open'.[47]

Given these early alarums and excursions, it is not surprising
that 'spy' stories and what the Prime Minister called a
'ridiculous spy fever' should proliferate. The *Cambridge Chronicle*
of 28 August 1914, in a typical report referred to the 'contagious
affliction known as "spy mania" having made its appearance in

the vicinity of that city: 'stories of pursuits and arrests have reached the office of this journal daily and in wholesale numbers. . . . The military authorities, too, are very much on the alert, and from the camps emanate several stories of "suspects" being very badly "wanted".' Some of the 'scares' were of a ludicrous character, like the Maldon, Essex, man whose home fell under suspicion because a carrier pigeon had landed on the roof of the house, 'causing a crowd of 200-300 persons to assemble'. Eventually the police searched his house and found nothing — certainly not the store of coded messages which they presumably suspected the pigeon was bringing in. The pigeon's owner was subsequently traced and the whole mystery solved by the simple explanation that the bird had lost its way.[48] Similarly, in Norfolk a vigilant territorial officer discovered what he thought were suspicious signalling lights from the top of a village church tower He assembled his men and they cautiously made their way with fixed bayonets through the pitch darkness until they reached the churchyard. They were just about to fire when they realised that the suspected 'spies' on the steeple were their comrades from another company, who had seized the opportunity to carry out a little signalling practice.[49]

But occasionally these unsubstantiated fears could have tragic consequences. At the small village of Henham on the Norfolk/Suffolk border, the schoolmaster fell under suspicion as a German agent, apparently because some years before a German friend of his son had stayed at the house. Although he had lived a blameless existence in Suffolk for thirty years and had been born in Devon, the stories continued to circulate until eventually he was ordered to leave the parish by the police, under the provisions of the 1914 Defence of the Realm Act. This was because 'suspicious persons' were not allowed to reside in coastal counties where they could presumably give succour to the enemy, should a landing take place. The threat of expulsion so preyed upon the master's mind that he committed suicide, shortly before he was due to leave. Although his innocence was subsequently established, this vindication came too late to save him and his family from disaster.[50] As Lord Stradbroke, the principal landowner in the area, indignantly wrote, by spreading tales which they knew to be untrue the villagers had killed their victim just as surely as if 'they had drawn the knife across his throat with their cowardly fingers'.

Fortunately, most such affairs were far less serious than this. At Stondon Massey the Rector noted in his journal that on 26 June 1915, men of the Cheshire regiment, who were stationed in his parish, thought they had detected a spy. The man concerned was observed walking with an Ordnance Survey map of the area and although he angrily explained he was an Oxford graduate who had regularly used such maps to guide him on his holiday hiking tours, they were not convinced. Eventually he appealed to the Rector for help, since he was being 'shadowed' by several of the soldiers as he walked along. The Rector unhelpfully replied that while the soldiers 'should not have proclaimed him the King's enemy without proof... he had been drawing suspicion upon himself by his unguarded action in these troubled times'.[51] In the end, the man had to endure this petty persecution until he reached Ongar, when they apparently left him.

But nervousness was probably greater at Stondon than at some other places because it had been selected to form part of a defensive ring of reinforcements and trenches to be constructed to thwart a possible advance on London, should an enemy landing take place. By November 1914 some hundreds of navvies had been brought in to help local labourers carry out the construction work. Eighteen months later, the project was still incomplete, though now soldiers had been recruited to undertake the building operations. Fortunately for all concerned, these elaborate preparations were never put to the test. For as the Rector realistically observed, the arrangements would never have withstood anything more powerful than 'a hastily-executed invasion of infantry'. Experience in France and Flanders had already shown that 'no trenches [were] able to meet successfully the onset of heavy guns'.[52] By December 1917, ironically, the first steps were being taken to demolish the fortifications through the removal of the barbed wire barriers that surrounded them. But it was not until February 1920 that the trenches were finally filled in, at a time when initiatives were being taken to dismantle similar fortifications elsewhere.[53] The whole thing had been a time-wasting, expensive and pointless exercise, whose main purpose seems to have been to occupy hundreds of navvies and soldiers for months at a time and to have led to the requisitioning of valuable farm land.

Even in more remote areas, military preparations manifested

themselves. At Rudston in the East Riding of Yorkshire, Winifred Holtby remembered the nervous young sentries on picket duty in the village and the 'bored Territorial officers perpetually craving for light entertainment'. The Holtby family responded with ready hospitality. They plied the young sentries who were watching for Zeppelins with nightly supplies of hardboiled eggs and mugs of tea, and arranged impromptu concerts for their off-duty hours. On mild autumn evenings the young men 'fought duels with oranges across the wide stretch of semicircular lawn'.[54]

But alongside these almost frivolous aspects, the War had its bleaker side. Already there were the personal tragedies of young men killed or injured in action, though few could have envisaged at that stage that the total death toll would reach nearly 723,000, or almost one in eight of the six million men serving in the British Army, Navy, and RFC/RAF between 1914 and 1918.[55] About 1.67 million were to be wounded. It was in these circumstances that C.F.G. Masterman was later to claim with emotion that in the retreat from Mons and the first battle of Ypres, during 1914-15, the 'flower of the British aristocracy' had perished. Many youngsters had joined up straight from public school, like the poet, Robert Graves, or Lady Cynthia Asquith's brother, Yvo, youngest son of the Earl of Wemyss, who volunteered straight from Eton. Only a few weeks after reaching the front he was killed, shortly after his nineteenth birthday. Indeed, what was to prove the most dangerous rank in the army — the subaltern — was initially recruited from current or former students of the public schools and the older universities. Graves himself was eventually to record that one in three of his generation at school died during the hostilities, 'because they all took commissions as soon as they could, most of them in the infantry and Royal Flying Corps. The average life expectancy of an infantry subaltern on the Western Front was, at some stages of the war, only about three months.'[56] Masterman, too, noted that at many aerodromes the average span of life of the individual was at times little more than a fortnight. He then added despairingly: 'In the useless slaughter of the Guards on the Somme, or of the Rifle Brigade in Hooge Wood, half the great families of England, heirs of large estates and wealth, perished without a cry. These boys, who had been brought up with a prospect before them of every good material thing that life can give, died without complaint, often through the bungling of Generals'.[57]

Already by the end of 1914, the dead included at least three peers and fifty-two peers' sons, as well as a large number of baronets and their sons. Winchester, typical of the public schools, sent none of its boys to Oxford in 1915, while of its former pupils one in six of those born in the 1880s and one in four of those born in the 1890s were destined to die in the conflict. Similarly, of 5,588 Etonians who served, 1,159 were killed and 1,469 wounded.[58] Some families, like that of the Earl of Wemyss, Lord Desborough, Lord Chalmers, and Lord Cawley, lost two or more sons within the space of about twelve months. In the first two of these cases that included the heir to the title. In all, of the peers and their sons under the age of fifty who served in the Great War, almost one in five was killed.[59]

These heavy losses inevitably had significant social and economic consequences. Although special war-time legislation reduced the burden of death duties levied on the estates of those who died at the front, for the largest properties, substantial sums could still be payable.[60] In some cases, estate sales became necessary, especially if an owner's death were quickly followed by that of his heir, killed at the front, or if, through these double deaths, the property passed to a distant relative who had no strong ties to the land. F.M.L. Thompson quotes the case of Sir Edmund Antrobus, whose death was closely followed by that of his only son, in action. This led to the Amesbury Abbey estate being put on the market in 1915, and the farms being purchased by their tenants.[61]

Aristocratic life styles, too, changed radically for those who remained behind, as a result of higher taxes, general shortages, the stagnation of rentals from agricultural land (partly the result of war-time restrictions), and a lack of domestic servants. Gardens lost their formerly immaculate appearance as workers were called up, and lawns were turned over to potato growing, especially in the difficult later stages of the War. At Aynho Park in Northamptonshire the gardeners were reduced from nine employed in 1914 to four three years later; of these, three were too old to serve and the fourth, aged sixteen, was too young. Despite his inexperience, he was given charge of the greenhouses. Disciplinary attitudes were also changing, and whereas before 1916 it had been laid down that every employee on this estate should attend Morning Service on Good Friday, or else forfeit a day's pay, after that date such ideas were abandoned. On other estates, similar adjustments were taking place, as the old order crumbled.

The wives and daughters of estate owners, anxious to play their part, also found outside employment for the first time in their lives. Many undertook nursing and canteen duties, even if, as with Lady Diana Manners, daughter of the Duke of Rutland, and Venetia Stanley, youngest child of Lord Sheffield, their stint of caring for the sick and needy was interspersed with a feverish social life. But at Cheveney, Colonel Borton's wife took her role so seriously that she became matron of the small convalescent home which she and her husband established. By 24 October 1914, the home had its first inmates — four wounded Belgian soldiers.[62] It remained in operation for the duration of the War. She also attended work parties to make bandages, and, like many other squires' ladies, continued to visit the cottagers to dispense charity and advice, when needed.

Rather incongruously, it was only in the matter of field sports that the gentry appear to have tried to withstand the pressures of change and to carry on as usual. Admittedly in some cases, as with the Althorp and Pytchley hunt, women had to take over as masters, while in others, the field was periodically swollen by army officers on leave, or snatching a day's hunting away from military duties. The Essex, for example, attracted larger fields when yeomanry or cavalry regiments were stationed in the country. Certainly Lord Willoughby de Broke, a noted hunting enthusiast, regularly brought out the officers of the Warwickshire Yeomanry when they were stationed in Essex.[63] Similarly the North Warwickshire, anxious that fields would be reduced by men joining their regiments, decided to start 'cubbing' from the end of August 1914, in order to keep down the number of foxes. 'The committee of the North Warwickshire are satisfied that this method of reducing the numbers . . . will be . . . far more sportsmanlike than that of shooting foxes, either by men engaged at the kennels or by tenant farmers'. So reads the account in the *Kenilworth Advertiser*. But the commitment of the hunting fraternity to their sport is perhaps best illustrated by a report in the *Wiltshire Gazette* at the end of that year, announcing that a 'well-known Brigadier-General' had sent a donation to the fund of the Hunt in which he was interested, with the message: 'We soldiers out here (at the Front) doing our share to keep the flag flying, feel very grateful to those stalwarts who are doing their share to keep fox-hunting on its legs'. In a similar vein, Lord Lonsdale poured money from his private resources into the Cottesmore to keep it going, arguing: 'What on earth are officers home from the front to do with their time if there's no hunting for them?'[64]

Gradually, however, the exigencies of war forced a change of attitude even among these enthusiasts. First, the Masters of Foxhounds Association had to agree to reduce packs of hounds by half, and lack of food forced some to cut down even more drastically. Then, during the summer of 1917 the cereal shortage posed a threat to the availability of feed for the horses. Eventually a compromise was reached, by which the horses were allowed a fixed ration, on the understanding that they would be placed at the disposal of the military authorities should they be required. But by this stage, the sport had been reduced to very small proportions indeed.

Shooting, too, continued to attract its war-time devotees, such as Lord Northampton, who on a short leave of four days from the Western front early in 1915, chose to spend one of them slaughtering pheasants on his estate at Castle Ashby. In the event, according to *Country Life*, the bag was not very large: 'we hear it said by all the soldiers who have come back and have been able to take a day or two's covert shooting, that the war seems to have a disastrous effect on their marksmanship. They are disposed to attribute it to a little natural "jumpiness" of the nerves after listening to the shells screeching and bursting around them for so many days'.[65] But in this sport, also, as the War continued, the shortage of keepers and of food needed to rear the birds led to a reduction in activity. Already by 1 May 1915, *Country Life* was reporting that on many estates where vast numbers of pheasants had formerly been reared 'no eggs at all are being set this year'. And on the Gorhambury estate in 1918 so few gamekeeping staff remained that practically no rabbits were shot, while the bag of partridges and pheasants was less than half of its pre-war figure. During 1917, under general pressure from farmers and the Board of Agriculture, anxious to prevent crops from being ravaged by hungry birds, tenant farmers were given powers to shoot those which came upon their land. It was a decision which at least two contributors to *Country Life* deplored as an undesirable break with tradition. But theirs was a minority view. Whatever the wishes of landowners, game preservation, like hunting, was to dwindle dramatically in the last two years of the War.

These attempts among the upper ranks of rural society to maintain a facade of 'business as usual' at least on the sporting front were, therefore, in the long run doomed to failure. Among the humbler country people, too, the pressures of War were changing attitudes. The euphoria of the early days began to give way increasingly to alternating moods of hope and pessimism. Already on 19 November 1914, George Sturt reported the town of Farnham as full of alarmist rumours concerning disasters to the Fleet and of the landing of sixty thousand Germans in Scotland.[66] Then there was the gradual realisation that many of the families of those who had joined up scarcely understood where or why their menfolk were fighting, so far outside the narrow course of their accustomed daily round were these major events. People who had never travelled beyond the nearest market town now had sons or husbands waging war in far off Flanders or France. Maps displayed at village clubs and inns were almost meaningless to most of them, and their imagination failed to grasp even vaguely the disposition of the far-flung battle line. F.E. Green recalled how one cowman whom he knew had asked whether Belgium was part of the British Empire. 'Is India this side or t'other of Egypt?' anxiously queried another old man, whose son had gone to the banks of the Nile.[67] Small wonder that a Buckinghamshire clergyman referred to the labourers in his parish as being 'dumbfounded by the happenings they but dimly understand'.[68]

Most distressing of all was the position of the wives and mothers, confused and distraught by the sudden departure of their menfolk for an unfamiliar destination, attended by incalculable risks and dangers. The *Mark Lane Express* in September 1914 described one woman waiting patiently by her cottage door for the arrival of the slow-moving carrier's cart coming from town. 'He had been amongst the newspapers and the special editions, and must know something.... He gives his answer ... and passes on, but informs another person sitting on the seat beside him that she ... has got two sons at the war and is naturally anxious.'[69] Even letter writing was a difficulty for many families, despite more than thirty years of compulsory elementary education. In most villages there were still men and women who had to rely upon neighbours to read letters sent to them by their relatives, and to write their replies. The message which these letters conveyed from the front was also bewildering to many recipients. 'You must not take too much notice of the reports of the soldiers in the trenches singing as if they had not a care in the world', wrote one young Northamptonshire man in September 1914. 'I heard more talk of religion — and from men from whom you would least expect it — than any popular songs! Some of the sights are simply shocking — you could not talk about them'.[70] In the following month the *Evesham Journal* summarised a letter from another recruit: 'sometimes the slaughter is terrific. It is often impossible to bury the dead and the stench from their decomposing bodies is very bad indeed. Sometimes . . . the bodies lie on the ground over the space of a mile as thick as sheaves after the self-binder in the harvest field. Sometimes explosions lift men eight or nine feet into the air and then they simply go to pieces'.[71] The impression made on families at home by such letters must have been shattering, so different was their tone from the generally optimistic line taken in the formal press accounts of the battlefield. Not surprisingly from mid-1915, the newspapers were forbidden to publish such unvarnished statements concerning life at the front. A gap was already beginning to emerge between those who were experiencing the horrors of war at first hand and those who merely read about them.

On a more mundane level, there was also the overturning of the accustomed routine for wives, especially those with young children, for whom the absence of their husband created a void which could not easily be filled. The incumbent of Dinton in Buckinghamshire was one who identified the feelings of drift and lack of purpose which this induced in some of them, when he wrote of his own parish:

> The dislocation of home life caused by the absence of the men seems to have unsettled the women in that they have no men to be regularly looked after & cared for. This disturbance of the routine of domestic life has taken from the women at any rate a part of the field duties & occupations which previously filled the daily life, and they seem incapable of adjusting themselves in such a way as to replace the lost duties by new

ones. Some of them work spasmodically on the land, but the majority have degenerated into an aimless existence, and their homes are far less clean and tidy than in pre-war days. Many of the young 'war-wives' without children are living in complete idleness on the [military] separation allowance. Carelessness or indifference seem to increase with the prolongation of the war. The children as they grow bigger are getting altogether out of hand, and the control of the father is seen to be very much missed.[72]

Religious observance was affected, too, with services of intercession proving popular in many parishes during the early months of the War. At Blewbury in Berkshire, and not untypically, the incumbent commented on the way that lapsed communicants had made 'their way back to the Altar & principally of course the wives of men serving abroad'. His colleague at Ashley Green, Buckinghamshire, noted that many people had learnt 'for the first time the value of intercessionary prayers. I have had letters from men at the front thanking me for our prayers & earnestly [asking] that they may be continued'.[73] Yet another cleric commented on the unusual quietness of those villages which were unaffected by the growth of army camps or munitions factories. With the departure of many of the younger men, the roads were less frequented, 'the places of public resort (we have two public reading rooms &c.) are empty, there are no gatherings for talk outside the church gates, on Sundays, and the side chapel, usually given up to the young men at service time, is untenanted'.[74] George Sturt had much the same impression: 'the roads, are almost emptied of stray young men now.... I never see youths, once so numerous on the Farnham road, in charge of horse and cart — the young careless men with flowers stuck in their caps. The cripples, the halt and the maimed, are now and then to be met; but for the most part the men we meet are rather elderly;...the jolly reckless outlook of young men is rare'.[75]

A more favourable cause for comment was the decline in drunkenness which accompanied these developments, resulting from restrictions on the supply and strength of alcohol, rising prices, and the gradual war-time limitation of opening hours. Another positive aspect was the growing sense of comradeship which manifested itself, both in a willingness to help neighbours in times of distress and in an anxiety to contribute to collections for the Red Cross, or to provide eggs for the wounded, and to give 'to Special collections of any kind'.[76]

But it was not just the social and spiritual aspects of village life which were affected by the War. Economically the demands of the military seriously disturbed production on the farms — a subject considered in a later chapter — and also the business prospects of country tradespeople. Inevitably the diversion of materials and men to war purposes reduced the supplies available for civilian use. As early as 12 August 1914, George Sturt commented on the difficulties experienced by businesses in Farnham, which had led to much short-time working, including in his own workshop: 'the builders are in want of materials: the gravel company cannot get trucks (railway) to send their gravel away, and scarce know how to keep their men at work. Half the motor cars, and more than half the horses in the neighbourhood have been commandeered by the military. The milkmen cannot get their milk delivered'. Much the same complaint was made by an Essex saddler and harnessmaker from Burnham-on-Crouch when he noted in his diary on 16 September: 'Trade is quiet here & I guess this is the position of many towns'.[77] In the years which lay ahead such dislocations and difficulties were to intensify as the economy was transformed to a war footing.

Chapter 3

Guarantees, Price Controls and the 'Plough Up' Campaign

'Nineteenth-century farmers learned to value their independence and prize their freedom. Yet during the last two years of the Great War they accepted the sacrifice of both. They submitted to State control; they co-operated with the Government in the effort to increase production: in spite of harassing difficulties, they raised more human food than had been produced from the land during the previous forty years'. Lord Ernle, *The Land and Its People*, London n.d. (*c.* 1925), 99.

Immediately after the outbreak of War, the Government's response to anxieties about the future course of food production had been to rely on exhortation and persuasion to achieve its ends, rather than to take any more positive action. Admittedly precautionary measures were adopted to buy up sugar supplies in the West Indies, to compensate for the loss of imports from Central Europe. A secret reserve of wheat was also built up, and control was assumed over the food crops of India. But beyond this, no steps were taken to protect grain supplies or to give financial encouragement to British farmers to produce more. Instead appeals were made to their patriotism to carry out a 'plough up' campaign. Unfortunately, many of them, mindful of the long years of depression which had affected cereal producers during the last quarter of the nineteenth century, were reluctant to act unless they could secure guaranteed prices, or at least a firm government commitment to cushion their industry from foreign competition, should the War end quickly. As a Leicestershire farmer told the February 1915 annual general meeting of the National Farmers' Union, it was the duty of NFU leaders to express to the Government their opposition to a policy which asked them to grow wheat and then refused to offer them a guaranteed price of even 35s. a quarter: "To my mind,' he declared bluntly, 'they consider farmers a lot of asses'.[1]

Nevertheless sufficient agriculturists were persuaded by the urgency of the situation, and by a growing confidence in the prospect of higher prices, to increase the acreage of wheat sown in the autumn of 1914. Although the total tillage area in 1915 was ultimately to fall below the level of the previous year, that for wheat was 20 per cent higher and was the largest acreage cultivated since 1891.[2] The oats acreage, too, rose slightly, in response to the greater demand for fodder crops. In these circumstances the Government's *laissez-faire* approach seemed justified.

Their complacency continued until the summer of 1915, when the effects of rising prices, reinforced by German submarine attacks on British shipping and a consequent uncertainty about food imports, gave rise to fresh worries. By July, retail food prices had risen by over 32 per cent in a year, and there was concern that in some industries, including agriculture, wages were failing to keep pace.[3] In these circumstances a special Departmental Committee was appointed under the chairmanship of Viscount Milner to consider the future course of food production in England and Wales, with particular reference to the harvest of 1916 and beyond.

The Milner Committee completed its deliberations with commendable speed, signing an interim report on 17 July, about a month after it had been appointed. This marked the first positive break with the philosophy of relying on market forces to achieve necessary adjustments in output levels. In the view of members, if farmers were to be persuaded to increase wheat production, they required the security of a guaranteed price of 45s. per quarter for a minimum of four years, to compensate them for abandoning the profitable livestock products which had served them well in the past. Many basically pastoral producers also lacked the machinery and manpower needed for a more labour intensive arable programme and this, too, had to be taken into account:

To obtain any substantial increase in the production of wheat, oats and potatoes . . . it will be necessary for farmers to sacrifice the comparative certainty of their present profits, to change some of their methods, to alter their rotations, and to increase their area of arable cultivation in the face of a shortage of labour. In addition, they will have to run the risk, not only of uncertain seasons, but also of a fall in the price of wheat at the conclusion of the War.... in order to ensure a general movement in that direction we consider it essential to guarantee a minimum price for home-grown wheat for a period of several years.[4]

The Committee stressed that the offering of a guarantee should not be regarded as an excuse by landlords to increase rentals. Instead encouragement should be given to farmers to pay higher wages, so as to compensate workers for war-time inflation. Finally, to ensure that agriculturists were given proper guidance on the crops they should grow, a network of county organisations must be created, based upon existing County Councils, and aided by smaller committees for each of the rural districts. It would be their task to liaise between the Board of Agriculture and the individual producer.

Although the Milner proposals had the backing of the President of the Board of Agriculture, Lord Selborne, who was particularly concerned at the threat from German submarines, he was unable to persuade his ministerial colleagues to act. After the matter had been discussed in Cabinet on 4 August, Herbert Asquith, the Prime Minister, informed the King that 'Lord Selborne's proposal to guarantee British farmers a setting price of 45/- per quarter for wheat during the next four years... found little favour, and will probably not be mooted again'.[5] It seemed to ministers that the immediate danger from submarines had waned, whilst the 1915 harvest both in Britain and the United States was likely to be well above average. In these circumstances a policy of inaction seemed justified. The only part of the Milner Committee report to be adopted was that creating County Agricultural Committees, but since in the early days these were large, unwieldy bodies, on which farmers served alongside members of the County Council who had no practical experience of agriculture, even that initiative had limited value.

Clearly this muted response disappointed the Milner Committee, and when its final report appeared in October, proposals were limited to such piecemeal suggestions as the necessity for increasing fertiliser supplies, the need to retain skilled labour on the farms, the importance of organising women's labour on a more effective basis, and the necessity for a continuation of the policy of releasing soldiers to assist at the busiest periods of the agricultural year.[6]

Farmers were thus left to their own devices to produce those commodities which were most profitable to them. And given the uncertainties of the grain market, plus the shortage of labour and the problems of securing machinery to till extra land, those men who had hitherto concentrated on pastoral farming made little effort to change their policy. Livestock numbers remained virtually unchanged and in 1916 not only did the wheat area fall back but the overall arable acreage dropped below the pre-war average.[7] Unfortunately, too, the 1916 harvest was not merely smaller in extent than that for 1915, but poorer in quality. At the same time the German submarine attack intensified once more and food prices rose sharply. By 1 July 1916, they averaged 61 per cent above the level of two years before, and this had increased to 68 per cent three months later.[8] In these circumstances, the Government's *laissez-faire* policies were no longer tenable, and even the possibility of food rationing was being mooted in Whitehall, though nothing came of it at the time. By the middle of November, demands for an official control of prices were growing, and on 27 November the first of these was introduced — for milk. During the following months the system of establishing fixed maximum prices was extended to virtually all agricultural products and regulations were imposed on their sale and distribution. The 4-lb loaf, for example, which had reached 11½d. by September 1917, was fixed at a maximum of 9d. in that month, while a maximum price for meat was also established. Milling ratios were successively raised, to secure the greatest possible amount of bread from a given quantity of grain, and the use of additives like potato flour was permitted.[9] By the end of September 1917, maximum prices were in operation for a whole range of commodities, including cheese, butter, jam, bacon, pickled herrings, meat, milk, potatoes and bread. In 1918 the list was extended further, to cover poultry, game, and eggs. The stabilisation of bread prices was achieved partly at the expense of British farmers, whose wheat was taken at lower prices than were being paid on the world market to foreign producers. The best and the worst qualities of home-grown meat were also sold at the same price, in order that 'the long and the short purses might in this respect be on an equality'.[10]

The inauguration of a policy of price control in the interests of the consumer was thus one early example of a departure from *laissez-faire* attitudes by the Asquith Government in the autumn of 1916. Another was the announcement by the President of the Board of Trade in October that a Wheat Commission was to be set up to take over all dealings in wheat, both home grown and imported. A third initiative was the appointment of an Agricultural Policy Sub-Committee, under the chairmanship of Lord Selborne, to advise on the post-war policy to be adopted for agriculture and to consider what steps were needed to meet the immediate food emergency of the winter of 1916/17. However, it was only following a change of administration in December 1916, with the appointment of David Lloyd George as Prime Minister, that a real sense of urgency was injected into the proceedings.

First, under the terms of the Defence of the Realm Act, powers were taken to decide upon land usage, in the national interest, and upon the crops which were to be grown. To carry out this policy small Executive Committees were to be formed by each of the County War Agricultural Committees. They were to have a maximum membership of seven and were to be appointed partly by the County Councils and partly by the ministry. Recruitment was to be confined largely to practical farmers, reinforced by a few landowners and land agents. At local level they were to be assisted by district committees and in some cases by parish representatives. Later the Executive Committees set up specialist groups to cover such topics as land cultivation, the supply of labour, the provision of machinery and, in 1918, the supply of recruits for the Army and the retention of those men needed on the land for essential work.

But in the initial stages during the winter of 1916/17, the main task of the Committees was to ensure that farmers cultivated their holdings efficiently. Where necessary in the national interest, this could mean the compulsory conversion of grassland to arable purposes. Ultimately the intention was to increase the arable area by 3m. acres compared to the 1916 position and to return to the position of the early 1870s when the land of Britain had fed 26m. people instead of the 16m. fed under the predominantly livestock regime of 1914.[11] The policy of limiting Government action to encouragement and exhortation adopted in 1914 had given way to a far sterner approach two years later.

Under the first Cultivation of Lands Order issued in January

1917, powers were given to the Committees to enter upon and survey land, to waive restrictive covenants on its cultivation imposed by landowners, to issue directions as to the crops to be raised in the future, and to draw up schemes for the tillage of derelict or waste land. As a last resort, if an occupier proved unable or unwilling to raise his husbandry standards, he could be evicted from his holding and the land cultivated under the aegis of the Committee itself. It was an unprecedented interference with private property rights and was reinforced by the fact that any farmer who refused to comply with notices relating to the crops to be grown on his holding could be fined or even imprisoned.[12]

By the end of January 1917, most of the Executive Committees had begun preliminary surveys of their particular county and were taking steps to stimulate cultivation of the desired cereal crops and to regulate the stocking of land. The first report to arrive was that for West Sussex, and its details can be regarded as fairly typical. Out of 123,000 acres investigated, it was discovered that 28,000 were inadequately cultivated and would have to be improved. In addition, a total of 4,370 acres of permanent pasture were to be converted to arable purposes for the growing of oats and potatoes.

However, to farmers accustomed to tilling their holdings as they thought fit, subject only to such restrictions as their landlord might impose, these new initiatives seemed an intolerable infringement of their freedom of action. Many argued that even if grassland were broken up, it would be unsuitable for the growing of wheat, because of the vulnerability of that crop to attacks by wire-worms and other pests on newly ploughed pastures. They condemned the advocates of the increased tillage programme as 'plough-maniacs', and pointed to the loss of meat and dairy produce which would follow such policies. Others resented the fact that carefully maintained grassland or acreages devoted to specialist crops like hops or bulbs might have to be converted to cereal growing without the occupier having even the right of appeal to an outside arbitrator. Hop producers were particularly affected, with the Government assuming control of the brewing industry in 1917, and cutting back on the barrels of beer brewed by something like two-thirds compared to the 1914 level.[13] In counties like Kent and Herefordshire, where hop cultivation was of major importance, the outcome was clear.

Hop acreage in the former county had dropped from 22,626 in 1914 to 9,739 in 1918, while in the latter the respective figures were 5,507 and 2,331. Over the same period the acreage of wheat in Kent had jumped from 46,464 to 71,912 and in Herefordshire from 24,264 to 45,982.[14] This was the kind of result the corn production programme was designed to achieve.

The manner in which the restrictions and regulations worked out at farm level is shown by the records of the various Executive Committees. Thus, in May 1917, the Bedfordshire Committee informed nurserymen at Biggleswade who were using 'good land for the purpose of flower growing' that the soil must be prepared for a cereal crop in 1918, with notice to that effect served forthwith; 'also informing them that the further growing of flowers during the War must be discontinued'.[15] This Committee was much bothered by the depredations of game, and even employed its own expert to catch rabbits on the property of offending landowners. The estate of Mr Francis Pym at Everton was a frequent recipient of attention in this connection.[16] But complaints were also made to many other landowners.

In Essex, entries in the Minute Book of the Executive Committee for 4 December 1917, include an agreement to take over a farm whose occupier had 'more land than he could manage', and the issuing of an order to another man 'forbidding the planting of black currant bushes and requiring arable cultivation of 6 acres'.[17] On a further occasion a farmer was firmly informed that he must take action within a fortnight to clean ditches, and bring his land back to an acceptable state of cultivation. But sometimes more drastic measures were needed. On 10 April 1917, an Essex land agent wrote to the owner of one farm, informing her that the County Committee was dissatisfied with production levels achieved by the occupier:

It has been necessary for me to attend before the Committee in London to explain the matter and also to go to Purleigh to see Mr. Wilkin [the errant farmer]. As the latter is 85 years of age and very short of labour it is not possible for him to improve matters, but he quite agrees more ought to be done with the land, and he is quite willing to give up under the pressure of the Committee, and let another tenant take it on who will do better in the National interest at the present crisis. . . .

I have been aware for some time that poor old Wilkin has got behind with his cultivation, but it is very difficult to do anything with an old gentleman of his age, and I knew you would not wish me to turn him out until we were compelled to do so. I can assure you that the present crisis has not arisen through any action of mine, but is entirely due to the Agricultural Committee, and this Mr.Wilkin quite understands.[18]

The agent was able to arrange for another tenant to take over the holding, and by September was reporting a rapid improvement in cultivation standards. Six fields had been ploughed up which 'old Mr. Wilkin had allowed to "tumble down" to grass. They looked very good and clean, and will no doubt produce good crops of wheat next year'. In such cases landowners were doubtless glad to get rid of an incompetent tenant without themselves incurring the odium of evicting him.

But in most instances less severe action was needed. Existing occupiers normally agreed to mend their ways when their deficiencies were pointed out to them. To help in this direction the Executive Committees were allowed to recommend the granting of credit to farmers for a period of nine months — at 5 per cent interest — to enable them to purchase fertilisers or to hire essential equipment needed to comply with the orders. In other cases Committees would hire out equipment under their own direction to assist farmers in need, while in Bedfordshire a farm foreman was recruited, presumably to supervise the tillage of holdings in hand or to provide guidance for the less efficient cultivators.

By the end of 1918, the Executive Committees on a national basis were farming about 125 holdings of more than 50 acres in area, the total acreage in hand being almost 24,000. Essex with 2,500 and Kent with 1,900 acres were at the head of the list. In many cases the Committees preferred to entrust the management of the holdings to a skilled local farmer, 'who took a natural pride in the task of converting a wilderness into a cornfield'. In that way some of the worst managed farm land in the country was brought back into cultivation.[19] This policy also continued for a short period after the War had ended, and it was not until the spring of 1919 that the Committees were instructed finally to hand back to the owners land taken into temporary occupation, and to sell the horses, tractors, and machinery they had acquired to assist with the tillage programme.[20]

Overall, something like 100,000 notices, requiring farmers to increase their arable acreage, were issued by the various Executive Committees. In the vast majority of instances the orders were carried out willingly, once the seriousness of the situation was understood. Nevertheless most Committees, under Board of Agriculture guidance, followed the example of Essex, where a target 'plough up' acreage of 85,000 was set for 1917 and of 64,000 for 1918. Here it was decided that in order to ensure 'that occupiers and owners who agreed voluntarily to the breaking up of grassland should be in no worse position to claim for any compensation which might be awarded', formal notices under the terms of the Defence of the Realm Regulations were to be issued to all.[21] There was also concern to give tenant farmers protection against post-war claims for breaches of the terms of leases which forbade the ploughing of established pastureland. Landowners were left instead to claim for damage done to their land from the Losses Commission set up to deal with all cases of damage to civilian property.[22] The signing of thousands of ploughing orders by the chairmen or executive officers of the various County Committees inevitably became a considerable burden on their time and energy during 1917 and 1918. Yet, out of more than 100,000 orders issued in the nation as a whole, prosecutions for non-compliance had to be instituted in 254 cases only. In 236 of these convictions were obtained.[23] Nevertheless, as the President of the Board of Agriculture sadly admitted, it was unavoidable that this kind of vigorous policy, persistently pursued, should make enemies: 'it caused hardships and loss to individuals. Carried out on an extensive scale with the utmost speed, it was inevitable that there should be mistakes. In some districts... the ploughing of pasture was pressed when the season was too advanced for the land to be cropped with reasonable prospects of success'.[24] Examples of poor cereal yields on newly ploughed land were publicised widely in both press and Parliament by critics of the 'plough up' programme. But in the long run the Board itself considered that the campaign had been justified, with output of wheat, barley, oats, rye, mixed corn, peas, beans and potatoes in 1918 amounting to over 18m. tons, compared to about 14m. tons produced in 1914. In other words, British agriculture at the end of the War was feeding the population for the equivalent of 155 days in the year, as compared to only 125 days at its outbreak.[25]

The 'plough up' campaign, with the regulations and restrictions which accompanied it from December 1916, was perhaps the clearest indicator of the Government's determination to control food production for the remainder of the War. As the instrument for that interventionist approach, a special Food Production Department was set up within the Board of Agriculture in January 1917. It had the task of overseeing the distribution of labour, machinery and supplies of feeding stuffs, fertilisers, and other essential commodities. It also informed the County Committees of the acreages they were to plant with grain and potatoes, and the grassland which would consequently have to be ploughed to secure that output. It was their duty to decide on priorities at local level. The Food Production Department was to remain in existence until 31 March 1919, when its remaining duties were incorporated in the Board of Agriculture.

In the long run there is little doubt that farmers suffered financially from the new policies. During the first two years of the War, paying little tax and free to raise the crops and livestock which paid them best, they had seen their incomes rise sharply. But in 1917-18 that position changed as cropping restrictions, rising input prices for fertilisers, seed, and machinery, and a firmer tax policy were applied. Under the 1918 Finance Act it was decided that farmers' taxable income should be fixed in future at double their rental, unless they could produce proper accounts which would demonstrate the actual income earned.[26] Up to 1915, taxable income had been assessed at a mere one-third of the rental, and even in 1915 this had been raised to the equivalent of rental payments only. Although angry cries were heard in farming circles during 1918 that this constituted a levying of 'double income-tax', most observers recognised it as a belated attempt to impose a fairer distribution of the tax burden. It also had the side effect of encouraging farmers to keep satisfactory accounts, in order that they could produce an accurate statement of taxable income to replace the rough and ready calculations of the double rental approach. Greater cost consciousness could only be in the long term interests of the industry.

Overall, one recent historian has suggested that real farm profits in 1915 were 22 per cent above the levels of 1914, which were themselves 6 per cent above the pre-war average, and that these continued to rise until 1918, when a change of direction occurred. Although still well above the pre-war level, or indeed of the position during the early War years, real farm profits in 1918, he suggests, were 9 per cent below those for 1917.[27] Contemporary financial records, scanty in number and often unsatisfactory in presentation though they may be, tend to bear this out. Thus in 1918 material collected from twenty-six farms, covering just over 8,000 acres in different parts of the country, reveal sharply rising gross profits in 1915-16, as Table 1 demonstrates. Of the acreage covered by this survey, 46 per cent was arable in 1913-14 and 49 per cent in 1917-18:

Table 1: Gross profits per acre on twenty-six farms

	Per Acre	Cash Increase/ Decrease on 1913-14	% Increase/ Decrease on 1913-14
	£ s. d.	£ s. d.	
1913-14	5 10	—	—
1914-15	4 7	(1 3)	− 21.4
1915-16	1 13 8	1 7 10	+ 477.1
1916-17	1 11 10	1 6 0	+ 445.7
1917-18	1 11 9	1 5 11	+ 444.3

N.B. These figures were calculated by subtracting each farmer's payments from his receipts. Although input prices like fertilisers, feeding stuffs, seeds, machinery, etc. were rising sharply, e.g. fertilisers rose by an estimated 123 per cent, feeding stuffs by 172 per cent, and seeds by 219 per cent between 1913-14 and 1917-18, shortages and changes in farming methods led to farmers buying smaller quantities of these than pre-war. Some of their profits were thus achieved by policies likely to leave the land in a poorer state of fertility at the end of the War.

Calculated from *Report of the Committee Appointed by the Agricultural Wages Board to Enquire into the Financial Result of the Occupation of Agricultural Land and the Cost of Living of Rural Workers*, P.P. 1919, Vol. VIII, 15. Hereafter cited as *1919 Report*.

But perhaps the most far-reaching sign of the interventionist approach adopted by the Lloyd George Government came in February 1917, when the new President of the Board of Agriculture, Rowland Prothero, introduced his Corn Production Bill. Prothero had been a member of the Milner Committee and had supported the system of guaranteed prices proposed by that Committee in July 1915. His commitment to the policy was reinforced in January 1917 by the signing of the Interim Report of the Selborne Sub-Committee which had been appointed five months earlier to draw up plans for the future development of British agriculture. Selborne called for a system of price guarantees to be applied to both wheat and oats and to remain in operation for at least four years. Barley was omitted — both then and later — partly in deference to the views of the temperance movement. Alongside this, plans were to be made for a permanent increase in the area of arable land compared to the situation before 1914. In a passage which marked a clear break with the earlier *laissez-faire* approach to farming, as well as a willingness to learn from German experience, the Sub-Committee demanded a permanent role for the state in the nation's agricultural affairs.

Nothing in agriculture [it declared] can be done by the wave of a magician's wand. Results can only be produced in the United Kingdom as in Germany by a constant and consistent policy. The State must adopt such a policy and formulate it publicly as the future basis of British agriculture, and explain to the nation that it is founded in the highest considerations of the common weal. It must be explained to landowners, farmers, and agricultural labourers alike that the experience of this War has shown that the methods and results of land management and of farming are matters involving the safety of the State, and are not of concern only to the interest of individuals. They must be plainly told that the security and welfare of the State demand that the agricultural land of the country must gradually be made to yield its maximum production both in foodstuffs and in timber ... much grass land must be reconverted into arable; the sugar-beet industry and the manufacture of potato products can be introduced into British agriculture to its great advantage; estates must be managed with a single eye to maximum production; capital must be attracted to the industrial equipment and improvement of the land and to the operations of intensive farming; agricultural labourers must be provided with an adequate supply of good cottages; small holdings both of owners and of occupiers must be fostered to provide a "ladder" for the agricultural labourer and for the demobilised sailors and soldiers; the organisation of agriculture must be developed; the country must be permeated with a complete system of agricultural education.[28]

The Sub-Committee also recommended that the Board of Agriculture should retain in perpetuity some of the powers to control land usage which had been assumed under the Defence of the Realm Act. If price guarantees were to be offered, then the nation should require in response a minimum standard of efficiency in the tillage and management of its soil. Where tenants defaulted on their obligations to farm efficiently, their occupation of the land should be terminated, or the Board should arrange to take over any estate which was neglected for a minimum period of five years. Only by the promotion of an active partnership between landowners, farmers, and the Board of Agriculture could an improvement in farming be secured.[29]

For the workers, Selborne recommended that a minimum wage should be fixed in each county, in order to compensate for the very sharp rise in prices which had already taken place. Significantly, in spite of the piecemeal attempts at controlling the price of milk and some kinds of potatoes, average retail food prices at the beginning of February 1917 were 89 per cent above the level for July 1914, with potatoes particularly scarce after the bad harvest of 1916. Wage rates, on the other hand, were in most counties only about 60 or 70 per cent above the 1914 level, and in some, like Cambridgeshire and Wiltshire, the advance was smaller than that.[30] Table 2 gives details of changes in wages per acre on the twenty-six farms covered in Table 1. The difference between the sharp rise in profits and the slow increase in wage costs which those two tables demonstrate is very clear. Viscount Milner's hope that market forces and the greater demand for labour created by war-time conditions would force up workers' wages had thus been disappointed. More positive policies were clearly needed.

Table 2: Wages per acre on twenty-six farms

	Per Acre s. d.	Cash Increase on 1913-14 s. d.	% Increase on 1913-14
1913-14	28 7	—	—
1914-15	29 8	1 1	3.8
1915-16	31 10	3 3	11.3
1916-17	36 10	8 3	28.8
1917-18	44 1	15 6	54.2

N.B. By the summer of 1917 a national minimum wage of 25s per week had been established for able-bodied labourers. The period covered by the accounts ends at Lady Day 1918.

Calculated from *1919 Report*, 15.

Armed with the recommendations of the Selborne Sub-Committee, therefore, and with knowledge gained as a member of the earlier Milner Committee, Prothero acted. In February 1917 he introduced the Corn Production Bill to Parliament. After lengthy debates it passed into law in August. In Part I provision was made for the offering of guaranteed minimum prices for wheat and oats, albeit at levels below the current buying price of the Food Ministry for the harvest of 1917 and 1918, and on a descending scale for four further years. Separate arrangements were made to provide a guaranteed price for potatoes:

Table 3: Guaranteed prices for wheat and oats in 1917 Corn Production Act

	Wheat Price, per quarter	Oats Price, per quarter
1917	60s.	38s. 6d.
1918 ⎫ 1919 ⎭	55s.	32s. 0d.
1920 ⎫ 1921 ⎬ 1922 ⎭	45s.	24s. 0d.

N.B. In April 1917, the current buying prices offered by the Ministry of Food were 78s. per quarter for wheat and 55s. per quarter for oats.

In practice, the guarantees were little more than gestures to engender confidence in the industry, for throughout the War, market prices remained above the guarantees offered, and no deficiency payments were needed.

Part II of the Act dealt with the question of workers' wages. A Central Wages Board was to be established, on which would serve representatives of the farmers and the labourers, together with independent members nominated by the Board of Agriculture itself. It would be aided in its task by district committees, and would have as its objective the establishing of minimum wages for each county in England and Wales. Under the Act, any employer who paid his worker less than the minimum could be fined up to £20, plus a fine up to £1 for each day 'on which the offence is continued after conviction therefor'.[31] This arrangement, which provided for a continuing review of wage rates, linked to a standard working week, was something for which the agricultural workers' trade unions had been pressing for more than half a decade. Its effect in raising living standards in rural areas will be considered in chapter 9. Suffice it here to point out that an immediate national minimum wage of 25s. per week was established, leading to an increase in earnings for labourers in some of the worst paid areas. In addition, with the agricultural unions now brought into the wage negotiating machinery at national and district level, there was a rapid rise in membership, with the National Agricultural Labourers' and Rural Workers' Union increasing the number of its branches from 350 in 1914 and 402 in 1917 to 1,537 in 1918 and 2,583 a year later. By the latter year this Union was claiming a membership of 170,749, while the other major trade union, the Workers' Union estimated its agricultural membership to be well over 100,000 by the summer of 1919.[32] At the start of 1917 that union's organisation in agriculture had been almost extinguished. It seems likely that the figures were exaggerated, but even more conservative estimates suggest a five-fold increase in National Union membership between 1917 and 1918.[33] George Dallas, the Workers' Union chief organiser for London and the Home Counties, set the mood when he called on labourers to take advantage of their new bargaining position to show 'farmers and landlords that the workers of England mean to end the tyranny of the countryside'.

The third Part of the Corn Production Act related to farm

rentals. Tenants were to be protected from all increases in rent which were attributable to the introduction of guaranteed prices, and any tenant faced with a demand for a higher payment could insist upon arbitration to ascertain whether the claim was justified or not. Unfortunately, the legislation did not give security of tenure where estates changed hands, and in the upsurge of land sales during the final year of the War, many farmers were faced with the option of receiving notice to quit from a new owner, anxious to raise rents, or else buying their farm for themselves. A large number chose the latter in a spirit of optimism engendered by the prosperous war-time conditions. Only in the difficult years of the early 1920s and beyond did they discover the true cost of the burden they had incurred.

Equally, on those estates where land did *not* change hands, landowners often felt cheated as they saw rents pegged at a time when their own outgoings were increasing sharply and farming profits were advancing steeply. 'You can see the profits oozing out of the farmers', wrote the agent of the Burton Constable estate in Yorkshire bitterly during 1917, 'but the unfortunate landlord doesn't get any look in, though I admit he gets his rent paid in full and punctually. However with one old enough, as I am, to remember what happened in the lean years of the late 80s and early 90s, the tenants ought to be weighing in with 10, 15 or 20 per cent added to their rents to make it anything like square'.[34]

Finally, Part IV of the Act reaffirmed the powers of the Board of Agriculture and the County War Agricultural Executive Committees over land cultivation and stocking, and the issuing of compulsory cropping orders. The only change was that following complaints from a minority of farmers and landowners, who felt themselves aggrieved by the stringent directives of the Executive Committees, proposals were included to introduce an appeals procedure involving an independent arbitrator. This was to come into operation either at the end of one year or at the close of hostilities, whichever should be the sooner.

In practice, even that concession proved illusory. In the summer of 1918, with the Germans engaged upon their last great offensive of the War, it was decided that to allow appeals against cropping orders, however few these might be, would seriously hamper the work of the Board of Agriculture in increasing food output.[35] For this reason, Rowland Prothero decided to introduce a fresh Bill, postponing until after the end of the War the introduction of an independent appeals procedure. He admitted that it broke promises made the previous year but argued that nothing must be allowed to interfere with the vital food needs of the country. The only compensation was that because of existing labour shortages and the difficulties of carrying out further compulsory 'plough up' campaigns, the issuing of fresh orders to break up grassland would be ended, though continuing emphasis was placed upon the need to increase cereal acreage wherever possible. In addition, the right of appeal to an arbitrator was to be allowed to those tenants who were in danger of being displaced for unsatisfactory husbandry.

These gestures were insufficient to satisfy his critics, and the legislation was greeted with considerable hostility, both in Parliament and outside. The familiar arguments were deployed that hastily ploughed and inadequately prepared former grassland had already failed to yield worthwhile crops. There were also disagreements over what constituted 'bad farming'. One critic declared: 'All farmers differ with regard to the best methods of cultivating their land and all farms differ.... It is impossible for any man, however capable, to go round the country and by merely walking over a field decide whether or not it is being cultivated in the proper way.'[36] Another man claimed that many agriculturists were jealous of one another, and did not like fellow farmers who were members of the Executive Committee in their area 'going on to their farms and saying how they ought to farm the land'.[37]

There is little doubt that the frank comments passed upon the cultivation standards of some farmers by the Committees aroused resentment among their recipients. A survey of southeast Derbyshire carried out in 1917, for example, concluded that of eight farms reported upon in the parish of Sandiacre only one could be described as good. Of one man, cultivating 107 acres of grass and 40 acres of arable, it was stated: 'This farm is in a shocking state. The tenant would require mechanical cultivation, considerable labour & also financial aid to get it into anything like condition.' Despite that disapproval, he weathered the storm, and was still in the parish in the early 1920s. Similarly another Sandiacre cultivator, with 16½ acres of arable, was said to have allowed his land to get into a 'pitiable condition, full of weeds, & no attempt . . . made to eliminate them. . . . He has also a large field in Risley parish: been in his possession 3 years, already depreciated badly. It was in excellent condition when he took it. . . . A very strong line ought to be taken with this man'.[38] Doubtless Committee members had every justification for their strictures, but such honesty was hardly likely to win them friends among a large segment of the farming fraternity.

Prothero was unmoved by all the protests, however, pointing out that the Executive and District Committee members normally comprised some of the most experienced and efficient farmers and land agents in a county, and that they were well able to judge husbandry standards. He also maintained that charges of crop losses caused by attacks from pests were exaggerated, and pointed to the overall increase in food production which had been secured.

> Without the forward policy of the plough, [he wrote later] agriculture must have dwindled under the pressure of the war. The tillage area would have continued to contract . . . the land would have been stripped of labour; and the industry would have suffered injuries from which the present generation would have found it difficult to recover. . . . The national value of the industry, for the first time for many years, was recognised. The sight of crops for human food, growing all over the country in exceptional abundance was encouraging. It gave a sense of security. Upon a people whose nerves were strained by prolonged effort, the psychological effect was important. During the anxious months of the spring and early summer of 1918, the influence was especially useful.[39]

But his critics were not persuaded, and their dissatisfaction was reinforced by the issuing of the final report of the Selborne Sub-Committee early in 1918. For this recommended that powers similar to those included in the Corn Production Act should be continued indefinitely. 'Our conception of the Board of Agriculture', the Report declared, 'is as of a great department of State charged with the care of agriculture in its widest sense, and with the promotion of the welfare of rural as distinct from urban life. Its duty should be to assist and stimulate agriculture by every possible means as a basic national industry'. After the War a network of statutory committees must be set up to replace the War Agricultural Committees of the County Councils, and with each Committee empowered to form District Sub-Committees. In Selborne's view there should be a permanent adoption of policies likely to increase the nation's self-sufficiency in agricultural products: 'the Corn Production Act has been passed as a war measure, and is therefore a temporary Act. We must renew our assurance with all the earnestness at our command that, unless after the war the principles of that Act are . . . embodied in a permanent statute, there can be no hope of the people of the United Kingdom becoming emancipated from dependence on supplies of foodstuffs brought from overseas, or of the increase of our rural population'.[40] As Edith Whetham has pointed out, the ultimate aim was to remove the incompetent and the drunkard, while 'the "practical man who practised the errors of his forefathers" would be eliminated in favour of technically trained young men, who had been taught not only the wisdom of their predecessors but also the agricultural sciences and the mysteries of book-keeping, so that they could calculate their costs of production to a fraction of a penny per gallon of milk'.[41] To this scheme would be linked plans to establish a 'farming ladder' and to combat the pre-war problem of rural depopulation by setting up colonies of smallholders. Many of these would be recruited from ex-soldiers, largely financed by government loans, and established on land reclaimed from formerly under-utilised moorland and marsh. It was hoped that unlike the individualistic small farmers of the older generation, these newcomers would support co-operative marketing and buying societies, and would carry into civilian life some of the discipline they had learned in the armed forces.

Whatever the virtues of such a comprehensive plan, however, most landowners and farmers objected on principle to proposals which might mean that after the War they would be subjected to controls which could involve 'the loss of their land, their homes, and their livelihood'.[42] The nebulous claims of national advantage and improved efficiency were not regarded as sufficient compensation for such a programme of intervention.

Nor was it only over the question of cropping regulations and husbandry standards that friction arose between farmers and the State. Some of the maximum price regulations, however popular among consumers, were disliked by farmers — notably that under which British bread-making wheat was purchased at a lower maximum price than was paid for supplies secured from abroad. Restrictions on the price of seed potatoes, introduced early in 1917, were also resented by the growers, and a number of cases occurred where farmers were prosecuted for selling above the authorised price. Thus in the autumn of 1917, one producer near Wisbech was fined £140 for selling seed potatoes at more than the maximum price of £13. 'On four transactions he made a profit of £108 17s. 6d.', reported the *National Food Journal*. 'The defence was that [the man], who is only in a small way of business, was ignorant of the fixed price. The fine was £35 in respect of each of the four cases'.[43] The same issue of the *Journal* included details concerning another farmer, also charged at Wisbech with selling seed potatoes at above the controlled price, by which he made an illegal profit of £12. In this case the fine was £80. Similarly a Lancashire farmer was fined £15 for selling milk above the fixed price, and a Huntingdonshire man, £20 for 'failing to furnish information' to the relevant Executive Committee 'as to sales of his produce'.

Elsewhere milk retailers might refuse to make deliveries to customers as a protest against what they considered the inadequate payments they were receiving. This happened at Sawbridgeworth in the late autumn of 1918, with one farmer firmly stating that the maximum price for delivered milk should be raised to 3s. per gallon, 'this being the price at which it was being sold in adjoining parishes. If the price was raised as he... desired he would do all he could to increase production but otherwise he would not trouble & would sell one or more of his cows'. After due deliberation, the Food Control Committee decided to accede to his demands; the price of delivered milk was raised to 3s. a gallon, while for undelivered it remained at 2s. 8d., as before.[44]

Other problems arose when farmers defied the regulations prohibiting the feeding of grain suitable for human consumption to livestock, or when they had to apply to the authorities for permission to feed tail or damaged corn to their own animals. Restrictions on the slaughtering of livestock, designed to regulate supplies of meat to the consumer, also limited sales outlets and interfered with the marketing arrangements of producers. They meant, too, that during the autumn of 1918 cattle and sheep sent for slaughter were sometimes returned to farmers, even where the shortage of feeding stuffs meant that the animals would lose condition before an approved market could be found for them.[45] Small wonder that in September, the Dunstable branch of the National Farmers' Union passed a resolution protesting at the 'innumerable arbitrary Orders and restrictions constantly issued by ever increasing hordes of officials' and agreeing 'to refuse to send in applications for permits to use their own grindings and tail corn necessary for feeding their own stock. We consider that a large number of the Orders lately issued imply that the farmer is not to be trusted and does not know how to conduct his business as well as the inexperienced officials placed over him'. A similar resolution was passed by the nearby Tring and District Branch in Hertfordshire at about the same time.[46] But not until November 1918 were the restrictions on meat slaughtering eased.

Alongside these were cases of men who combined farming and milling and who failed to maintain a sufficiently high milling ratio. On the latter score, a farmer and miller from the Worksop area was fined £23 for offences against the flour orders — £10 for extracting only 48.5 per cent instead of 71.25 per cent of flour from an admixture of barley and wheat, and £1 each on 13 summonses for failing to make returns. A Bedfordshire man who allowed his stack of wheat to be damaged by rats, so that out of sixty or seventy quarters, five or six bushels had been destroyed, was fined £50. Even after the War had ended the restrictions remained in force for some time, and early in January 1919, an 81-year-old woman farmer from Great Holland, Essex, was fined the substantial sum of £227 for using wheat to feed to poultry, despite repeated warnings. Accordingly to the report in the *National Food Journal*, she 'claimed to obey the laws of God', and presumably felt free to ignore those drawn up by mere mortals at Westminster![47]

Significantly some of the Executive Committees, too, came to resent the endless stream of orders and directives to which they were subjected. As early as July 1917, the Bedfordshire Committee passed a series of resolutions expressing its view that;

> The multiplicity of Orders, affecting Agriculture, which have been issued have undoubtedly caused irritation, confusion and distrust amongst farmers, and have at least in some cases been unnecessary and arbitrary....

The Sale of Horses Order 1917 needs further amendment to enable persons carrying on trades and businesses of National importance to purchase horses and to retain them for the purposes of such trades. . . .

There should be no commandeering of property or produce without fair and full payment or compensation.

Security and confidence are two great incentives to food production and it is necessary that the Government should act with the greatest caution in all matters affecting Agriculture, thereby commanding the confidence of farmers, if the greatest possible output is to be obtained from the land.[48]

Nevertheless, despite such reservations, there is little doubt that a combined system of regulation and punishment was needed to combat the desperate food situation in which Britain found herself during the last two years of the War. But to farmers, unused to keeping records, or even to following any directions but their own inclinations and perhaps their landlord's covenants, in cultivating their holdings, this upsurge of bureaucratic interference was highly unwelcome. It was something which they were determined should cease with the ending of hostilities. And although many continued to value the security offered by guaranteed prices, a number were prepared to forego even these in the interests of recovering their independence of action, once the Armistice came.

This was made clear by the Majority Interim Report of the Royal Commission on Agriculture, which stated in December 1919 that a 'considerable body of evidence' had been received from farmers showing their doubts about the benefits secured from guaranteed cereal prices. 'It was said by witnesses speaking on behalf of the National Farmers' Unions, which represent together over 100,000 occupiers, that the farmers were prepared, if freed from control of their farming operations and permitted to make their own bargains in the labour and produce market, to carry on their industry in a manner satisfactory to themselves without guarantees from the State'.[49]

Significantly, however, the Majority Report, signed by twelve Commission members, came out in favour of continuing the system of guarantees and, indeed, extending it to cover barley, despite the views of the temperance movement. They argued that over a considerable area of the country barley could be grown more economically than any other cereal. The Report then continued:

> We think it desirable that the State should possess the power of insuring that the objects for which guarantees are given will be attained. We recommend, therefore, that coupled with a system of guarantees should go definite powers of oversight and control of farming operations. We are of opinion that, if found necessary, the powers under Part IV of the Corn Production Act should be extended so as to enable the Boards of Agriculture, or the County Committees, to take effective action in the Courts or otherwise against any land-owner or farmer who impedes or neglects to carry out the orders issued by them for the better cultivation of the holding. Only in extreme cases do we think that these authorities should relieve a tenant of his holding. We consider that both the owner and the occupier of land owe the duty to the State of seeing that the holding is cultivated according to the rules of good husbandry; and that no land capable of cultivation should be allowed to lie unproductive, or should be imperfectly cultivated.[50]

These arguments, advocating action for the benefit of the community at large, were in marked contrast to the pre-1914 policy of relying upon market forces and individual judgment to govern farming affairs. They were an indication of the changed opinion engendered in some quarters by the experiences of the War. But eleven members of the Commission disagreed with this interventionist stance and they produced a report of their own which argued that there was no immediate risk of grain prices falling to unremunerative levels — a most unhappy hostage to fortune. Consequently, there was no need for guarantees to be offered. The financial position of agriculture had already improved, and they saw little merit in embarking upon a policy which involved the expenditure of public funds 'in diverting agriculture into uneconomic fields'. Although they believed that the State had a residual right to require the holders of land to cultivate it efficiently, they were opposed to the close controls exercised during the War being applied to peacetime conditions. In their view the farmer should be free to use his own judgement as to what to produce and how to produce it. They concluded by recommending that 'farmers be informed that they shall be left free to cultivate their land in such manner as they deem best, in accordance with the rules of good husbandry'.[51]

Confronted by these conflicting arguments the Government decided to retain the guarantee system, and in 1920 introduced the Agriculture Act, which was designed to continue those arrangements. The new minimum prices were to come into operation from August 1921 and were to continue indefinitely until such time as four years' notice of their termination had been given by Order in Council.[52] However, in the following year grain prices began to move sharply downwards, and with the possibility of heavy deficiency payments being made to farmers for the first time, under the guarantees, there was alarm in official circles. The Act was abruptly repealed, with farmers given compensatory payment on an acreage basis for the 1921 harvest only. The sum involved was £19.7m. and after its disbursement the industry was abandoned to the pressures of world competition and a severe post-war depression.[53] For years to come that incident, and the failure to give the notice agreed in the Agriculture Act for the termination of the guarantees, was regarded by farmers as a cynical political betrayal. Even in the mid-1930s there were those who claimed to have purchased their farms 'on the strength of the Coalition Government's Corn Production Act', and then to have found their investment become a millstone round their neck when the cash buffer on which they had counted was swept away.[54]

For the workers, too, the 1921 legislation was a 'betrayal' since they lost the protection of the Wages Board machinery which had been so laboriously constructed less than four years before. Both the National Union and the Workers' Union organised protest meetings and warned that farmers were seeking to cut wage rates even before the legislation came into effect on 1 October. But all protest was in vain. Over the succeeding months workers' earnings inexorably fell, as farmers desperately sought to cut their labour bills.

Of course it could be argued that those agriculturists who had complained bitterly of the State's 'interference' in the good days were now able to see the weakness of their arguments once conditions turned against British farming. But there were others like F.D. Acland, who had acted as Parliamentary Secretary for Agriculture between May 1915 and December 1916, who saw the repeal Bill as undermining the trust and co-operation which were essential if agriculture were to flourish. The financial disaster which would inevitably face many arable producers after repeal would be blamed upon the Government and its successors rather than upon world competition: 'It is important that farmers should regard the experts of the Ministry of Agriculture, not as tricky or ignorant bureaucrats, but as anxious to assist them. Now the Board and all its servants will be handicapped for years.'[55] In chapter 10 the difficult position of farmers and their workers during the inter-war years will be examined in more detail. In the meantime, we must return to the broader problems faced within the countryside during 1914 and beyond, as increasing quantities of men and materials were sucked into the deepening conflict.

Chapter 4

The Farmers and the Military: 1914-18

'What immediately followed was a nightmare.... First came the engineers, and their needs meant that half the farmhouse was commandeered for offices and lodgings. The first camp site chosen and surveyed was on the new pasture land which lay opposite the farmhouse on the south side of the main road.... Then, a steady stream of traction engines began to haul material... and, as soon as some huts were erected to house them, a swarm of strange workmen arrived to build the camp.... In the midst of this welter of war preparations [the farmer] walked about, feeling that he had been suddenly dispossessed of everything in life which he valued. Every day came a demand for more land or the use of still another portion of his farm buildings. No one paid any attention to him, save to tell him that this or that piece of his property had been requisitioned'. A.G. Street, *The Gentleman of the Party*, London 1944 edn, 141-2, 149.

As the War proceeded along its remorseless course, rural life in general and agricultural activities in particular, became more and more affected by the military demands made upon them. That applied especially to labour, with around a quarter of a million men eventually recruited from farming to serve in the Armed Forces or in other areas of war production, such as the munitions factories and the construction and running of aerodromes and military camps. This compares with a total of about $1\frac{1}{4}$ million male farmers, bailiffs, labourers, woodmen, etc. recorded as employed on the land in 1911. Of these, 42.5 per cent were between 19 and 40 years, which was the age group most vulnerable to military recruitment.[1] Their numbers were subsequently supplemented by youngsters who reached the minimum age for enlistment during the War itself. Already by January 1915, an estimated 15.6 per cent of the farm labourers of England had left the industry for other employment, although the number of male labourers actually at work was only 12.4 per cent below the level of January 1914.[2] In these early days, farmers were able to make good a considerable part of the deficiency by the use of retired workers and those invalided out of the forces. But as the months went by that grew more difficult as rural and industrial communities alike were influenced by the recruitment drives. By 30 April 1915, around 40 per cent of the male population of military age in Dorset was estimated to have joined up, 35.5 per cent of that in Westmorland, and 34.6 per cent of that in Norfolk. Other rural areas making a major initial contribution included the Welsh counties of Flint (with 39.6 per cent of those of military age enlisted) and Brecknock (with 35.1 per cent).[3] They may be compared with recruitment figures of 36.3 per cent for London, 34.5 per cent for Lancashire, and 43.2 per cent for Northumberland, with its mixture of mining and agriculture. In Essex, too, cases were quoted of farmers who had seen the departure of more than half their workers.[4]

Inevitably this gave rise to complaints in agricultural circles. The *Farmer and Stockbreeder* plaintively pointed out in February 1915 that the wet winter season and the shortage of labour were preventing cultivators from responding to the appeals to grow more grain: 'they cannot work shorthanded on a system which tends to increase the employment of labour'. While from Brecon came the report: 'I do not know what we are going to do with labour so scarce. We must let other work, fencing, etc., stand for a year, and grow all the corn we can'.[5]

During the months and years which followed, these pressures intensified. Unfortunately no statistics exist to show the precise occupations of those who joined up, but Board of Trade surveys suggest that by January 1917, the number of permanently employed male workers in agriculture had dropped by 32 per cent from its July 1914 figure. Even in January 1918, when a number of substitutes had been recruited, including German prisoners of war and certain categories of soldiers, the level was still 28.7 per cent below that of three and a half years earlier.[6] But such estimates relate only to employees, and do not cover farmers and their relatives, for whom recruitment figures were far lower once the initial excitement had ended. Furthermore, the Board's statistics, based as they were upon a sample of larger farmers, who employed relatively substantial labour forces, scarcely gave an accurate national picture. For whilst the average pre-war holding employed about two male workers (including relatives), the average respondent to the Board of Trade survey in April 1915 — to quote but one example — employed over nine workers. In addition, the pastoral areas of the country were under represented, particularly Wales, where small family holdings were common.[7] It is for these reasons that a recent writer has declared that Board estimates of total labour losses are 'almost certainly much too high'.[8]

An added complication to any assessment was the fact that contradictory figures were put forward by the various government departments during the War. The Board of Agriculture, in particular, was anxious to make the case that the industry was suffering from severe labour shortage, so as to strengthen its hand in negotiations with other official bodies and especially with the War Office. Hence in a letter written to the Man-Power Distribution Board on 25 September 1916, the secretary to the Board of Agriculture claimed that the industry had by mid-July of that year already lost 280,000 workers, exclusive of those who had been called up as reservists or who had left the land for work in the mines, munitions factories, and the varying government construction projects. If these were included he estimated that 'at least 350,000 men' had been drawn from the land since 4 August 1914.[9] Clearly this was a gross exaggeration, and it is significant that the President of the Board of Agriculture himself claimed a loss of only a quarter of a million workers by December 1916.[10] But that figure, too, is far too high. It may be compared to the only estimate produced by the Ministry of National Service — for April 1918 — which suggested that since the outbreak of war, 273,000 agricultural workers had left to join the services or work in the munitions factories.[11] Yet another estimate suggests a total of 243,000 men enlisted by July 1918[12]

Quantitatively, therefore, the loss of labour from the land was considerably less severe than some of the propagandists once claimed, notably the Board of Agriculture. But *qualitatively* there can be no doubt of the serious losses experienced in many parts of the industry. As was the case within a large part of manufacturing production, where dilution policies also applied, even when substitutes were secured, they rarely equalled the men they were replacing. This was shown particularly clearly in the spring of 1918, when the government launched a scheme to recruit War Agricultural Volunteers from men who were either aged forty-five years or more or were in too low a medical category for normal military service. Although it was optimistically observed that many of the volunteers were gardeners or men who had had experience of farm work 'in their earlier days', their practical contribution proved of little value. In all, about 3,904 of these volunteers were placed on farms in 1918.[13]

Nor, as already indicated, was recruitment for the armed forces the only threat. In areas like Hampshire, Essex, Lincolnshire, Northamptonshire, Norfolk, Cambridgeshire, and East Suffolk, a major problem was the construction of aerodromes, with workers attracted by the high wages offered by contractors. In September 1918 the five aerodromes constructed in East Suffolk were alone employing five hundred men.[14] Similarly on the Brassey estate in Northamptonshire, the agent was instructed to enquire how many of the local farmers had lost men for the building of two nearby aerodromes. So angry was Major Brassey himself over the issue that he raised it in Parliament, pointing out that the contractors, secure in their financial arrangements with the government, could agree to pay far higher wages than farmers could afford: 'In one particular case motor lorries are sent to the villages for the men, who live some miles distant from the aerodrome, and they are taken back in motor lorries at night'.[15] But the Parliamentary Secretary to the Air Council was prepared to offer little more than sympathy, emphasising that as the work was being done by sub-contractors and not the government itself, it was difficult to regulate such competition.[16] The reality was, of course, that the service ministries were primarily concerned with pursuing of the war effort, and were not prepared to do anything which would delay construction of much-needed airfields.

In Wiltshire, it was the erection or extension of military camps which was the bogey. According to A.G. Street, when building operations commenced in his neighbourhood during the spring of 1915, the labour market was altered with a vengeance.

> Boys who were not yet of military age, were at a premium, and could get three times as much money as their fathers, by working for the contractors who were constructing the new camps. At that period the farms in our neighbourhood would have been denuded of almost all labour, but for the fact that the married men lived in the farm cottages. . . . Young carters being especially in demand for camp-hauling, we were hard put to it to man our six two-horse single-furrow plough teams.[17]

He and his fellows continued in business by the application of more machinery and by allowing husbandry standards to deteriorate. 'To see banks untrimmed, ditches uncleaned, field corners not dug, and one's farm generally untidy, hurt one's proper pride. But there it was. There was only barely enough labour for essentials, and the frills had to be cut out.' Equally damaging was the erosion of order and method in running the farm, which gave rise to deep frustration. The only compensation for him, as for many others, was the very high price paid for food during the War years. Despite increases in taxation and other outgoings, this meant large farming profits. Street subsequently claimed that on his approximately 300-acre holding near Wilton (nearly 170 acres of it arable), he was making about £2,000 a year by 1918.[18] As he frankly observed it was 'impossible to lose money at farming just then.'

In Yorkshire, as in much of the industrial north, the labour situation was also aggravated by the manpower demands of the mining industry and of munitions.[19]

It was when they lost their most experienced workers that farmers' worries over the labour question became especially acute. The government gradually recognised the validity of their fears on this point, and in order to ease the problem, agreed in the summer of 1915 to discourage recruiting officers from inducing skilled men to enlist unless there was evidence that suitable substitutes could be secured outside the recruitment age and fitness range.[20] Unfortunately the system was easier to formulate than to operate. The manpower needs of the military and the attitude of those in charge of recruiting in many parts of the country led to widespread breaches of the undertaking, as well as to some serious anomalies. The ill-feeling this engendered was made clear in a letter written by a Kentish farmer in October 1915 to the then President of the Board of Agriculture, the Earl of Selborne. His difficulties had arisen despite the fact that under the national registration scheme introduced in August 1915, for men between the ages of fifteen and sixty-five not already in the forces, skilled workers engaged in important areas of agriculture were to be 'starred' and neither accepted as volunteers for military service nor solicited for it.[21] In this case the complainant's holding had been visited by a recruiting officer who had

> persuaded against their will to join the Army, the second
> horseman, the thatcher and my first dryer under head hop-

dryer, he also went to two lads at the plough and tried to persuade them, also my first waggoner. Three were married men. If we are to have our farms depleted of workmen, it will be impossible to carry on the work.

I may add the same thing was tried at my farm in East Kent. I should be the last to try and stop men enlisting that could be spared, but when one sees so many single men not doing their part, I feel it is bad policy to enlist serviceable married men.[22]

The arrangement had a further serious weakness in that the single man employed on a small farm who was able to turn his hand to every job was excluded from the special arrangements, no matter how vital his contribution to the running of that holding.

By November 1915, widespread criticisms were being voiced concerning the whole process. One MP claimed that the methods used for starring had caused more difficulties in agricultural districts than any other. He quoted the case of a farmer of 80 acres who had managed to get his two sons starred as shepherds, even though 'nobody in the locality has ever seen a sheep on the farm at all'. Another man with six sons had secured 'stars' for five of them, while in a third instance the farmer himself had failed to secure 'starred' status although his employees had been so recorded.[23] It was in these circumstances that Lord Selborne condemned the entire operation as having been conducted with 'indescribable and criminal carelessness'.[24] In order to meet some of the criticisms, in the autumn of 1915 the War Office agreed to the appointment of local tribunals to hear applications by employers against the enlistment of men judged essential to civilian production. They were to be manned by representatives of county and borough councils, as well as farmers and other employers. Ultimately an elaborate three-tier appeals procedure was constructed, with the candidate allowed to be represented by a solicitor before the final tribunal.[25]

Yet, despite all efforts to achieve a fair balance, the conflicting manpower needs of the armed forces and agriculture continued to arouse controversy throughout the War and led to heated exchanges within the Cabinet and in Parliament. As early as April 1916, shortly after the introduction of conscription, Walter Long at the Local Government Board wrote to Selborne, vigorously condemning the way 'the Military Authorities are claiming for themselves a position to which they are not entitled and I know that in many cases the strain on agriculture has reached very nearly breaking point.'[26]

Further attempts to regularise the situation were made during the following October with the drawing up of a minimum scale of farm labour requirements, but even that did not end the skirmishing. Under the scale, one physically fit man was to be available for each plough team, or each herd of twenty cows in milk, or each fifty head of stalled cattle, or for a given quantity of sheep. The scale assumed assistance was available for lighter work, probably from women or boys, but made no explicit provision for this.[27] Yet, less than three months after it had been established, Selborne's eventual successor, Rowland Prothero, received what he called a 'staggering blow' when the War Office announced that it was going to take 30,000 additional men away from the land.[28] The Earl of Derby, as Secretary for War, stoutly defended the action and plaintively claimed that although they had recently recruited '10,600 men from agriculture, they were endeavouring from the ranks of the Army to send back men — not as strong or as skilled as those they had taken, but men, who, they trusted would make good the gaps that had been caused. . . . I rather resent the insinuation continually made that the War Office has only one idea and that is to get men and to pay no consideration whatever to agriculture or other fields of industry'.[29] That did not appease his critics, however, and the disagreements continued.

Discontent within the countryside was meanwhile being reinforced by two other developments. The first was the way in which the appeals tribunals worked, particularly after the introduction of conscription in March 1916. Although farmers were given exemption from military service under this scheme, a similar protection did not apply to their sons, or, in all cases, to smallholders. Evidence soon mounted that some tribunals were using their influence to grant exemptions to farmers' sons at the expense of agricultural labourers. The criterion they were supposed to adopt was the overall importance of the men concerned to the running of the farm, the object being to keep the most skilled workers on a holding. Farmers responded by nominating their own sons for these positions, rather than the men who had hitherto carried out the tasks. Or in some cases, they ostensibly retired from business and announced that their son had taken over the farm. Thus Horace West, the 36-year-old son of a farmer from Southleigh, Oxfordshire, successfully applied for exemption on the grounds that he was farm foreman and that the only other workers on his father's 530 acre farm were three men over military age, and three boys.[30] Significantly six men from this farm had already gone into the Army and none of the remaining workers was capable of doing the son's job. Altogether of seven appeals submitted by agriculturists to the Oxfordshire tribunal on 27 April 1917, five involved farmers appealing on behalf of themselves or their relatives, of whom four were successful in gaining some exemptions. Less fortunate were a hawker and smallholder from Minster Lovell and a carrier from Combe, who had applied to an earlier sitting of the same tribunal. They were aged forty and thirty-six respectively, and ran their own businesses single-handed. In each case they were given a month's grace to allow them to settle their affairs, which probably meant the sale of their businesses.[31]

Similarly in Wales there is evidence of farmers asking land agents to insert their sons' names in tenancy agreements to show that the farm was being run jointly by father and sons. There was also the case of a Cardiganshire farmer who in 1916 recalled his two businessmen sons from London and installed them as titular landholders in a small farm he had purchased especially for the purpose. He then hired solicitors to defend them against the Army — an action which caused great local bitterness.[32] In much of rural Wales there was, indeed, a readiness on the part of tribunals to accept applicants' pleas as to why they should not be conscripted. Tribunal members, themselves residing in an area of small peasant farms, doubtless shared many of the prejudices and anxieties of the men with whom they were dealing. Thus the Lleyn tribunal in South Carnarvonshire had by the middle of June 1916, considered 1,500 applications for exemption; all save 180 had been given this concession, and of the residual 180, 'more than half had been rejected unfit for Army Service and had returned to their civil employment'.[33] Many Welsh applicants stressed the ill-health and incapacity of the employing farmer, as a reason why they should not join up. Thomas Davies of Felinfach, aged 19, noted that his father was 'aged and helpless and depends entirely upon me to do all the farm work. The farm contains 65 acres, including 17 acres of ploughed land and

occasionally I assist as a cowman, because I have only my aged
parents with me and a small boy of 9 years old. I may also state
that I have a defective eyesight and injurious (*sic*) thumb'.[34]
Despite the vagueness of the appeal, he was granted exemption
and was able to retain that concession even at the end of 1917, on
the understanding that he remained in his existing employment.
There were many other successful applications couched in these
terms to tribunals in Cardiganshire, as hundreds of surviving
records bear witness.

Inequality of treatment was, however, not the only problem.
In Cardigan there were allegations in the spring of 1918 that
farmers had used the threat of military service to discourage
workers from joining a trade union, declaring they would
release for military duties 'any farm-servant who dared to join
the union. It was also alleged that at the last hiring season [1917]
certain farmers had used the same threat in order to prevent
young men from claiming wages to which their increased com-
petence and experience entitled them'. This had reinforced the
discontent already caused by the variability of application of the
Military Service Acts. The overall view gained ground 'that
justice for the labourer does not exist'.[35]

Obstacles were also put in the way of military recruitment at
hiring fairs by agriculturists anxious to retain their staff, as well
as by farm servants unwilling to join the ranks of potential
battlefield victims. In East Denbighshire, where recruiting
officers were ordered to attend fairs accompanied by the band of
the Royal Welsh Fusiliers, it was sourly noted that as the band
marched in 'the farmers marched their men out'.[36] Even when
recruiters went out to individual farms to see the men,
employers watched for their approach and sent the workers up
to the mountain pastures out of the way. The aim of recruiting
officers was to catch labourers before they had agreed to serve
for a six-month contract, since if they enlisted during that period
they were likely to lose the pay to which they were entitled. This
excuse was frequently used for the disappointing response at
hiring fairs held in the principality during the winter of 1914. 'A
haul of 25 recruits at Llangefni Fair at that time can be
adjudged very good, especially when compared to the
Beddgelert Fair of September 1914 when none volunteered, and
12 men at Pwllheli Fair in November 1914. In May 1915 parties
of troops distributed 30,000 recruiting leaflets at hiring fairs in

Lleyn, for a net gain of 23 men; at another where 200 men were individually canvassed, 10 recruits resulted'.[37] Similar difficulties were experienced at hiring fairs in Lincolnshire, Lancashire, and Cumbria, with the men encouraged to re-engage with their former employer in order to avoid enlistment. For the military authorities had warned that if 'farm hands [were] out of employment beyond a certain time they would be called up', even when prior to this they had held a post which warranted exemption.[38]

Such conditions inevitably strengthened the bargaining power of employers in negotiating with the men over wages and conditions of service. On the other hand, those young labourers *below* the Army age limit were in particular demand and were able to secure higher rates. In Cumberland during the spring of 1917, youths of seventeen were able to command up to £30 per half-year, with board and lodging, while in Lincolnshire they could obtain as much as £5 or £6 per annum more than in the previous year. Irish migrant workers of all ages also benefited from this arrangement since they, too, were exempt from conscription. Though the fact of their immunity aroused ill-feeling among many English families whose own sons were at war. Some farmers refused to hire them, while from Lancashire came reports of labourers objecting to working alongside them. At Skipton in Yorkshire, early in July 1918, feelings ran so high that fights broke out between the Irishmen and local people. A farmer summed up the attitude of many critics when he declared that all the migrants who had come over 'to demand unreasonably high wages at the present time ought to be conscribed on the spot, and the general opinion was that the men should not be hired if there was any other way out of the labour difficulty'.[39] But often there was no alternative, and so they were taken on. Nor was the Government prepared to tackle the thorny problem of conscripting a probably unwilling Irish male population, despite considering the matter closely in the last months of the War.[40]

A second difficulty associated with the exemption question was that where farmers were able to retain sons on their holdings they were reluctant to engage female substitutes in case this endangered their sons' position. From Somerset in the late summer of 1916 the organisers of women's work on the land complained of young men under thirty being exempted for months at a time, or permanently, while in Devon, the Women's

War Service County Committee claimed that women were not prepared to offer themselves for work 'until more of the farmers' sons [were] gone'.[41] During the later stages of the War this prejudice against women weakened, especially after January 1917, when the Army Council decided to treat female labour as supplementary to, and not as a substitute for, male workers. Reassured on this point, farmers gave them a trial. But the disputes over exemptions were not so easily resolved.

The methods applied in the recruitment programme also aroused dissatisfaction when it was seen that in some cases married men were being called up whilst certain of their unmarried counterparts stayed behind. Although promises had been made that single men would be called up first, the various loopholes in the system, plus the fact that not all unmarried men were fit enough to join, meant that the policy failed to work out that way in practice. The question was highlighted in a letter from a Cambridgeshire farmer, who angrily informed E.S. Montagu, the Chancellor of the Duchy of Lancaster and a Cambridgeshire MP, of problems in his community at the beginning of 1916. Not only had one fellow agriculturist turned a worker off 'before the tribunal, and then [got] his son off', but there were ten other single men working in nearby villages who were employed on tasks of no military importance and yet had escaped enlistment: 'I might say that I gave my two sons, one has been in and out of the trenches for eight months, and the other one was sent home again because he was to *(sic)* young. I think as this is a people's War, all should take their share'.[42] He then added bitterly: 'I might say I was one of the [military] canvassers . . . and I was asked repeatedly by the married men, if the single men would have to go first, and I told them that we had Mr Asquith's and Lord Derby's word, that every single man before married, and in most cases, they said they were willing to go up in there *(sic)* groups, when every single man was gone, and not before. I think that if there are single men left when the married men are called up to serve I feel I have done a great injustice to them, and if Mr Asquith don't keep his word to the married I feel I must sever myself from the Liberal party altogether'.

Despite such representations it was not until April 1918 that an attempt was made to tackle the worst of the anomalies. In an initiative which Rowland Prothero angrily condemned as likely to destroy the confidence of the farming community by ending agriculture's status as a protected industry, all the old exemptions based upon employment were withdrawn.[43] Henceforward these were to be fixed upon personal grounds only and related to the merits of each case. And although Prothero had resisted the measure, along with some of the County War Agricultural Executives, like that for Somerset — which openly adopted obstructive tactics — most people welcomed the change as a belated move towards justice and equality.[44] *The Times* captured this mood when it declared:

> In some parts of the country the unfairness which has marked the selection of men available for the Army has caused much bitterness, a large number of labourers having been taken for military service, while the farmers' sons have been allowed to remain.... "There is undoubtedly," said our correspondent, "a strong opinion in many parts of Somerset that farmers' sons have been too leniently dealt with. In Frome, Yeovil, Wells, Highbridge, and other centres where agriculturists meet, farmers habitually express dissatisfaction at the vigorous comb-out, but it is widely recognised to be a tardy act of justice to the labourers and smallholders. Many hard cases come before the tribunal, but instances in which a farmer has been allowed to retain several sons have occasioned much discontent, which the present comb-out is calculated to remove.
>
> From the neighbouring county of Wilts... many farmers have been allowed to retain an unfair proportion of their sons, and responsible men, even among the farming class, comment on the number of young farmers who, apparently fail to take a serious view of the claims of the country.[45]

In Wiltshire, the question had caused argument as early as December 1914, with one correspondent to the *Wiltshire Gazette* angrily noting the reluctance of farmers' sons to enlist: 'Above them the landed gentry have responded splendidly to the call of their country, and below them the labourers have done well, but the farmer's son simply stays at home'.[46] This he attributed to a lack of patriotism and to the fact that because most of them could not get commissions they refused to serve alongside the labourers, out of a snobbish sense of their own importance. Another writer replied to these allegations with equal vehemence, denying any neglect of duty by farmers' sons and pointing out that 'the man who helps to increase our home food supply is equal in importance to the man that goes to the front'.[47]

The senior ranks of the National Farmers' Union were similarly divided over the issue. Suggestions made in the early months of the War, that a list should be prepared of those farmers who had enlisted, were rejected, with one executive committee member firmly declaring there were 'other things besides killing Germans, and one thing was to see that there was not a shortage of food in the country'.[48] A colleague sourly added that to hold up to special honour those who had enlisted cast 'a reproach on those doing their duty at home'.

The Cabinet, for its part, admitted that in some counties, including Cumberland, Westmorland, and Durham, the quota of farmers' sons recruited had not been high, while the West Midlands regional director of the Ministry of National Service reported the widespread suspicion that farmers were refusing any kind of substitute labour in order to protect their sons: 'yet their retention from year to year is often a source of discontent in a parish'.[49] In Cardigan, farmers' anger at attempts to impose firmer regulations was so great that they threatened to turn cattle into the crops if their labour force were pruned further. Significantly this county, too, was accused of neglecting substitute labour and of failing to use that which it had recruited in an efficient manner.[50]

Within Parliament the government's spring 1918 comb-out earned predictably heavy criticism from the agricultural 'lobby'. So bitter did the debate become that Prothero, despite his private reservations over the issue, felt it necessary to remind MPs that agriculturists' difficulties were paltry compared to those faced by soldiers fighting on the Western Front. In an emotional speech, he drew attention to the way in which these men had 'every day to go down into a veritable hell and face death in its most appalling form. . . . Compare their condition with the condition of the men on the farms, working in their own familiar peaceful surroundings, not risking their lives, their limbs, their eyesight, and their health for all time. . . . We must remember that what we are asking from the men on the land is as nothing compared with what we are asking from the men whom we send to the front'.[51]

But few of his critics were disarmed. Indeed, it was often precisely because of their awareness of the horrors of trench warfare that they resisted conscription so vehemently. In the event their alarm proved short-lived. For on 26 June, it was decided to postpone the calling up of any more men until after the harvest. Of the 30,000 quota imposed in the spring, only 22,654 had actually been called up when the embargo was announced. The fortunate remainder escaped altogether, for after the harvest the easing of the military position in Europe and a reluctance to upset farmers any further led to the whole operation being suspended.[52]

The regional response to this quota scheme had, meanwhile, shown marked variations. In the northern district, where Cumbrian farmers and their relatives had earlier been accused of laggardliness, more men were recruited than were actually required, while another area of difficulty, the south-west, managed to achieve six-sevenths of its target. But elsewhere manpower shortages proved more severe than the authorities were prepared to admit or delaying tactics were more successfully deployed. The east central district, for example, produced only about four-fifths of its total, with the regional officer firmly adding: 'it is considered that the recruitment of a further quota of skilled agriculturists could not be undertaken without the possibility of endangering the industry and diminishing food production, and . . . it is doubtful whether men could be obtained if recruiting were confined to unskilled men in grade 1'.[53] In Wales, the situation was still more unsatisfactory, with only about half the target figure actually achieved. Significantly, Cardigan, which had been given a quota of 425 men, sent away only 114, while from Flint, where there were complaints of labour shortage and where early responses to recruitment had been good, a mere 88 of the 350 men required were posted.[54] Soundings by the Ministry of National Service as to future enlistment in the principality were met with firm discouragement, the local representative declaring that a fresh quota could only be met 'at the expense of serious dislocation of the agricultural industry failing man for man substitution, and strong opposition would have to be faced in such a contingency. In any case, a further programme cannot be arranged until after the termination of the winter ploughing which, in Wales, is frequently a prolonged operation owing to the winter conditions'.[55]

Thus it was that the unenthusiastic reaction of many farmers and their sons towards military recruitment persisted to the end of hostilities. Inevitably this attitude affected the total of those coming forward to enlist. Peter Dewey, for one, has suggested that whilst the adult male relatives of farmers employed on the land fell by perhaps 15 per cent over the war years compared to the pre-war position, for regular male hired workers it dropped by about 28 per cent, and for casual workers by over 41 per cent.[56] As he points out, the rapid rise in agricultural profits provided a strong incentive for farmers and their families to avoid military service, in order to secure the full benefits of the opportunities available. External pressure upon them from community leaders were also comparatively weak, since members of farming families were 'seldom coerced by social opinion or the recruiting officer into enlistment' in the way that a number of labourers were. Furthermore, after the introduction of conscription, farmers themselves were given complete exemption from military service, while their sons, as we have seen, were often able to arrange 'temporary' postponements which lasted for months and even years.

But if labour shortages and the implementation of recruitment policies continued to cause friction between the military and agriculturists throughout the war period, a third bone of contention was that of land usage. Within days of the outbreak of hostilities, property was being requisitioned for military camps and subsequently for aerodromes and munitions factories. This not only affected the local labour supply by encouraging men to flock to better paid employment on government contract schemes, as we have already noted, but it influenced general tillage standards. In some cases farmers were vaguely advised to put up red flags to warn off troops carrying out military manoeuvres in the area, so as to avoid damage to growing crops. But most instances of disruption were more serious than this. An east Sussex farmer complained to an Executive Committee Meeting of the National Farmers' Union in January 1915, that the military authorities had already commandeered 100 acres of land round his house:

It was all enclosed pasture, and had been covered with hutments. Roads had been driven all across the place, and the farmyard was like a rolling sea of mud. They had put up rifle ranges across the arable land and entrenched 30 acres at the

1. A farming family plucking geese, c.1900

2. The Fowler brothers of Brookhall, Norfolk, c.1907

3. Women shovelling potatoes for the sieving machine

4. Forestry Corps moving logs

south end of the farm. The whole place was turned upside down and torn to pieces in a way that was perfectly heart-breaking. No offer of compensation had been made to him... he was told he was absolutely at the mercy of the War Office, and that he had to accept what he could get.[57]

Wiltshire was another county seriously affected by the growth of military camps, about 100,000 soldiers being stationed in the Salisbury area alone by December 1914. Here, also, land was commandeered on a major scale, as A.G. Street has described in his novel, *The Gentleman of the Party*. In this case, the farmer saw his property transformed from 'an orderly, peaceful place, entirely under his direction' to 'a noisy whirlpool of mud, over which he, apparently, had precious little jurisdiction.... Cement, bricks, timber, window-panes, corrugated iron, drain-pipes, electric-light plants, surveyors, navvies, bricklayers, carpenters, beer, bad language, and many other ingredients which went to the building of a camp were hauled along the road'. Tracks and roadways became impassable for ordinary traffic during the wet winter months and it was common for the traction engines which were used for hauling building materials to the camps to become hopelessly bogged down in the mud.[58]

Nor were these the only difficulties. Ordinary farming activities became impossible on many holdings and yet agriculturists found great difficulty in extracting the relevant compensation from the authorities. Two farming brothers from Codford St Peter in Wiltshire, who had part of their land commandeered in September 1915, were among the victims of this particular bureaucratic tangle. Early in the following February their bailiff began to press for payment of rent by the military, pointing out that there would soon be the normal six months' rental to pay on the holding and he '*must* have your portion' before he could discharge his obligations.[59] Eventually a payment was agreed, but efforts to extract subsequent sums proved unavailing and in the end the brothers had to appear before the Defence of the Realm Losses Commission to demand settlement of a claim amounting to £984 13s. 1d. for a period of almost a year up to Michaelmas 1917. After some discussion, the Commission made an award of £377 2s. 6d., plus £4 4s. towards the cost of preparing the appeal.[60]

But delay in payment was not the brothers' only grievance. Broken fences, damaged gate posts, and the straying of military horses on to growing crops were other grounds for complaint, although often to little purpose. On 25 October 1917, the bailiff sent a letter to a camp of Australians protesting at the 'very serious damage which is being done to our Farm by the troops digging trenches etc. by the Rifle Range. Great holes are being made on some of the best land on the Farm, & it will be . . . a very great amount of labour to fill them.'[61] A month later there were fears that the rifle range itself was to be extended to include the only area of roots, '& where we intended lambing down 320 Ewes'. Preparations had been made for the accommodation of the sheep, but it had proved impossible to confirm whether the rifle range changes were to be implemented or not. In the end the County War Agricultural Committee had to be contacted to soothe the warring parties.

Elsewhere special arrangements were made during the harvest season for the temporary closure of rifle ranges during the day time so that crops could be gathered on nearby land 'in the danger zones'.[62]

Occasionally the requisitioning of land led to farmers losing their entire holding. During the early months of 1917, almost fifty farmers and smallholders in the Bristol area were required to leave in order that the military could take over. Compensation was paid but, as the *Mark Lane Express* pointed out, financial recompense was not everything 'when a man is called upon to vacate the farm which may be the only home he has ever known'. The paper called for the provision of fresh land somewhere else for the displaced farmers, perhaps in the Cotswolds, where before the War there had been much amalgamation of holdings.[63]

Another grievance was that when overall assessment of compensation for requisitioned land was calculated under the Defence of the Realm Act, payment was only calculated for crops destroyed. Other important considerations, such as the question of tenant right, were ignored and there was no independent system of arbitration.[64]

A less drastic but nonetheless annoying cause for concern to some farmers was the temporary utilisation of men and horses for short-term construction projects. This took place in parishes like Tarrant Launceston in Dorset, where a naval camp was under development by the autumn of 1914. It led to local farmers having to loan men and horses for weeks at a time, to the detriment of their own tillage plans. Small wonder that on 31 December, one man sadly wrote in his diary that work on the farm was 'very backward owing to so many Horses & Men being taken for the camp!!!' During the week ending 7 December he had had between eight and eleven horses per day on loan, plus waggons and carts. Although the authorities made payment at the rate of 10s. per horse per day, this was small consolation when work was falling behind. In all, building operations led to the hiring of horses and waggons from this farmer from 30 October 1914 to 9 February 1915.[65] (On the positive side, however, the camp provided a major outlet for the farm's milk, taking 2,790 gallons in July 1917.)

But the requisitioning of horses for the construction of camps was of minor significance when compared to military demands for horses to use in the waging of the War itself. Even though the internal combustion engine was beginning to come into its own, horses were still required in massive numbers both for riding and draught purposes. As the mobilisation arrangements got under way, army remount officers appeared at farm gates, armed with buff forms on which farmers could claim payment at market value for the animals they lost. But, as E.H. Whetham drily observes, buff forms could not pull the binders in the harvest fields, and once the horses had been taken there were often delays before they were paid for.[66]

The scale of the requisitioning seems to have taken most agriculturists by surprise. At Tysoe, Kathleen Ashby noted that a group of army sergeants arrived within a few days of the outbreak of War and took away horses on a considerable scale: 'Every farmhouse in Tysoe had some...shock and grief that day'. The Ashbys themselves lost an old and much loved carthorse named Captain, who despite his age was still useful, 'if you humoured him and knocked off promptly after his stint of work, but under new men and at hard tasks he must break down'.[67] Similarly a Derbyshire farmer's son recalled that many of the agriculturists in his area who had visited the Bakewell show a few days after the declaration of War had been forced to sell their animals, if they were of the 'right sort', whether they wanted to or not. Fortunately for the family, his father had left their horses at home and had gone with an uncle, whose animal was too old to be of interest to the Army.[68] So they had managed to escape unscathed, while some of their neighbours, less prudent or less fortunate, had found that their only horse had been commandeered.

The fact that the requisitioning was taking place at harvest time, when the demand for draught horses was at a peak, led to angry questions being asked in the Commons. More than one MP complained that the remount officers were acquiring animals in places where the harvest had only just commenced. In reply the Under Secretary of State for War soothingly promised that in future not more than half of any farm's horses would be taken, and 'if possible . . . a smaller extent than that'.[69] But the remount officers, charged with obtaining more than a hundred thousand horses within the first week of the War, requisitioned them from the nearest farms and private stables, irrespective of statements made in Parliament. As one writer puts it, this was 'the first experience of a common discrepancy between the public policy of the War Office towards civilians and civilian property, and the actions of local officers, working on rigid instructions to a short time-table'.[70]

By September, the point was being made defensively that the Army had only taken about nine thousand heavy horses from farms, or a little over 1 per cent of the number recorded as being used on the land in June 1914. But the process did not stop there. Already by 16 November, the total requisitioned had risen to 2 per cent of the June total, and by June 1915, when new statistics were collected, the figure was about 8 per cent.[71] For saddle horses on farms the drop in numbers had been a drastic 25 per cent. These changes presented particular problems for agriculturists in counties like Essex, Huntingdon, Norfolk, and Pembroke, where against the overall national trend, the arable acreage had increased and yet the heavy horses available to cultivate that extra acreage had fallen — by 9, 10.5, 9, and 8 per cent, respectively, in the case of these four. Each horse requisitioned meant the loss to its owner not only of power for harvesting, carting, and ploughing, but also the loss of a known and often well-loved character, skilled in carrying out the tasks required of it. Many of the animals taken at the outbreak of war went overseas with the expeditionary forces, were involved in the retreat from Mons, and, like the men who accompanied them, were killed and wounded in large numbers.

After the first months of the War, efforts were made to secure the bulk of Army horses from overseas, and the British stock gradually recovered. The proportion of unbroken animals under one year, which had accounted for just over 9 per cent of total agricultural horses in England and Wales in 1914, edged up to about 10 per cent in 1916, and there were also more older unbroken animals. It was not until 1918 that the total of horses used for agricultural purposes appreciably exceeded the 1914 level (by around 2 per cent at that date), and many of these were relatively immature. Ironically, they only reached their full working potential after the War had ended.

In the meantime, the arable acreage itself had increased by almost 13 per cent between June 1914 and June 1918, under the influence of the Government's 1916-18 'plough up' programme. Clearly without the use of tractors, including the 10,000 or so imported from the United States in 1917-18, to supplement horses, and the temporary loan of military animals at the busy seasons of the year, it would have been impossible to carry through the official tillage programme. In all, over 4,200 Fordson tractors had been distributed under government aegis alone by the end of 1918 and 650,000 acres were ploughed by state-owned tractors, out of a total tillage acreage of about 10,263,000 in England and Wales in that year.[72] This was an increase of 1,856,000 acres over the 1916 level and it was in helping to bring that extra land under the plough that the tractors proved so valuable. They were particularly useful in traditionally pastoral districts, where the need for horses in peacetime had been strictly limited, and comparatively few plough animals were kept.

Once they had requisitioned the horses, the military authorities had to keep them fed and littered. This applied not merely to animals in this country but also to those on the Western front, which were supplied with regular shipments of fodder from this country. In March 1915, the Prime Minister noted that there were already 160,000 horses in France, 'every loss being regularly supplied', and for them '[we] send out from here every day 1000 tons of hay'.[73] In the peace-time Army, oats, hay, chaff, and straw were normally obtained by competitive tender from corn and hay merchants. But, given the quantities needed from the autumn of 1914, it was more than the trade could supply at the permitted prices. Once again the War Office resorted to requisitioning, chiefly from farms which had the mis-fortune to be near military centres. Farmers, for their part, resented the commandeering process both because they felt they were inadequately paid for the crops taken and because they were losing the freedom to dispose of their produce as they saw fit. A Leicestershire member of the Executive Committee of the National Farmers' Union argued that in his part of the country the War Office was commandeering hay during the spring of 1915 at £3 15s. a ton, whereas on the open market it would have fetched £5.[74] Once the stocks had been requisitioned, they were officially marked and could not be used by the farmer even to feed his own stock. In addition, no payment was made for the produce until it had been taken away. Hence complaints from Essex at the end of 1916 that on some farms, hay which had been requisitioned a year before had still not been baled. It was taking up space in the stackyard and yet the farmers concerned were unable to utilise it, even if they were short of fodder.[75] Other critics noted the losses of farmers whose stacks were returned as being below standard.

Faced with a mounting wave of protests, the War Office began to make concessions. From November 1914 it agreed to purchase supplies chiefly through informal committees of farmers organised by the county councils. The committees were to act as 'a kind of arbitrators between the farmer and the War Office'.[76] But, in practice, the latter reverted to requisitioning from individuals when the need arose, and those affected found that they still had no legal method of appeal. Not until July 1915 did the War Office set up two forage appeals committees, one for the north and one for the south of the country, to hear applications from farmers concerning excessive purchases or insufficient prices.[77] These latter were still being calculated on the level ruling in the summer of 1914, despite the sharp overall inflation. Later the regulations were tightened further and by November 1917, not only had a maximum price scale been imposed but the War Office could enforce the sale of hay and straw where it was considered that farmers were needlessly holding up supplies.[78]

Yet if throughout these years of hostilities the military authorities continued to make major demands upon farmers for land, for men, and for horses, they were also prepared to give help where that proved feasible. The most significant initiative in this direction was the release of soldiers from the Home Defence Force to work on the land. It is to an examination of how that conciliatory gesture was applied that we must now turn.

Chapter 5

Soldiers on the Land

'It would have been utterly impossible in 1917 to carry on farming at all without a large supply of soldier labour, and this position is now very much emphasised by the additional ground which has been ploughed up.' *Report of the Board of Agriculture and Fisheries on Wages and Conditions of Employment in Agriculture*, Report on Northamptonshire, P.P. 1919, Vol. IX, 236. The Report was drawn up in March 1918.

There is little doubt that of all the issues causing friction between farmers and the military authorities during the War, that of the supply of labour was the one which aroused the greatest sense of grievance. It was to meet complaints on this score that the War Office gradually began to make concessions by temporarily releasing members of the armed forces to give help on the land at the busy seasons of the year. Indeed, as early as 28 April 1915, a Kentish member of the National Farmers' Union Executive Committee had suggested that as there were so many soldiers encamped in his county, the War Office should be approached with a view to securing their assistance for the harvest: 'Instead of as now, digging trenches, filling them up, and emptying them again.'[1] But at that stage his half mocking comments fell on deaf ears.

Not until early in June was the question examined seriously, with the Under Secretary of State for War admitting that 'immediate consideration' was being given to releasing men to help in the coming hay and corn harvests. Shortly afterwards it was agreed that soldiers from the Home Army would be granted special agricultural furloughs for periods of a fortnight between 11 July and 15 October.[2] Although the Labour Exchanges were to ensure that the proper conditions of employment were fulfilled, the finding of work and the rate of wages paid were largely left to private negotiations between the soldier and the farmer. Unfortunately, the scheme was of limited use, since only about half of the soldiers applied for by agriculturists were actually supplied.[3]

In the autumn, the scheme was further extended, with a view to assisting with the preparation of the ground for winter sowing. Under the new arrangement, where a local labour shortage was identified, men were to be supplied for a maximum of four weeks and were to be paid by the farmer at the rate of 4s. per day, if they organised their own board and lodging, and 2s. 6d. if these were provided for them. Railway travel to their destination was free and the only transport expected from the employer was in taking them from the nearest station to his farm.[4] The Army, for its part, gained by being relieved of the cost of the soldiers' keep at a time when they were not required for official duties.[5]

Alongside this, farmers who lived near to a military depot could apply at short notice direct to the Commanding Officer for soldier labour to be made available for a period of up to six working days. This concession was intended to allow them to take advantage of occasional fine days to get on with their ploughing and planting. Convalescent troops, too, might be engaged, providing their health was not adversely affected thereby. They were to be paid at a rate about seven-eighths of that offered to their fit counterparts.[6]

Throughout this period, therefore, no definite programme existed to release soldiers for continuous work on the land. Everything was planned on an *ad hoc* basis to meet specific seasonal needs. The only limitations were that men serving abroad could not be brought home for the purpose, whilst those under training were also excluded. Throughout it was understood that each helper was liable to instant recall, should the military situation demand it.

Among farmers, meanwhile, there was much suspicion as to the value of men recruited in this haphazard fashion and, as with all substitute workers, an anxiety not to employ staff who would jeopardise their right to retain permanent employees. Thus in June 1915, the Cardiff Divisional Office Labour Exchange complained that in Wales when circulars were issued advertising the availability of soldier helpers, 97 per cent of farmers ignored them completely, 2 per cent refused them, and most of the remaining 1 per cent asked for specific men to be released — usually ex-employees or members of the family.[7] In north and west Wales it was also quite common for agriculturists to specify that the soldiers must be Welsh-speakers and experienced in the kind of work carried out on small peasant holdings, including the ability to use a scythe. Neither of these conditions was easy to meet from the ranks of the British Army.

The first major change in the arrangements came early in 1916, following the introduction of the new Military Service Act, which brought in conscription. Now farmers were allowed to use soldiers at any time of the year, provided they made application first to the local Labour Exchange. This was to ensure that unemployed workers in an area received first preference if any jobs were vacant.[8]

In theory all of the soldiers supplied under these arrangements were supposed to have a knowledge of general farm work. The reality rarely matched up to this, but despite their disappointment, by the spring of 1916, tillage pressures were such that many agriculturists were anxiously seeking military aid. Ploughmen were in particular demand, with 15,000 men sent out on short furloughs to assist with the spring sowing.

Later, with the approach of harvest, there was a growing need for troops to be supplied for general farm duties. In all, between 3 and 30 June, applications were received for 13,391 soldiers to carry out these tasks. But, given the exigencies of war, with preparations under way for the start of the battle of the Somme, the military were reluctant to release such large numbers. The total actually supplied during that period was, therefore, a mere 3,795.[9] The plan was that they should be sent out in squads, equipped with tents, and allowed to camp in the districts where their services were needed. But in view of the small numbers allocated, the Board of Agriculture protested at the inadequate arrangements, and the allotment was increased to 14,000 men by the end of July. Even that was considered unsatisfactory and after a heated Cabinet discussion on 1 August 1916, it was decided that if the harvest were not to be lost, more recruits must be found. This time the War Office agreed to release a further 12,000 to 15,000 men to supplement the 14,000 already on offer. However, within days, thanks to further confusion over figures, that offer was withdrawn, only to be partially reinstated shortly after. In total, between 12 August and 3 October 1916, 16,690 men were supplied for harvest and other work (7,679 of them being men who had been specifically asked for by name by the farmers and were presumably family members or former employees.) This compares with a figure of 28,805 applied for by farmers.[10] It was a substantial deficit.

Throughout, the scheme was plagued by administrative misunderstandings between the Board of Agriculture and the War Office as to the actual numbers required, with the latter complaining in the summer of 1916 of the 'very large discrepancy' between requests put forward by the Board and those proposed by the local centres to which farmers applied.[11] Another difficulty was that many of the soldiers who were sent out proved to be of little use, never having worked on the land before. According to the War Office, approaching 1,500 of those dispatched during the summer of 1916 proved so bad that despite the labour shortage farmers refused to keep them.[12] 'Two men were sent from Shrewsbury to Mr Wm Prydderch, ... Ty Croes, who knew nothing about farm work and are useless to the farmer as workers at the Corn Harvest', angrily reported the Secretary of the Anglesey War Agricultural Committee, on 26 August 1916. 'I have advised him to send same back. . . . It is absolutely necessary if men are sent at all to Anglesey, that they must be capable of using the scythe and other operations in connection with the Corn Harvest'.[13] A fortnight earlier he had similarly noted that where farmers had applied for specific men to be supplied, it was useless to send substitutes, without further negotiations, since the farmers would simply return them: 'in cases where the Military Authorities are unable to release the men applied for, they should correspond with the farmers and ask them if they are prepared to accept other soldiers in their stead. One of the main reasons why farmers ask for particular men is that they have no room to accommodate others who are not from the district. In the great majority of cases where they ask for specific men they are previous servants whose homes are in the district and in all these cases the farmer is not required to provide sleeping apartments'.[14] The imposition of such conditions was partly a sign that labour shortages in Anglesey were not severe, but it was also a symbol of the independent attitude of the farming community. It was an approach they shared with many agriculturists elsewhere, and it further added to the difficulties of the military as they struggled to satisfy the conflicting needs of the battle front and the harvest field.

An added complication was that the rates of pay offered to the soldier harvesters varied regionally. In the arable eastern counties they amounted to 6s. for a working day of ten hours, where the soldier provided his own board and lodging, and 4s. 6d. where he lived in, with 6d. an hour overtime. [15] Elsewhere in the country the rate was 5s. for a ten-hour working day without board and lodging, and 3s. 6d. per day where these were provided, plus 5d. an hour overtime. On military grounds it was also necessary to keep a large proportion of the men in the eastern counties, so that they were available either to be shipped to France or to be used to oppose a possible German invasion of this country. Though, in any case, demands for their help at harvest time were likely to be at a peak in the grain growing counties.

During the period a soldier received civilian wages from the farmer, his Army pay (which was a smaller amount) was included in this sum, and he was only credited with Army payments on those Sundays during the furlough on which he received no civilian wages. But a major cause of discontent on a number of farms was that under these arrangements the soldiers were often paid as much as their skilled civilian counterparts, such as shepherds or horsemen, even though they were only able to carry out unskilled tasks. They also worked shorter hours. [16] Even Rowland Prothero himself admitted that the introduction of these and other forms of subsidised labour by the government was, in effect, the supply of 'State-assisted "blacklegs" ', whose appearance weakened the ability of the civilian workers to bargain for better pay. [17] The troops were also provided with the clothing in which they worked, whilst the civilian labourers had to supply this for themselves. The families of the married men, in addition, received separation allowances, like all members of the armed services.

Some farmers solved the grievance between their regular employees and the soldiers over the length of the working day by declaring that the latter must put in 'the same hours as the other men or go'. [18] But the earnings anomaly was more difficult to tackle, and it was only at the beginning of 1917 that serious attention was turned to it. This followed the creation of the Food Production Department in January of that year. One of the major features of the programme then outlined was the forming of a coherent scheme for the deployment of soldiers, to replace the existing haphazard arrangements. At the same time it was decided that pay must be based on the local rates offered to civilian labourers in a given area and was to be determined by the relevant County War Agricultural Committee. Only for harvest work did the old system continue to apply, with minimum rates fixed by the War Office. It was a plan which initially caused confusion among employers and led to complaints about the official requirement to pay a higher rate for the corn harvest than for haymaking. In the eastern counties, the military grain harvest rate was fixed at 7s. per day, as opposed to 6s. in the rest of the country, while the payment for haymaking in all regions was 5s. per day.[19]

Nor did these changes eliminate completely the friction between civilian workers and their soldier colleagues. Even the introduction of agricultural wages boards in the spring of 1918 failed to achieve that, following the implementation of the 1917 Corn Production Act. For whilst these substantially raised civilian minimum wages, soldier labourers, too, were entitled to the enhanced rates, and their dependants still enjoyed the normal military separation allowances. In Monmouthshire, for example, it was reported in the spring of 1918 that on one farm a soldier labourer with three children was securing a wage of 25s. a week, while his wife and children obtained 25s. 6d. a week separation allowance. This gave a weekly total of 50s. 6d. for the soldier and his family, whilst a civilian labourer, also with a wife and three children, received a total of 28s. a week in wages and allowances.[20] Cases were quoted, too, of former agricultural labourers in low medical categories who had been conscripted and then, after a few weeks' training, had returned to their home area under military auspices to work permanently on the land at full civilian rates, while their wives received the appropriate army allowances. This even applied when their husbands were able to live at home. Not until the summer of 1918 was that brought to an end, with the withdrawal of separation allowances from all such workers living at home. Henceforward they were to receive civilian earnings only, plus an allowance from the Army for Sundays. However, it was also laid down that should these sums not amount to the equivalent of ordinary Army pay, the difference would be made up from military funds to that basic minimum.[21] The families of workers who were not resident at home continued to receive their allowances as before.

The bitterness to which these discrepancies gave rise among

civilians is shown clearly in a letter written by a Hampshire carter's wife in late August 1918, when she angrily declared:

> The Food Controller says the people are not drawing all their meat rations. The simple reason is that the poor lack means wherewith to get it. .... If 22s. 6d. is not sufficient for a soldier's wife and one child, how is a farm hand expected to keep himself, wife, and, say, six to eight children, on less than 37s. a week.[22]

But the grievances were not all on one side. Apart from the natural dissatisfaction of those men whose wives had lost separation allowances under the summer 1918 initiative, there was a minority of soldiers who even under the earlier arrangements had experienced difficulties in collecting the sums due to them from employers.[23] In east Sussex during May 1917, the military authorities had to inform farmers that a minimum weekly wage of 25s. must be offered to all soldier labourers, since some of the unskilled had been paid only 20s. Out of this one farmer admitted retaining 15s. a week for his worker's keep. He then sent 2s. per week to the military authorities at Chichester, and paid the soldier 3s. Another man complained that his two skilled ploughmen helpers, to whom he was paying 25s. a week, had pointed out that they were entitled to extra amounts for overtime and for Sunday working. The sums involved totalled 11s. per week per man, but the farmer clearly felt aggrieved that they had demanded their rights.[24] In Essex, the County War Agricultural Executive Committee even had to warn that soldiers who were engaged in farm work and were paying for their own board and lodging should not be charged more than 15s. or 16s. a week out of the basic 25s. per week they were earning.[25] Eventually clear-cut rules were drawn up by the military authorities, covering the pay and conditions which were to apply, and warning farmers against granting leave to workers without formal approval being given by the relevant military headquarters.

Meanwhile, alongside this belated rationalisation of pay and conditions for soldier labourers, a still more significant development was the creation of special agricultural companies. These were drawn from men who were physically unfit for active service in the Army, or who, in a few cases, were considered suitable for consideration on other grounds. Among the latter group proposed for transfer by the Essex Agricultural Executive Committee were a private in the Essex Yeomanry, whose farmer brother had died and who was now required to take over the running of the family holding, and a farmer-private who was to be transferred to agricultural duties whilst the cowman he employed was called up instead![26]

The proposal for the deployment of the agricultural companies was made as a compensatory gesture by the military authorities less than two months after that calling up of 30,000 more men from the land in January 1917, which had so shocked the President of the Board of Agriculture, Rowland Prothero. It also followed pressure in the House of Commons for some such initiative.[27] Originally about 11,500 soldiers were made available under the new scheme, including 4,000 transferred from Infantry Works Battalions. Most were men from category CII or CIII, who were unfit for normal Home Defence purposes and were to be formed into companies of between 100 and 250 men each, stationed at forty-three suitable distribution centres. Every centre was to be under the command of an officer with agricultural experience, and the distribution of the men to the farms was to be arranged by the County Agricultural Executive Committees.[28] Save in the most desperate military circumstances, they were to remain on the land for the duration of the War, although periodic medical examinations were to be arranged to ensure that they were still below the minimum health level for conventional soldiering.[29] The first men went out early in March but during the hay and corn harvest of that year the zeal of the medical teams was such that they had to be ordered to cease work because they were disrupting agricultural activities. They were not allowed to recommence their examinations until the end of September, when most harvesting had ended.[30]

Farmers, for their part, were angered and dismayed that they were to lose fit, skilled men with whom they were used to working and were to be asked instead to run what some contemptuously designated 'infirmaries' rather than farms. But most responded to the Government's appeal that they should train 'the Kitcheners of a new agricultural army', and over time they were rewarded for their persistence. Those who at first sent back men because of their ignorance of the work required soon heard from colleagues in the district that these unskilled workers were, under careful teaching, rapidly becoming useful farm labourers. The commandants of the distribution centres and the county labour officers also attended markets and farmers' meetings, and persuaded those who were short of labour to give the men a trial. Farmers were encouraged to visit the centres to interview potential recruits.

Over time the men improved in physique and developed some aptitude for the work, though clearly those who had suffered serious injuries at the front, such as the loss of an eye, were destined to be gravely handicapped for the rest of their lives. And as the Director of National Service unsentimentally pointed out to the Cabinet early in 1917, the heavier the fighting the more men the Army would have to 'degrade' from Category A of the health code to Categories B, C, and E, and 'consequently the greater... the volume of the return flow to civil life', i.e. of potential recruits to the agricultural companies.[31]

Not surprisingly in such circumstances, members of the Cabinet themselves had a low opinion of the 'companies'. In late November 1917, Sir Auckland Geddes referred disparagingly to the 'large number of men technically in the Army, and wearing uniform, who were of no military value, and were not part of the Home Defence Force or of draft finding units... He did not suggest any immediate disbandment of the Agricultural Companies... but he suggested that recruiting for such should cease, and that a gradual disbandment should take place'. Lord Derby agreed, declaring that 'nothing was more detrimental to the Army than the keeping on the books of the Army men of no military value... However, he recognised the great importance of maintaining agricultural work, and he feared that if the men now in the Agricultural Companies were set free they would leave agriculture and enter munitions work, where wages were so much higher and conditions so much easier'.[32] On these ignoble grounds, therefore, the companies were retained and, indeed, increased in size over the final months of the War. But such debates, had they been known to farmers, would surely have confirmed their suspicions that they were being sent men 'who [were] no use as soldiers'.[33]

The civilian labourers, too, resented this further augmentation of the military contribution. Early in February 1917 a conference of Norfolk union delegates passed an indignant resolution 'emphatically' protesting 'against CIII men being handed over in battalions under military command to work on the land, this being a direct violation of pledges given on behalf of the Government by Lord Derby & others'. But their indignation, like the resentment of the farmers, was ignored by the authorities, and arrangements for the formation of the companies continued without interruption.

It was, therefore, from the spring of 1917 that the military began to make a major contribution to the food production effort. In addition to the creation of the agricultural companies, the Army Council agreed to release 12,500 members of the Home Defence Force on a special furlough, to last to 30 April, in order to help with spring ploughing upon the newly extended arable acreage. Early in March, men from this group began to arrive at the distribution centres. Unfortunately of the 24,000 men initially allocated, in agricultural companies or for ploughing, only about 3,000 proved to have had any experience of the latter operation. The rest were almost useless. The situation was now growing desperate as the sowing season was drawing to an end, the wet, cold winter having already seriously hampered tillage plans. On 12 March, therefore, the military authorities took the unprecedented step of ordering that all skilled soldier ploughmen in the United Kingdom were to be returned to their depots on furlough up to at least 30 April. These proved to be the calibre of men needed. By the end of the first week of April, about 40,000 men of the three classes were at work, 18,000 of them skilled ploughmen from Category A of the military fitness code. When their furlough officially ended on 10 May, however, the pressures of the War were such that they were promptly withdrawn and within ten days all had returned to their units, even though the ploughing programme was still incomplete. As part compensation, the furlough of the other groups was extended to 25 July, and thereafter for the harvest season as well.[34] In June 1917, they were joined by 17,000 extra men sent to distribution centres for the hay and corn harvests.

Other ways in which the military assisted during 1917 included the release in January of that year of three hundred men skilled in handling steam plough tackle. At the same time a census was taken of the steam tackle available, and arrangements were made for the supply of tractors, with nearly six hundred of these on offer under government auspices by the end of March. Of that total, 118 belonged to the Government and the bulk of the rest were privately owned machines lent to the authorities to ensure maximum usage.[35] By the end of the year, the number of government-owned tractors had risen to about 1,600. Similarly, in May, one month's furlough was given to skilled shepherds to enable them to help with the sheep shearing.

From April 1917, plans were also in hand for the 1918 harvest. In order to plough up the additional three million acres deemed neccssary, around eighty thousand more soldiers would be required, plus the loan of sixty thousand Army horses and the provision of at least five thousand tractors — almost ten times the number currently available. Throughout the summer of 1917 the Cabinet deliberated, unable to decide whether to accept this major programme or not. In the meantime the farmers and the Board of Agriculture waited impatiently on the sidelines. Eventually in late June, it was agreed that just over 2½ million extra acres should be brought under tillage over the 1916 total, with each county allocated a share of that target. To assist with the plough up campaign a further fifty thousand soldiers would be released on a short-term basis, half of them being skilled workers and the other half unskilled. They were to be released at the rate of five thousand a week, starting on 7 July 1917. On this basis, it was estimated the full fifty thousand would have arrived at the distribution centres by early September.

Then came the appalling losses of Passchendaele and the Army's desperate need for more men. The earlier commitments to agriculture were shelved and by December 1917, only thirty-five thousand of the promised fifty thousand troops had actually arrived.[36] From Essex, came reports early in October that a mere seven men were available at the distribution centre to meet the demands of the county's farmers for sixty-one extra workers.[37] So desperate had the situation become by the end of the year that special agricultural furloughs of three months' duration were arranged for 1,500 soldier ploughmen serving overseas, who were to be brought home especially for that purpose.

Not until March 1918 did the full complement of soldiers reach the farms, by which time the sowing season was almost over. To add to the problem, many of the new arrivals proved to be totally inexperienced and from the late autumn of 1917 about thirty plough training schools had to be set up hastily by the Food Production Department. A three weeks' course of tuition was provided, with more than 4,000 men trained in this way to work with horses. Most had been van-drivers or carters from towns in civilian life, and so had some horse-handling skills. Other schools were established to train tractor drivers, these being men who knew how to drive motor cars or had knowledge of petrol engines. A two weeks' course at the school was followed by two weeks' apprenticeship on the farm, working with skilled drivers, before they were allowed to take charge of their own vehicle. In all, 4,093 soldiers were supplied for this work, with about two hundred more sent out for training with steam plough and threshing sets.[38] Farmers who co-operated in the scheme and provided two weeks' training for the men could use their services for other tasks free of charge when weather conditions made ploughing impossible.[39] Inevitably, however, with such hasty training arrangements the quality of work achieved proved very variable.

As a result of these expedients, by January 1918 around forty thousand soldiers of one kind or another were on offer for work on the land. By the following November that number had more than doubled. Yet, except for members of the agricultural companies, it was a shifting labour force, with soldiers withdrawn or moved on to other farms, as the pressures of war or the vagaries of administration dictated. Many farmers would doubtless have agreed with the Gloucestershire agriculturist who glumly declared in 1918 that 'soldiers selected to do agricultural work should be sent to the district from which they had been taken to join the Army'. His experience of military labour had been unfortunate. Of two men sent to him, one had been a barber and the other a stationer in civilian life. Neither was of the least use. 'They would never turn out in the morning, and seemed to consider that they had come to the farm to enjoy a holiday.' He had also applied for a man to do hedging, and yet the recruit sent to him 'knew nothing about it.'[40]

In Herefordshire, similar complaints were heard. Among the soldiers sent to work on the land there, were men who in civilian life had worked as a lift attendant, bricklayer's labourer, ship's painter, brass polisher, needle maker, chocolate maker, cabman, ladies' tailor, and musical conductor. From the Loughborough area of Leicestershire it was bitterly observed that very few soldier labourers had any idea how to work with horses, 'and it is an exception to get a soldier who can milk. They are poor substitutes for the skilled men taken from the land.' In that district the value of work performed was calculated in the ratio of three soldiers to two ordinary agricultural labourers.[41]

Punch, too, joined in the criticisms, depicting in its cartoons the CIII members of the agricultural companies as ineffective weaklings who were the despair of their farmer employers.[42] And anxious clergymen commented upon the adverse influence on the female population which was exerted when they were billeted in the villages. 'I believe... the presence of stray "soldiers" working on the land does not tend to "moral" improvement', commented one solemnly.[43] Others were worried that the radical social views of some of them would foment discontent in rural communities. At Drayton St Leonard in Oxfordshire, three men stationed there in the spring of 1918 were classed as 'Socialists from the towns', who were stirring up 'the muddy water & [giving] the people courage to protest against, e.g. bad housing conditions'.[44] This was clearly felt to be an unwelcome departure, however justified the villagers' grievances might have been.

The soldiers, for their part, often had little enthusiasm for their unsolicited agricultural chores, though most no doubt preferred them to the dangers and discomforts of the trenches. However, in Carnarvonshire, a farmer was frankly informed by one unwilling recruit that he would 'rather be in France than on a farm', while in Holland, Lincolnshire, other men flatly refused to remain in the sheds which were offered to them as sleeping quarters.[45] The need to feed and house them satisfactorily was also underlined by the Government. In May 1917, the Financial Secretary to the War Office warned that unless farmers catered for the soldiers in a suitable manner they could not 'expect to get the best work out of them, and... it would be natural that the men should want to come back to military service'. Later, as food supplies grew tighter, there was a growing reluctance among cottagers to offer billeting facilities to the military. This was a factor hampering the use of soldier labourers in areas as far apart as Yorkshire and the south-east of England, as well as in much of Wales. A Glamorgan farmer claimed in the winter of 1917-18 that he would have employed soldiers but the villagers would not lodge them 'owing to the difficulty in obtaining food'.[46] Even the introduction of rationing in the early months of 1918 did not solve the problem entirely, for supplies often remained short and not all food was covered by the new arrangements, bread being one notable exception.

To those soldiers who had been born in towns the unfamiliar and laborious grind of land work proved particularly unattractive, especially if they were sent to a critical and unsympathetic employer. There were also occasions when disputes arose between them and their employer over matters which were not their fault. Tractor drivers, for example, might be unable to plough as and when required because of the wet condition of the soil, or because the machine had broken down — a common problem in the early years. The following extract from the minute book of the Pembrokeshire Machinery Sub-Committee of the War Agricultural Executive, dated 22 May 1918, illustrates this aspect:

> *R.B. Prettyjohn, Heathfield*
> The Committee received a letter from Mr. R.B. Prettyjohn, complaining that the men on the Tractor did not commence work until 10 o'clock and that one of the men Pte. Mather had been grossly insolent. A report on the matter was also received from Mr. Green, Tractor Representative. The Committee being satisfied with the report, it was decided to reply to Mr. Prettyjohn regretting the unpleasantness but [they] did not consider it was any fault of the men being late starting work, and under the circumstances they were justified in leaving before finishing the field.[47]

During that week, in the county as a whole, eight of the thirty-two tractors provided by the Government had been out of commission, and one of the remainder had been able to work for only two days.

Some of the farmers also had unreasonably high expectations as to the range of duties which the soldiers could carry out. The War Office commented sharply on the complaints of one farmer about the deficiencies of his military helper:

> Mr. Goulding required a skilled farm hand who could work young horses, manage a horse hoe, grass mower, self binder, stack and thatch, and help to carry corn. He omitted to mention that he also expected this man to milk cows and to be

a poultry expert. . . . We have already asked Commands to send the best men they have at their disposal and who are available for agriculture. We cannot do more.[48]

Similarly on the Brassey estate at Apethorpe in Northamptonshire, the agent first of all asked for a soldier to be sent who could work with a steam plough; he then changed his mind and requested a man who could also act as a foreman, and when the military were not immediately able to supply a suitable candidate, he abruptly cancelled the whole arrangement.[49] Often, too, demands were made for military assistance at extremely short notice. On 30 January 1918, the Apethorpe agent asked for '12 horses and 4 soldiers to work them' to be sent 'at once'. The Horse Officer for the County Agricultural Executive Committee meekly replied the following day, regretting that he had insufficient animals on hand to meet this request, but promised to supply them the following week.[50] This kind of abrupt request was by no means unusual.

Yet, despite all the difficulties, without the contribution of the soldiers it would have been impossible to carry through the food production programme. Most farmers came to recognise this, particularly after the middle of 1917, when greater efforts were made by the military authorities to select suitable candidates.[51] Soldiers were by far the largest group of substitute workers used on the land, contributing perhaps 45 per cent of the total. Their numbers had risen from 61,000 at work in late March 1918 to around 87,000 by November of that year, of whom 79,000 were men in agricultural companies, 5,000 were specialist ploughmen who had been sent out on two months' furlough, and 3,000 were engaged in potato harvesting.[52] Even in December of that year, when farming activities had slackened for the winter, there were still 72,247 at work. This may be compared to 11,529 members of the women's land army and 30,405 prisoners of war also employed in agricultural work at that date. At this stage approximately one soldier was employed on the land to every nine civilian male workers.[53]

To supplement the contribution of the agricultural companies and the groups of soldiers released to help on a seasonal basis, farmers were also able to secure temporary aid from specifically named members of the armed forces. Often they were relatives, although sometimes a farmer who had himself volunteered was allowed to return to his holding for the harvest.

In Anglesey, for example, during mid-June 1916, eighty-five applications were forwarded by farmers for men to help with the haymaking; all save seven gave the name of a particular man and declared their unwillingness to consider a substitute. A high proportion of the soldiers mentioned had the same surname as the applicant and were presumably part of the family.[54] This kind of arrangement not only continued throughout the War but persisted after the Armistice. Thus of eighteen applications for assistance received by the Pembrokeshire Agricultural Committee on 13 November 1918, eleven were for men with the same surname as the applicant.[55] These arrangements, needless to say, applied in England as well as in the principality.

The way family linkages were used to bring back sons is also made clear in correspondence, as in the two following extracts from the Pembrokeshire Agricultural Committee letter book. Both were written early in August 1918, the first being addressed to the Officer Commanding the 15th Battery of the Welsh Regiment in France:

> Mr. T. Cousins, Whitlow farm, Martletwy, has applied to the Executive committee for temporary leave for his son Lance Cpl. Cousins over the corn harvest. Mr. Cousins Senr. has a large farm with more than 40 acres under corn, and as there is no skilled labour available in his district, the committee strongly recommend that if possible temporary furlough should be granted to his son.
>
> The Committee understands that Lance Cpl. Cousins has not had leave for twelve months.[56]

The second application was sent to the Officer Commanding the Welsh Regiment at Pembroke Dock:

> Mr. W. Evans, Hencoed Farm...has applied for temporary leave over the Corn harvest for his son Pte. J.B. Evans. Mr. Evans has a farm of 239 acres of which 67 acres are under cultivation, he has 86 cattle, 11 horses with only one man employed. It would be practically impossible for Mr. Evans to harvest his corn unless his son is granted furlough.
>
> As Pte. Evans has for the last three years been in sole charge of the Agricultural Machinery including the Binder on the farm, the Executive Committee strongly recommend that if possible Mr. Evans' application should receive fair consideration.

As a result of the appeals, Cousins was allowed the temporary furlough requested, and Evans was given one month's leave. Where successful, these arrangements gave the man concerned a short spell of welcome home leave. But the whole system was something of a lottery. Of ten applications submitted on behalf of Pembrokeshire Agricultural Executive Committee on 12 August 1918 (four of whom were for family members), *none* was successful. Yet of eleven applications submitted on the previous day (four of them again for family members), eight were successful. Most of those put forward on 12 August failed because the worker applied for was a Category A soldier and, as such, classed as ineligible.[57]

Only after the Armistice did matters become more relaxed. The cessation of hostilities could not be followed by immediate demobilisation, and complaints of shortages of agricultural labour continued. Consequently men of low medical category who were experienced farm workers and were serving at home were at once attached to agricultural companies and made available for land work. In January 1919, this provision was extended by an Army Council instruction allowing any agriculturist serving at home, no matter what his medical category, to be attached to one of the companies, pending his demobilisation. Under this arrangement, over twelve thousand men were sent out to their former employers on furlough.[58]

Meanwhile, demobilisation of agricultural workers was proceeding apace. The first to be released were the so-called 'key men', and within a week of the Armistice some of these were on their way back to the land. At the same time, plans were drawn up for the immediate release of those who had recently been called up and who were still in the country. By 12 February 1919, these various schemes had led to the demobilisation of fifty-four thousand agriculturists, most of them 'contract', 'pivotal', or 'slip' men, whom a farmer was ready to employ immediately they were demobilised.[59]

With such arrangements under way, labour shortages grew less acute. But even in the spring of 1919, there were still twenty-seven thousand soldiers at work.[60] And suggestions by the Government that the agricultural companies should be disbanded were greeted by howls of protest, farmers claiming that it was impossible to replace them. The matter was raised repeatedly in Parliament, and although on 16 April the Leader of the Commons declared it was impossible to keep men 'unde-mobilised if they [were] not required for military reasons', early in May it was decided to make certain concessions to the agricultural lobby. Under the new scheme, 20 per cent of the members of agricultural companies were to be retained temporarily. The late sowing season, caused by bad weather, was the principal reason put forward for this change of policy. [61] Eventually, as the demobilisation process moved towards its final stages, the labour shortage disappeared and the remaining soldiers were withdrawn. It was ironical that farmers, who had greeted the formation of the agricultural companies with derision, should prove in the end such enthusiastic advocates of their retention.

So far attention has been concentrated on those members of the armed forces who were released to help farmers with the general cultivation of their land. But there was another group of military men who were also widely employed in agriculture — the members of the Forage Corps, whose duty it was to bale hay and straw for the vast numbers of Army horses used in the war effort both in this country and overseas. Throughout these years they travelled round from farm to farm, working on ricks previously commandeered by the authorities. Their work was tiring, repetitive, and dusty, and they were expected to carry out their duties in all except the coldest or wettest of weather. One man who was employed as a baler in Kent during the autumn of 1916 later described the routine expected of them:

> We were divided into gangs of twelve and sent into various parts of Kent in charge of a sergeant. . . . Let me give you an idea as to how our party was formed.
>
> First of all was Jim Jephson one of our transport drivers with his pair of horses and wagon. He had two of the boys with him for company, then followed the train composed of the following, Traction engine, Hay-baler, Transport Wagon, Living Van and lastly Water Barrel, and then followed the other transport wagon driven by Bill Davis. Rather an imposing procession, as we went through the various villages on our route. Our men either rode or walked just as they wanted, and as we only travelled about 4 miles an hour we could easily keep up with the "train". The only order we got was that 2 men had to ride on the water barrel to look after the brake when going down hill. [62]

Once they had reached their destination, the team set up the machinery in the rickyard and began work. On good days they would bale as much as ten tons of hay, although often they were hampered by the machinery breaking down. This was scarcely surprising in view of the inexperience of the men working it. The hay was compressed into bales, each weighing about 200 lbs. and fastened with wire.[63] A female clerk travelled with the team, her job being to record the quantity of hay and straw delivered to the nearest railway station for onward despatch to military distribution centres.

The villagers, meanwhile, made the baling teams welcome. The Kentish party mentioned was based for some weeks in 1916 at the parish of Keston and soon made friends with local people. Some of the men were billeted with a shopkeeper and spent part of their leisure hours helping in the shop: 'we used to go just where we liked. The village club was thrown open to us, and several concerts and parties was (*sic*) arranged for our bene-fit. . . . A few days before leaving Keston the friends we had made got a concert and dance up for us and we had a fine time. The chairman made a speech saying 'how pleased he was that we had been staying in their village, and hoping we should have as fine a time wherever we went. Mr. Marder [the farmer] also gave us a small party at his house and . . . said how sorry he was to part with us'.[64]

In the later stages of the War, most of the duties of the male members of the Forage Corps were taken over by female sub-stitutes recruited from the women's land army, and the men were assigned to other duties. By 1917-18, indeed, women were being seen as an essential part of the nation's farm labour force, and appeals were issued to them to offer their services, through such diverse agencies as the offices of the Board of Agriculture and the pages of *Punch*. It is to that growing female contribution to the agricultural war effort that we will now turn.

Chapter 6

Women and Girls on the Land: 1914-18

'... since the food production campaign began the number of women on the land has been increased from something like 91,000 to over 300,000, that is to say whole-time and part-time workers. The local organization in each county consists of a women's war agricultural committee, of district sub-committees, an outfit officer who distributes the outfits, and a village registrar. All these are volunteers and unpaid.... Besides the village women included in the 300,000, there are what we call the land army. These are women who have undertaken to work on the land and to go wherever they are sent.' *Hansard*, 5th Series, Vol. 108, speech by the President of the Board of Agriculture, 18 July 1918, col. 1280-1281.

For most of the half-century before the First World War the number of women employed in agriculture had been falling. In 1871, 58,112 female labourers and farm servants were recorded in the population census, but by 1911 that total had fallen to 13,214. Only in areas devoted to market gardening, fruit and hop growing, and in more remote communities like those in Northumberland, Durham and parts of Wales, where women's involvement in land work was traditional, did the permanent labour force remain at a high level. In 1911, women comprised 22 per cent of Northumberland's agricultural labourers, and almost 11 per cent of those in Durham. In the former county, with its isolated, scattered farmsteads, it was still customary for a farmer to expect his hind to provide a woman worker as part of his conditions of employment.[1] Single women or widows, too, were sometimes hired as independent labourers, to help with the cattle or in tilling the soil.

West Wales, with its multiplicity of peasant holdings and its pastoral husbandry likewise employed many women and girls. Indeed, certain of the smaller hill farms were run by the female members of the family whilst the men were engaged in mining or quarrying, or away at markets and fairs negotiating for the purchase and sale of produce. In Cardiganshire, where women and girls formed almost 25 per cent of the total population engaged in agriculture in 1911, youngsters were trained for their duties from an early age:

> by the time they have attained the age of fifteen many of them are competent to perform all the lighter tasks that generally fall to the lot of women on farms. Amongst the classes of work invariably undertaken ... are milking, butter- and cheese-making, feeding of calves, pigs, poultry and cleaning of pens.[2]

Other tasks included loading dung carts, planting and harvesting potatoes, hoeing and gathering turnips, and, in the spring, driving the harrow. Only from ploughing were they exempted.

But elsewhere the contribution of permanent women workers was in decline. The main reasons for this were probably the low pay earned by most of them, which scarcely made the effort worthwhile, changing farming methods, and the improved real wages of male labourers, at any rate up to the end of the nineteenth century. It is perhaps significant that in the decade 1901-1911, when average real wages in agriculture were falling, the number of female farm servants and labourers increased by about 10 per cent. There were, in addition, a large number of part-time employees, who assisted at the busy seasons of the year, but probably did not declare their occupation to the census enumerator. The 1908 Census of Agricultural Production suggested that there were about 32,000 women in this category, but its figure of 68,000 for *permanently* employed workers possibly included female domestic servants who would rarely or never expect to work outside.[3] Certainly it is a figure far higher than any recorded in the Population Census returns between 1871 and 1931.

Other factors which reinforced the women's distaste for outdoor employment included the improvement in educational provisions, which made girls aware of opportunities outside the narrow confines of their own community, and a dislike of the drudging nature of the job itself. Male workers, too, were often unwilling for the female members of their family to go out into the fields, since this would not only disrupt home life but might undermine their own wages and employment prospects, if farmers were able to rely on a supply of lower-paid females.[4]

So it was that on the eve of the First World War, the employment of women on the land was well below its mid-Victorian level. At the same time, in arable areas or fruit growing districts, they still played a major part in seasonal activities. Even in 1914, these could last for many months in the year in some counties. Thus in the Holland division of Lincolnshire, work usually began with hoeing and weeding in the potato and corn fields in April. In the fruit and market garden areas, which covered a major part of the district, this was followed by the picking of soft fruit and the cutting of cabbage in May, and then continued on until the potato harvest, which might itself last to about Christmas.[5] Much the same conditions applied in the neighbouring counties of Cambridgeshire and Norfolk, with harvest work still of importance in the latter, despite the growing use of self-binders. Arthur Randell of Wiggenhall St Mary Magdalen in the Norfolk fens remembered his mother going with her younger children to help in the corn fields: 'There she would tie and shock sheaves . . . as fast as any man. About four o'clock she would take some of us back home, and when my father and the others came in about half-past seven the tea would be on the table'.[6]

Such was the general position, therefore, when the Great War broke out in August 1914. It was followed by that rapid fall in the number of male workers which has been noted in an earlier chapter. But initially, and perhaps surprisingly, this outflow did not immediately lead to any compensatory rise in the total of full-time females. Board of Trade statistics even suggest a *fall* of more than one-quarter in the women permanently employed on the land between July 1914 and 1915.[7] This can be attributed partly to the fact that more attractive and remunerative posts now became available to them as shop assistants, packers, delivery girls, railway workers, waitresses, and many others. In Leicestershire, in 1918 it was sourly observed that few labourers' wives would work on the land because of the greater opportunities offered by town factories and the munitions industry. In the county town itself women conductors on trams could earn 52s. for a 52½ hour week, plus a free uniform and one week's paid holiday, while in the factories 20s. to 40s. a week could be secured. Similarly, in Lindsey, Lincolnshire, the attractions of the local ironstone works were such that one large farmer claimed 'he could not get any girls over 15 years' to work for him. And in Warwickshire, where munitions factories were widespread, there was great difficulty in persuading females to take on any kind of land work.[8] The low esteem in which that employment was held before 1914 doubtless reinforced their determination to remain aloof.

For those married women whose husbands had joined up, there was a further economic reason behind their failure to seek agricultural employment. This was the separation allowance which they all received.[9] In October 1914, the wife of a private or corporal with two children obtained an allowance of 17s. 6d. per week, and with three children, 20s. — figures which compared well with the average weekly earnings of 17s. 10d. to 22s. 6d. secured by general labourers on farms in England and Wales in 1912-13.[10] Out of that the labourers had had to support both themselves and their families, whereas the allowance was for wives and children only. In the early months of the War, therefore, the military allowance alone provided a satisfactory income for many rural households. It could also be supplemented in counties such as Sussex, Essex and Kent, where large numbers of soldiers had to be accommodated, by income from billeting. An Essex woman recalled that when her village became a training centre not only was every available piece of ground suddenly covered with marquees and tents but the whole parish was canvassed to provide billets.[11] Similarly in Northamptonshire and parts of Norfolk the military allowance system and income from soldiers' lodgings were put forward as major factors in the failure of women to volunteer for field work.[12]

Only in the last months of the War, as food supplies tightened, did the enthusiasm for billeting wane. By this time, too, the value of the separation allowances had been eroded by inflation, the cost of living in July 1918 being about double the level of four years earlier while the amount paid to the wife of a private or corporal with two or three children was only about 70 per cent higher.[13] It is clear from War Cabinet discussions in January 1917 that one of the reasons for the failure to grant appropriate all round increases in the allowances was the fear that generous treatment might reduce the incentive for women to work. Significantly the rate paid to wives without children remained unchanged from October 1914 to the end of the War — at 12s. 6d. per week, while the childless widows' pension rate in October 1914 was fixed at only 6s. 6d. a week, even though some Cabinet members had pressed for 7s. 6d.[14]

But if economic considerations hampered the recruitment of female workers in some counties during the early stages of the

War, a further important stumbling block was the attitude of the farmers themselves. There was a widespread belief that women were incapable of performing the heavier or dirtier jobs on the land, or those involving the use of horses, and that they would refuse to work in bad weather. An Essex man claimed in March 1916 that although he had employed women during the summer, they were unable to meet his labour needs all the year round. He had lost twenty-five of his forty-three permanent male workers, and expected five more to be called up shortly. But 'it would take a good many more than thirty women to fill the vacant places. . . . The great difficulty he had to contend with in regard to women was discipline. It is no use for the women to run off home when a shower of rain came on'.[15] Likewise in Hampshire as late as January 1918, it was reported that many agriculturists had resolutely set their faces against women's labour: 'They will take on anything that comes along, boys, old men, cripples, mentally deficients, criminals, or anything else; . . . they will not have women'.[16] But in most places by that date such determined resistance was rare.

Another hurdle was that under the recruiting system the number of men allowed to remain on a farm was proportionate to its arable acreage or to the stock that it carried. Initially farmers feared that if they engaged unskilled, inexperienced women, they would lose their skilled men. Eventually the War Office removed this objection by issuing orders to their representatives that female labour was to be treated as only supplementary when assessments of farm needs were made. But the instructions were slow in filtering down, and some mistakes did occur, thereby reinforcing farmers' suspicions.

Opposition was encountered, too, from male workers who feared that they might be forced into the Army if women proved effective substitutes, or who saw tham as an unacceptable form of cheap labour. Their fears on the former point were given extra weight by certain of the more enthusiastic promoters of female labour, who stressed the ready availability of women to take the place of men.[17] Such initiatives were, however, discouraged by the Secretary to the Board of Agriculture. He took the view that they would merely infuriate the farmers and would have the effect of setting them against 'the whole of the women's organisation.'[18]

The farm workers' hostility, meanwhile, manifested itself in a resolution approved at the annual conference of their trade union in February 1916, which unequivocally condemned 'the introduction of...Women Labour into the Agricultural Industry'.[19] The delegate who seconded the resolution angrily declared that to his mind there was 'nothing more shocking...than to see women drabbling about in the fields. Their wages were half as much as the wages of men. If the women were allowed to work on the land, down would go the wages of the men'. Significantly, the patriotic gesture made by the union's first general secretary, George Edwards, in writing to the *Eastern Daily Press* early in January 1916 to appeal to the 'working-women of Norfolk' to offer their services for spring work on the farms, caused great offence to many members. It was a major factor behind the ill-tempered debate at the February conference.[20]

Alongside these problems, there were the difficulties caused by fluctuations in the demand for female labour. Apart from unavoidable variations caused by seasonal and climatic considerations, there was uncertainty as to the extent to which farmers could secure other kinds of help, including soldiers on furlough and prisoners of war. When these became available, requests for women workers fell away.

Initially the Government confined its own role concerning female labour to encouraging the formation of county committees to organise their employment under the aegis of the Labour Exchanges Department of the Board of Trade. In the early summer of 1915 a grant of £1,000 was also placed at the disposal of the Labour Exchanges to enable them to provide rudimentary training for suitable candidates. But the impact of these piecemeal schemes was limited. By July 1915, only nineteen special Women's Committees had been set up, and most counties were still without them at the beginning of 1916.

Nevertheless, during August 1915 the Labour Exchanges Department started to issue a series of 'notes' on war service for country women which, among other things, recommended the drawing up of village registers listing those interested in field work. Three months later the President of the Board of Agriculture also issued a circular recommending the establishment of short training courses by the newly-created County War Agricultural Committees, to familiarise potential workers with their duties before they were sent to a farm.[21] This following the pioneering example of Cornwall, where women's committees had already been formed in every parish, and arrangements made for instruction to be given in milking and dairy work.[22] At the same time the propaganda campaign was intensified. Between December 1915 and November 1918 every issue of the *Journal of the Board of Agriculture* included information on the work being carried out by women land workers. Alongside that, recruitment among the better off sectors of society was encouraged, with the Board appealing for women and girls of 'high standing socially, who live in a dairying district' to learn to milk. It was argued that if other inhabitants saw them going to and from work each day, they would be encouraged to follow their example, while employers would begin to take female labour seriously.[23] Such propaganda was in interesting contrast to the pre-war approach to middle-class girls and women, which had frequently placed its main emphasis on the importance of their acquiring 'appropriate' feminine skills and accomplishments, suitable for future wives and mothers, rather than for seeking independent employment outside the home.

This appeal to the well-to-do to play their part met with some limited success. Although the state was slow to intervene, a number of voluntary organisations appeared to make good the deficiency. Before the War only two bodies, the Women's Agricultural and Horticultural International Union (or the Women's Farm and Garden Union, as it became in May 1915) and the National Political League, had existed to train educated women for land work. The former, established in 1899, was concerned with females engaged in working their own land, or those in salaried posts in horticulture and agriculture; the latter, formed in 1911, had grandiose notions of promoting land settlements where trainees could learn poultry farming and similar tasks on a co-operative basis. Now they were joined by other bodies, including the Women's Legion, which formed an agricultural branch under the influence of Lady Londonderry, and the Women's Defence Relief Corps, formed by a Mrs Dawson Scott, which began to arrange for the seasonal recruitment of female land workers during the early summer of 1915.[24]

Most of these organisations were to prove of little value. The Secretary to the Board of Agriculture glumly concluded in the autumn of 1916 that the Women's Legion was expensive to run in comparison with the results it had achieved, while the National Political League was criticised for pursuing its

5. Forage Corps and Army Service Corps loading hay bales

6. Royal Garrison Artillery leaving Ivinghoe for France

SERVICE ON THE LAND.

The New Recruit. "SIR, I HAVE FINISHED FEEDING THE NON-RUMINANT PACHYDERMS. HAVE YOU ANY FURTHER ORDERS?"

7. Lack of soldiers' farming skills

8. Soldier operating mowing machine

objectives through the use of unspecified 'mischievous' methods. It, too, had little practical utility.[25] Confirmation on this latter point can be obtained from its surviving records, which suggest ambitious plans but little achievement. The Women's Defence Relief Corps was almost as useless. At its peak in the summers of 1916 and 1917 it sent out less than five hundred workers, mainly hop-picking, fruit gathering, and the like, and it seems to have been hampered by a perennial shortage of cash, despite its use of volunteer workers and its receipt of a small government grant of £50 in 1917.[26] Its members often had to endure uncomfortable living conditions when they reached the farms, being expected to sleep on the floor in outhouses upon chaff-filled canvas bags, and to eat off trestle tables and benches. Rates of pay were poor, many farmers refusing to give more than 13s. 6d. a week for the unskilled help they provided, and this scarcely met their basic expenses. When coupled with the arduous nature of the work they were required to undertake, it soon led to a falling away of support among would-be volunteers.[27] The organisation's over-optimistic and amateurish character is exemplified by the comment of one of its founders that farm work was so 'easily learnt... that all that would be required... to acquire what knowledge was necessary would be three days under the direction of a capable farmer'.[28] The reality proved very different.

Much the same charge of ineffectiveness could be levelled against Lady Londonderry's Women's Legion, even though the Board of Agriculture made an annual grant of two hundred pounds during 1915 and 1916 to assist its work. As the Secretary to the Board sourly observed in September 1916: 'It is all very well for say, the local duchess to be brought into a new movement at its inception, mainly because her name is of value in an advertisement and because her purse is useful to provide the necessary funds, but when the movement has once been started, unless the duchess has the good sense to efface herself as quickly as possible and allow the project to be carried on by the people who are primarily interested in it, in nine times out of ten the scheme is bound to fail'.[29] Eventually the work of both the National Political League and the Women's Legion was terminated by the Board of Agriculture on grounds of inefficiency, with matters between the Board and the Legion reaching crisis point in October 1917 over the deficiencies of the Rutland branch, its major sector.[30] Ultimately Lady Londonderry was persuaded to confine the Legion's 'agricultural' efforts to fruit bottling and horticulture. But it was small wonder that on 13 December, a Board of Agriculture official should complain of the mass of unco-ordinated private schemes: 'The country is full of these irresponsible training(?) centres for women, and they are doing great mischief'.[31] Part of the blame for that undoubtedly lay, however, with the Board's own slowness to take an initiative in this sphere.

It was, indeed, not until February 1916 that a comprehensive government plan for the use of female labour at last began to emerge. Under this, the Board of Agriculture was to urge the formation in every county of a Women's Farm Labour Committee, which would operate in conjunction with the County War Agricultural Committees, and would have its own network of district committees and village registrars. House to house canvasses were to be undertaken and lists of women prepared who were ready to volunteer on a full or part-time basis for land work. Within six months, the proposal had been adopted and sixty-three county committees set up, along with the appointment of 1,060 district representatives and over four thousand village registrars. Each woman who registered and began work was issued with a certificate which proudly proclaimed that the volunteer who helped in agriculture during the war was 'as truly serving her country as the man who is fighting in the trenches or on the sea'.[32] Efforts were made to arouse a sense of patriotism, and in order to promote comradeship, those who had completed thirty days' approved service were given a bottle green baize armlet, marked with a scarlet crown, as a sign of their commitment.

During the spring and summer of 1916 an estimated 140,000 women came forward in response to these appeals, of whom seventy-two thousand received certificates and sixty-two thousand armlets. However, by the end of the year, support had dwindled, and a confidential report issued at that time suggested only 60,000 women were now registered.[33] But these volunteers were supplemented by a large number of females who, although working on the land, refused to be registered. They feared that by so doing they might become liable for compulsory service, or would have to work for employers whom they disliked. In the Braintree area of Essex, for example, women were said to be refusing to register because they were 'terrified about being taken away from their own villages', while in Cheshire, where by 1918 females comprised about one-third of the total agricultural labour force, the fear of compulsion and dislike of the armlet were put forward as the principal reasons for non-registration.[34] The armlet may have been objected to because of its military overtones.

In order to simplify the organisation of part-time workers and to provide continuity of service for the farmer, special group-leaders or forewomen were also appointed. They were responsible for maintaining the time and pay sheets of their group — thereby relieving farmers of a tedious chore — and for arranging the payment of wages. In addition, so that married women with young children might work, efforts were made to persuade housewives who were unable to go out, to care for these youngsters and to give a helping hand with the washing, cooking, and sewing of the workers.[35] In some areas crèches were established for the youngest children, with the War Agricultural Committee of Holland in Lincolnshire proving a pioneer in this regard. An unfurnished house was hired at Holbeach and was fitted out partly by gifts and partly from a fund of £25 collected from local farmers. It accommodated thirty children and charged 6d. per day for an infant up to three years and 4d. per day each for a second and third child.[36] Similar nurseries were set up at Long Sutton and some other places under the general supervision of the local district nurse.

But if family and household commitments hampered the recruitment of some village women for work on the land, a major barrier for many was their lack of suitable clothing and footwear. Some of the more enthusiastic volunteers in Norfolk were said to be wearing their husband's boots while the menfolk were away in the Army.[37] But not all women favoured this solution. Consequently, in the spring of 1916 the Board of Agriculture entered into arrangements with the Co-operative Wholesale Society for the supply of appropriate clothing at specially low prices to the relevant Women's County Committees. Advice was given on the kind of clothes to be worn, the suggested outfit consisting of a drabett coat and skirt, knickerbockers, an overall, boots or clogs, leggings, and a hat. A price list of the articles was supplied to village registrars, who were to be responsible for placing orders. However, in view of the low pay of most part-time workers, with 3d. or 4d. an hour common during the summer of 1916, it is unlikely that the Board's suggestions were widely adopted. Even with the special price arrangements, a drabett coat and skirt would have cost 15s. 9d., while overalls were 6s. 11d. each and black leather boots, 7s. 8d.[38] In any case, at the end of 1916 the Co-operative Society withdrew from the scheme on grounds of labour shortage. Later, arrangements were made by the Women's Branch of the Board of Agriculture to allow the sale of certain articles of clothing and boots at low prices to those village women who had worked on the land for twenty-four hours a week over a given period. A Treasury grant of 5s. per pair was offered on the boots, with the women expected to refund the remainder of the cost.[39] In Hampshire alone during the seven months to February 1918, 589 pairs of boots, 48 pairs of gaiters, 29 overalls, 33 hats, and 19 pairs of breeches were sold to the county's two and a half thousand registered female workers under this scheme.[40] But apart from providing cheap footwear, the arrangement can hardly be said to have made a major contribution to the women's war effort.

Alongside these attempts to increase the employment of village women, the Board belatedly began to encourage the recruitment of a more permanent and mobile force of female workers, drawn principally from the middle-classes. In January 1916 it agreed to finance a training scheme run by the Women's Farm and Garden Union, and, at the same time, to help establish with that body a new joint association to be called the Women's National Land Service Corps (WNLS). As with the contemporary campaign to attract villagers, great stress was placed upon the patriotic importance of the work. Women were exhorted to join the WNLS in order to preserve the nations's food supply and, above all, to promote a favourable attitude towards female employment in agriculture by making a good impression upon sceptical farmers.[41] Within a year about two thousand had joined and after undergoing six weeks' training on one of the farms made available to the Corps, they were sent to their new posts. Often they went in groups of two or three, so that they could live in a cottage together, though others lodged with villagers or with their employer. In all cases they were expected to earn sufficient to cover their living expenses, and steps were taken to ensure that they did not undercut or supplant local women.[42] According to the second report of the

Corps, issued in the autumn of 1917, most of the trained workers obtained posts as carters and milkers, though several undertook milk rounds, and a number became ploughwomen — including some who drove tractors.[43] Throughout, the aim was to ensure that the women worked on equal terms with male labourers and did not seek special concessions. For only so, it was believed, could the latent hostility of farmers and labourers towards female landworkers be overcome. By their example, they could also encourage the village women to volunteer. One girl noted that when she first arrived at the small village to which she had been posted, all the females except two considered that farm work was beneath their dignity: 'when I appeared on the scene it astounded them beyond measure, but they have got over their shock to the extent that five are now helping on this farm alone'.[44]

For many middle-class girls, bored by a narrow pre-war round of small-talk, tennis parties, and dances, within a limited social circle, the WNLS offered an opportunity to display independence and self-reliance. The pride with which some of the members described their daily round makes this very clear. One enthusiast informed Corps headquarters:

> I have now worked on this farm over a year, and find I am able to do practically everything that comes round. My work begins at 5.30 a.m. with milking ten cows, feeding the young calves, and washing up the milking utensils. After breakfast I take part in whatever may be going on. We have been manure carting all last week, myself and one man keeping four carts going. I am able to manage the horses myself, and can prove that girls are quite capable of unloading the manure from the covered yards where beasts have been tramping it all the whole year. . . . I can take a team of three horses and lorry to the station and unload a truck of wet brewer's grains and also unload it again into the grain hole; also manage to fetch two tons of cake with the lorry and pair, and unload it out of the railway truck into the lorry . . . I have cut off and unloaded mangels, cut and camped swedes, take (*sic*) the beast to the sales, and get them numbered and penned. I helped to put the wheat in and harrowed it myself. During the hay and corn harvest I took my whack (as the men say) with the rest, on the rick or in the field with the machines,

and I unloaded every other load of corn from the first to the last load, ... and I took my turn whether unloading down on a low rick or right high up on the highest stack, nor did I keep the wagons waiting.... I end up the day by milking the ten cows again, feeding the calves and washing up. It is now about 5.30 p.m. and my time is my own, though in the long evenings we generally move the beasts from one pasture to another, and I do some gardening and mow the lawns and paths.[45]

Needless to say, among most farmers and male workers there was as much initial scepticism about these volunteers as there had been about many of their predecessors. Two recruits who eventually proved very successful land girls described how in their first post the farmer's assistant had been 'very much against the idea', saying 'it was no use employing "ladies," they wouldn't do any dirty work'.[46]

Despite the valuable momentum given to women's employment by the WNLS, however, in the long run it proved unable to meet the demands made upon it. In a confidential report issued at the end of 1916, it estimated that an additional forty thousand full-time female workers were needed, and these it could not supply. A more comprehensive programme was required.[47] A deputation from the Corps anxiously interviewed Rowland Prothero soon after his appointment as President of the Board of Agriculture in December, and suggested that the Government should initiate a Women's Land Army, with a special Women's Department at the Board to organise it. It also submitted a draft scheme for this, based on its own experiences, and although that was not adopted, the idea of a Land Army was.[48]

The first step in the plan was the appointment in January 1917 of Miss Meriel Talbot as director of the newly created Women's Branch of the Board. The year before she had been appointed the Board's first woman inspector and so was well qualified for her new task. Two months later an appeal for recruits for the Women's Land Army was issued. Initially the proposal was for ten thousand workers, but in the event thirty thousand applicants came forward, of whom two thousand had actually been placed on farms by the middle of July 1917. The Land Army differed from its WNLS predecessor in a number of ways.

Firstly, it was not confined to 'educated' women, though many of these did offer themselves for enlistment. Secondly, in the early days members had to sign up for the duration of the War, though in January 1918 this was changed, with commitments of one year or six months only required. Recruits also had to be prepared to move to any district if required, and to agree not to leave their job without the consent of the County Women's Agricultural Committee. Thirdly, a free uniform was provided, along with a recognised wage scale, free training (where necessary), free travel to the place of employment, and free maintenance in a depot for a period of up to two weeks if a girl were out of employment through no fault of her own.[49]

When a recruit had been medically examined — and according to Prothero, out of forty-five thousand women who eventually responded to the appeal, 50 per cent were rejected on this ground alone — she was measured for her outfit before going to the training centre or, if this were unnecessary, to the farm where she was to work. The outfit comprised two overalls, a hat, a pair of breeches, a pair of boots, a pair of leggings, a jersey, one pair of clogs and a mackintosh. A second issue of an overall, a hat, a pair of breeches, a pair of boots, and a pair of leggings was made six months later. The wearing of breeches, although eminently practical for women working among wet crops or on heavy ploughland, was regarded as particularly controversial, and in the early stages girls were ordered never to appear in public wearing them unless they were covered by an overall. Warnings were given against wearing jewelry or lace frills, and great stress was placed upon the need to uphold the high moral standards and good name of the Land Army. As the *Handbook*, which was given to every member, carefully pointed out:

> You are doing a man's work and so you are dressed rather like a man; but remember that just because you wear a smock and breeches you should take care to behave like an English girl who expects chivalry and respect from everyone she meets. Noisy or ugly behaviour brings discredit, not only upon yourself but upon the uniform, and the whole Women's Land Army. When people see you pass... show them that an English girl who is working for her Country on the land is the best sort of girl.

The cost of the clothing was considerable. Out of £230,273 spent by the Board of Agriculture on the Women's Branch during its first fifteen months, £130,037 had been expended on uniform. But suitable clothes were 'absolutely essential' if they were to carry out their work efficiently.[50]

Wages were fixed initially at 18s. per week, rising to a minimum of 20s., once a recruit had passed an efficiency test. In March 1918, the commencing wage was raised to 20s., with 22s. now paid to those who had passed an efficiency test, and in April 1919, a further increase was secured, with the minimum weekly rate raised to 22s. 6d. for the first three months, which included the training period, and afterwards advancing to a minimum of 25s.[51] Women who trained as motor-tractor drivers — a role they began to take on from November 1917 — were paid at least 25s. a week, rising to 30s. after a fortnight's successful work on a farm, and increased further after a month's employment by the payment of a bonus of 1s. for every acre ploughed after that date.[52] Out of these sums the girls had to pay for their own board and lodgings.

The WNLS meanwhile continued its operations, catering for those girls who did not wish to give a formal commitment to serve for a specified period, or who found other aspects of the Land Army regulations unacceptable. By the end of 1919, when it was wound up, it was estimated that it and its sister organisation, the Women's Farm and Garden Union, had placed over nine thousand women on the land (of whom 812 were still working on 30 September in that year).[53] However, possibly the most important aspect of Corps work in these later stages was in organising seasonal labour, under the aegis of the Board of Agriculture. Much of its contribution in this sphere took the form of recruiting women from the universities and the teaching profession to meet special demands during the busy summer season. In 1918 it enrolled over three thousand women from these sources to work in flax-pulling camps in Somerset, Northamptonshire, and elsewhere. But workers were also supplied for other tasks, including fruit picking, potato setting, weeding and hoeing, unskilled market gardening, and potato gathering. Wages were fixed at 20s. a week, or 18s. if free accommodation were provided, with the girls doing their own catering.[54] Finally, the WNLS continued to supply group leaders or forewomen for the organisation of village women, as well as candidates to head the Government training hostels in connection with the Land Army.

In the early stages, training was, indeed, a major pre-occupation of the latter organisation. Many new recruits proved extremely raw, and a network of training centres was needed to cater for them. These ranged from specially selected farms where two or three women were trained by the farmer at government expense, to practice farms on which groups of women worked together, and, finally, to the agricultural colleges and farm schools, which had been stripped of most of their male students by the War. These were now turned over to providing short courses for women.

At first instruction was given for a month only. But as Rowland Prothero subsequently admitted, this did little more than harden the students' muscles and give a rudimentary knowledge of the use of tools. Later the training was extended to six weeks, and efficiency tests were introduced.[55] Special attention was paid to milking, the care of horses, and, in the later months of the War, tractor driving for a few candidates. Thatching, in which women became very successful, was also taught. Even mole catching seems to have been within the scope of some.[56]

Much ingenuity was needed to instil into the recruits the rudiments of their future employment in the brief time available. At one training farm in Essex, two wooden 'cows' were provided with rubber udders on which the girls could practise milking. From these they moved on to goats, and only when they became fully proficient were they allowed to milk the valuable dairy cows. They were also taught to care for the farm livestock and poultry, and, at the appropriate seasons, to hoe, make hay, harvest crops, and to harrow.[57] Others learnt to plough, while some joined the special forestry section, despite initial doubts as to their suitability by the director of timber supplies.[58] Here they worked under the aegis of the Board of Trade and were taught to fell timber and saw it into lengths for pit props, trench poles, railway sleepers, and barbed-wire poles. Bark stripping and hauling the felled trees on special horse-drawn sledges were other tasks undertaken. A number also volunteered for the forage department, where they were engaged in teams upon the laborious task of baling perhaps eleven tons of hay per day for animal fodder. Later both of these sections were made into a separate Forestry Corps and Forage Corps, respectively.[59]

At first farmers and their wives looked askance at the Land Army recruits, partly because they were 'foreigners' and partly because of doubts as to their suitability for the work. A former maid who worked on a farm near Chichester recalled the amazement of local farm workers when she proved a proficient ploughwoman. Her prowess even formed a topic for conversation at the village public house: 'one farm hand from a different farm would go back and would tell his boss what he heard at the pub about land girls who ploughed. Two or three farmers wouldn't believe it. And they'd come on this farm and they'd see me doing it'.[60] Their scepticism was shared by some Members of Parliament, one of whom declared firmly that, on average, women were not worth 'more than 60 per cent of men; and in the main operations of farming there is much work they cannot do at all'. Even the Board of Agriculture seems to have concluded that a woman was only capable of performing two-thirds of the work of an average man.[61]

A further obstacle was that on small farms it was sometimes difficult to accommodate girls, especially if there were resident male farm workers as well. This was the case in North Derbyshire, while in Devon the farmers preferred to billet soldiers rather than Land Army workers. In Cardigan the difficulty was reinforced by the fact that smaller farmers tended to regard them as mere substitute domestic servants. They expected the girls to scrub floors, cook, nurse the baby, and do household work, as well as help in the fields, and were 'rather perplexed at being met with a blank refusal', as an official report put it in 1918.

Elsewhere it was the loneliness of the task or the unsympathetic reaction of local people which caused most unhappiness. One organising secretary reported visiting a recruit in October 1917 who had been bluntly informed by the farm bailiff that women were of no use on the land. Added to this, the girl had been taunted by villagers that she was 'taking a man's place and driving him to the Army'. Her landlady, a former housemaid at the Hall, disapproved of land girls and did not hide her dislike: 'I am not allowed into the house without taking off my boots.' In civilian life, this girl had been a milliner and after such a discouraging start she wanted to leave the Land Army. Fortunately the organising secretary managed to arrange a new posting for her, where she was able to work with other girls, and she settled down quite happily.[62]

Even with the best will in the world, however, long days spent hoeing crops or planting potatoes could prove monotonous and physically taxing to women unaccustomed to such unrelenting toil. Two girls who worked on a Devon farm recalled the aching backs and arms they endured for the first few months, as they lifted potatoes and mangolds, or spent the whole day 'shaking out heavy manure on the fields'.[63] Another middle-class girl who worked on a farm near Godalming in Surrey, along with three companions, made clear the arduous nature of the tasks undertaken, in entries in her diary. At the same time, she found consolation in observing the countryside and the wild life, as the following extracts make clear:

1917

18th June: Weeding in the oats in Big Field. We watched the hay-sweep and the swath-turned go out to Hidestile and presently they sent for us.

We had 9 o'clock lunch under an ash within sound of the snipe and by a cold spring of water. We were in the hay until 3 p.m. when a thunderstorm came on. We rode home to the farm. . . .

20th June: Haymaking at Ashlands. There was enough wind to make it difficult to round the cocks as you could only put up the swaths on the one side. We were in the hay until 3 when we were sent on the rick. We worked on the rick in a gale of wind which drove the seed into our eyes and filled our pockets and our clothes. At 9 p.m. when we stopped the wind had died down a little and there was a lovely sky. Clear golden light in the west but very stormy.

23rd June: The oats are nearly weeded at last and everybody's hopes are rising of a new job. The thistles have been like a young forest. Peggy did her best to cheer things along by reciting to us as we hoed . . . However, we've nearly finished those oats and it has made us all feel cheerier. . . .[64]

In the end this girl injured her wrist while potato-picking and had to resign, after working for about six months.

For many of the better-off recruits, the standard of accommodation offered on small farms was also a trial. A Somerset doctor's daughter described how at her first job on a farm near Totnes in Devon, she had to take her meals in the kitchen with her employer, his wife, their eight children — and nine cats.

These latter sat in a circle near the farmer and 'he used to spit out his bacon rind at them . . . He was the dirtiest old man I think I have ever seen in my life'. Her sleeping quarters comprised a small scantily furnished room, and for washing she was rationed to one pint of hot water a day.[65] But if she found her situation uncomfortable, the farmer's family probably regarded her as impossibly 'stuck up'.

Village women, too, often looked upon the land girls with a wary eye, and in Staffordshire it was claimed that they were 'working much better than usual to prevent farmers employing' these unwanted outsiders.[66] Similar hostility was reported from a number of Essex farms, though in Rutland, Land Army members were the subject of 'great interest', and local women there were encouraged to make enquiries as to the possibility of joining up themselves. But often the land girls had little sympathy for their cottager counterparts. The forewoman of a forestry gang working on the Welsh borders described how she had under her direction a group of land girls, who were acting as fellers, and some village women, who were responsible for clearing away the undergrowth. These latter she dismissively described as 'quaint old bodies, who have days off periodically to kill their pigs — always at the new moon, for evil will befall anyone who performs the deed except at the new moon . . . the next day the old lady returns to the woods, bearing with her a fearsome-looking concoction called pig's pudding — a kind of sausage composed of pig's blood and onions — and at lunch time all the old bodies gather round and have a great feast.'[67] It is almost as if she is describing the members of a remote foreign tribe rather than her own compatriots. It was this patronising approach which was roundly condemned by *The Times*:

> So if you chance to be billeted with a 'village woman,' young lady of the Land Army, bear in mind that she is a hostess worth knowing and one who can teach you much. And as for [a] fuller social life — may not yours and hers be the fuller and better for the sisterhood?[68]

The article had been provoked by the issuing of an appeal for more entertainment facilities to be provided for land girls, including invitations to country house parties and tennis club tournaments.

The authorities, for their part, remained primarily concerned to maintain the high moral reputation of the Land Army, and there were repeated calls for tighter controls to be exercised in this regard. From Leicestershire, the County Women's War Agricultural Committee proposed the imposition of fines or punishments upon those who behaved in an unruly manner or who absented themselves without notice from the farms to which they had been sent.[69] Similar sentiments were expressed by Lady Mather Jackson, chairman of the Monmouthshire Committee, when she noted that one major problem was that the girls were 'constantly asking for week-ends off, and [showing] their opposition to the order with regard to their time of coming in at night... They stay out late and often do not return to their Farms until 12 and one in the morning and this is of constant occurrence if they are within distance of a Town, and naturally they are very much talked about... No doubt we have here an absolutely different Class of Girls to deal with than in most Country Districts as they are drawn from Industrial Centres and from Colliery Districts, where they have been under no control or discipline whatever, and have been brought up to practically do nothing, their Fathers earning big wages as Colliers'.[70]

In Hertfordshire, the following rules were drawn up by an anxious County Committee in August 1918:

1. No member is allowed to enter the bar of a public-house.
2. Members must be in their billets for the night by 9.30 p.m. If prevented, they must satisfy their landlady that they have a really good reason for staying out later.
3. Members are not allowed to smoke while at work, or in any public place when in uniform.
4. When in uniform, members must always wear the overall in any public place.
5. Members are not allowed to have any communication whatever with German Prisoners of War, whether on or off duty.[71]

Even Meriel Talbot, the Director of the Women's Branch, gloomily predicted that 'at any moment some scandal about the Land Army' would 'break out and the Department blamed for its inadequate supervision'.[72] But she recognised that as the Land Army was not truly an army and the girls were working for private employers, any attempt to impose military discipline such as applied in the Women's Army Auxiliary Corps (WAAC) would be doomed to failure.[73] Happily, too, in almost every case the alarmists' anxieties proved groundless. Nonetheless, during the summer of 1918 the Women's Branch did appoint eighty full-time welfare officers, whose duty it was to visit the workers and to ensure that their conduct was above reproach. They were also to organise clubs and arrange carefully supervised leisure activities such as concerts, amateur theatricals, sewing classes, reading circles and evening lectures.[74] From January 1918 the Army even ran its own monthly journal, called the *Landswoman*. Through its columns women in remote country places could get shopping commissions carried out for them in London, a correspondence club was established, and news was given of Land Army rallies up and down the country. The exchange of day-to-day experiences which its columns provided gave a sense of 'belonging' even to the most solitary girl.[75]

But if concern for workers' welfare was one important factor in the Land Army's success, another was its ability to overcome the doubts of farmers as to its members' efficiency. To this end organisers arranged competitions and shows where they could demonstrate their skills. The pacemaker was Cornwall, where the first competition, privately arranged, was held at Launceston on 9 March 1916, a year before the Land Army itself was launched. It was followed soon after by similar demonstrations at Trure (on 7 April), St Austell (on 11 May), and at Helston (on 12 June 1916). All three of these last were organised by the County War Agricultural Committee. Competitions included ploughing matches, harrowing, rolling, horse raking, harnessing horses, driving waggons, hand hoeing roots, preparing seed beds, and many other tasks.[76] The idea soon spread, especially after the Land Army made its appearance. In July 1917, for example, what was billed as a national competition for experienced women workers was organised at Bishops Stortford, with 340 participants. *The Times* waxed almost lyrical over the event:

> Across the sun-scorched fields, with a pleasant breeze coming occasionally to lighten their labours, the land women, bronzed and freckled, strode with easy step, walking from the hips, splendidly healthy... With bill-hook and stick they cleared out the ditches, bending to their work after the

manner of the various counties whence they came. Strong of arm, they piled their carts with manure... and then they tilted their load in its place and set it out. They hoed, drawing the earth well up around the plants... They harnessed horses.[77.]

Milking, the plucking and dressing of poultry, and harrowing were other tasks undertaken, all with great success.

Through these initiatives and with the steady improvement in the training and skill of the women recruits, the value of the Land Army was slowly recognised by farmers. Although as late as the winter of 1917/18 there were still many who considered them 'more as aids to men than substitutes', and regarded them as relatively expensive compared to their male counterparts.[78] They also found difficulty in obtaining winter employment unless they could milk. And if the Board of Agriculture's estimate that on average they could only do about two-thirds of the work of men were accurate, the claims of their high cost would seem justified. For in January 1918, while the average weekly wage rate of ordinary male labourers in the Midland, Eastern and Southern counties ranged between 25s. and 27s. per week, the lowest paid Land Army girls received 18s., rising to 20s. per week when they had acquired some experience.

But despite allegations of their costliness, the women earned admiration for the determined way they stuck to their work despite bad weather and the arduous nature of many of the tasks they tackled. Northamptonshire farmers described them as 'very plucky' and as 'always very keen and... very patriotic, and always try as hard as they can'.[79]

They certainly needed all the resolution they could muster to overcome the discomforts of inclement weather, strained muscles, and dust and dirt. An Oxfordshire girl who worked in the Forage Corps recalled how some of the hay ricks purchased by the Army had been 'left standing for years... sometimes we found the centre full of white powder and we were sneezing, weeping, etc. At one village [we] bought a red-spotted handkerchief, and we knotted it round our necks and stopped the dust getting down our necks'.[80] Similar difficulties were encountered by the threshing gangs, with many improvising masks of muslin or light canvas as a protection against the dust and smoke.

Alongside the general drudgery, there were also acts of

individual bravery, like the girl who went into a box where a cow, mad with pain after calving, was killing her calf, even though none of the men would go near. She pacified the animal and saved the calf. Then there was the woman who saved a fellow worker from being gored by a bull by kicking the animal violently on the nose, so that it backed away long enough for the man to get up and escape. As a recognition of these contributions, a special distinguished service bar, awarded by the director of the Women's Branch, was introduced in October 1918, with a total of forty-six bars eventually awarded.[81] The Land Army badge, to which the bar was attached, was itself awarded after two months' satisfactory service.

Overall between March 1917 and October 1919, around 23,000 women were placed on the land by the WLA, 15,000 of them after receiving some form of training. In July 1918 alone 2,775 were under instruction. And of the 12,657 women whose subsequent career was recorded, 5,734 obtained positions as milkers, 293 as tractor-drivers, 3,971 as general field workers, 635 as carters, 260 as ploughwomen, 84 as thatchers, and 21 as shepherds. The remainder were distributed among the other branches of the agricultural industry.[82] And as the labour shortage intensified following the military recruitment campaign of the spring of 1918 and as the Land Army became accepted even by conservative farmers, so the number of recruits employed rose. On 24 November 1917, there were 6,672 at work. This had increased to 7,665 by March 1918, and reached a peak of about 16,000 by September in that year.[83]

The President of the Board of Agriculture, Rowland Prothero, subsequently described the way that farmers' attitudes shifted. In March 1917 any allusion to women workers at meetings attended by agriculturists

> was received in silence or with disapproving grunts. Three months later, there were interjections for or against their employment. Then came an interval when the subject was received with applause, more or less slight. . . . The final stage was reached, when the real gratitude of the farmers was expressed in the call for "three cheers for the women." The Land Army and the village women had won.[84]

That was perhaps too sanguine, for a large proportion of agriculturists regarded them as poor substitutes for men even at the end of the War.[85] But Prothero's claim of a softening of hostility was clearly valid.

Especially in the early days, the use of Land Army workers also showed significant regional variations. In March 1918, out of 7,665 women under WLA jurisdiction, four thousand were employed in Norfolk, an arable county where they were needed for field work, and just over one thousand in the dairying counties of Lancashire and Cheshire. A later survey, for the week ending 26 April 1919, showed 10,103 at work throughout England and Wales. Once again, Lancashire and Cheshire featured prominently, with 784 recruits between them. A third major user was Kent, with 802 workers, of whom 267 were engaged on threshing in the west of the county.[86] But now the girls were much more evenly spread throughout the country, with fourteen counties having between two hundred and three hundred members at work.

After the Armistice, totals inevitably dwindled, although as late as October 1919 there were still eight thousand WLA women at work. Not until 30 November was the Land Army at last disbanded, after the end of the potato harvest.[87] Significantly, some of those who were still working at the end of 1919 wished to stay in agriculture. In order to help them, the Government offered free passages to the dominions for those desiring them, while land settlement facilities in this country were made available to a few. But most who stayed on did so as ordinary employees, and merged into the general female agricultural labour force.[88]

Village women, meanwhile, largely returned to their domestic duties when their menfolk returned from the front or from government work. In July 1918, 90,900 females had been *permanently* employed in agriculture, according to Board of Trade estimates; this compared with 57,000 women so engaged in July 1914, and 79,400 two years later.[89] But by June 1921, when the first post-war Census of Population was taken, only 32,265 females classed themselves as agricultural labourers and farm servants, along with 19,440 women farmers (11,485 of these last being widows). Admittedly, the total of labourers had increased sharply compared to the 1911 figure of just over 13,000, but it was well below the position in mid-Victorian England, let alone that of the war years.[90] And of those still at work, 2,156 were in Northumberland, a traditional centre of female activity, where they now comprised over a quarter of the total agricultural work force. Lincolnshire, another traditional area, had 2,592, and Kent, with its hop-picking, market gardening, and fruit growing preoccupations, had 3,114.[91] Elsewhere it seems that the old attitudes towards female employment on the land had rapidly reasserted themsleves. In the years of growing unemployment which followed, this became still more evident. In 1922, the biennial conference of the farm workers' union unequivocally passed a resolution declaring that 'where male labour is available female labour should be discouraged'.[92] By 1931, the number of female agricultural labourers and farm servants had fallen to under eighteen thousand (compared to 476,984 male workers employed at that date). (See Appendix 1). Even among farmers, the women's total had dropped to 17,367 (10,448 of them widows); this was lower than it had been before 1914. During the War the situation had been very different. For then, despite the importance of the Land Army and the other middle-class organisations in raising the status and perhaps the efficiency of women land workers, it had been the ordinary villagers who on a full-time and part-time basis had borne the brunt of the additional work load.

Nor was the contribution of village women during those difficult years confined to farm work. In a number of areas, arrangements were made for them to cultivate waste land or allotments, particularly where farmers were initially unwilling to experiment with female labour. In Cornwall, such initiatives were undertaken in the summer of 1916 because many of those registered for landwork had been unable to obtain it.[93] And in Monmouth and Devon, derelict farms were handed over by the County War Agricultural Committees to the Women's Committees to be cultivated entirely by female labour.[94]

The Board of Agriculture, in its notes on 'War Service for Country Women' took a similarly broad line when discussing the contribution they could make:

> nearly all of us could help in picking fruit, both wild and garden varieties, for jam, and in making as much jam as possible... some of us could go out weeding and hoeing for the farmers; many of us could start keeping fowls or take more pains with the fowls we have already got, so that they shall be more productive; all of us can see to it that no ground is

wasted in our own gardens that might be used for growing more vegetables for use in the winter ... let your neighbours know that you are ready to help them; it may be that War work for you will be in minding the children next door while their mother works in the fields or goes out milking, because all the farmers' men have joined the Army.... If you know of an allotment or bit of garden that is not being used, try and get it for growing more vegetables for your own use, or for sale during the coming winter.[95]

These appeals were reinforced by references to the tasks carried out by French and Belgian peasant women, often under the most difficult conditions. The Essex Women's War Work Association, for example, pointed out that Frenchwomen were taking on all the work of their farms even though shells were bursting around them. 'It must not be laid to the door of Englishwomen that because the men have left to fight for them and their children, fewer cows are kept, fewer chickens are reared, fewer potatoes grown and less land cultivated, so that in consequence food becomes ever dearer and dearer'.[96]

However, perhaps the most significant development for the female members of village communities to emerge from the War was the growth of the Women's Institute movement in this country. Women's Institutes had started in Canada in 1897, though it was not until September 1915 that the first was opened in Britain, in Anglesey. It owed its existence to the influence of a Canadian widow, Mrs Alfred Watt, who had settled in this country. By Christmas 1915 there were four Institutes formed in Wales and three in England, and at this stage great stress was placed by their leaders on the need to conserve and increase home food supplies, as well as to promote a spirit of co-operation and comradeship among members. During the following year the movement spread steadily, with forty Institutes in existence by the beginning of 1917. The Government, too, had now become interested in the project and in September of that year it agreed that the Women's Branch of the Board of Agriculture should take responsibility for forming new Institutes, although once established they were to be free to make their own rules and to operate independently, within their national and county federations.[97]

An examination of the first reports of the Institutes indicates their wide range of activities, although in the long run perhaps the most valuable of these was their social role. For the first time, village women were able to meet together to discuss common problems and to manage their own affairs on a non-religious, non-political basis. To *The Times*, the new movement was a major plank in the regeneration of rural life: 'one of the most satisfactory consequences resulting from the formation of a Women's Institute,' it declared, ' is the number of village women who learn to give expression to their ideas and who themselves become lecturers and demonstrators of no mean order'.[98] Lady Denman, the first chairman of the National Federation, also stressed the need to promote village industries if the pre-war exodus from the countryside were to be checked. Already by the summer of 1918 a number of Institutes had embarked on soft toy making, basket making, rush mat weaving, and similar crafts upon a commercial basis.[99]

Nevertheless, during the War years a major part of the Institutes' energies was concerned with food production. Among the various projects set in hand were those at Bibury, Gloucestershire, where a branch of fifty-four members had not only bottled a large quantity of fruit during their first year of operation, but had cultivated extra garden ground, and purchased seeds and chicken food on a co-operative basis: 'Herbs have been collected. Several Members have started rabbit-rearing and goat keeping'.[100] Similarly at Criccieth in Wales, where membership had reached 149, demonstrations were held and lectures given on fruit and vegetable bottling, with a canning machine and equipment purchased co-operatively. 'At least five extra acres have been cultivated, seeds and potato sprayer were bought co-operatively. The co-operative selling of produce has been transferred to a registered Co-operative Society. Spagnum Moss and wastepaper have been collected, sugar has been distributed to fruit growers, and a Red Cross Working Party has been held'. Market gardening and poultry production were undertaken on a commercial basis, with a special wholesale market organised from the summer of 1916.[101]

At Llanfairpwll in Anglesey, the Institute was instrumental in getting a nurse-midwife for the village and in organising and equipping a girls' club, while at Downton in Wiltshire activities included the provision of school dinners and the co-operative purchase of coal. A year later, this latter community had extended its horizons further, with the establishment of a children's boot club and the holding of weekly meetings on law, government and social problems by request of the members, 'since the granting of the vote to women'.[102] Another village expressed its determination to get members elected to the parish council in order that they might bring about an improvement in housing conditions, and by the summer of 1919 reports were coming in of success in this direction. As one Surrey institute proudly proclaimed, thanks to its efforts three women, all WI members, had been elected to the parish council where formerly it had consisted only of men.[103]

But on a more mundane level, many Institutes clearly regarded their food raising activities and rabbit, goat, and pig clubs as the principal features of their existence during the War years.[104]

Ironically, then, of all the war-time societies and associations set up to cater for women in rural areas, it was the Women's Institutes alone which were destined to endure and to flourish. By October 1919 there were already more than 1,200 of them, with Hampshire alone registering 87, Essex 70 and Dorset 57.[105] Certainly Rowland Prothero, as President of the Board of Agriculture, saw them playing a major part in the Board's overall plans for improving the quality of rural life, and there were proposals for them to act as the focus for local education authority courses in domestic economy and for health improvement schemes in connection with the newly-created Ministry of Health.[106] These wider ambitions did not materialise, although many Institutes did concern themselves with child welfare proposals and subscriptions to local nursing associations and hospitals. Overall the value of the movement in improving the lot of country women, and in broadening their horizons remained considerable. The Board of Agriculture itself, meanwhile, withdrew from WI organisational work in October 1919, when it handed over responsibility to the movement's own National Federation. They have retained it ever since.

Chapter 7

Prisoners of War and Aliens

'At one time the sight of prisoners of war under guard working on the land caused considerable comment in the countryside, but we have got used to it, and no one now takes any notice of the captives as they go to and from their daily tasks. It may be added to the credit of German prisoners that many farmers we have spoken to are well pleased with the way they work and particularly the men who were engaged in agriculture before the war'. *Mark Lane Express*, 13 May 1918, 451.

'The help given by the prisoners of war during the 1919 harvest went far to overcome the difficulties which arose through the withdrawal of the soldier labourers'. J.K. Montgomery, *The Maintenance of the Agricultural Labour Supply in England and Wales during the War*, Rome 1922, 49.

Of all the substitute workers employed in agriculture during the last difficult months of the War, among the most valuable, and perhaps the most unexpected, were German prisoners of war. The number employed jumped from around five thousand at the beginning of 1918 to more than thirty thousand by the year's end. This compared with over seventy-two thousand soldiers, eleven thousand Land Army women, and almost four thousand War Agricultural Volunteers also at work under government auspices at the later date.[1] Nor did their use end with the Armistice. Even in September 1919 more than twenty-five thousand of them were still employed, and although this total had dwindled to 9,325 by the end of October, it was not until the following month that the repatriation programme came into full effect.[2]

The decision to employ enemy aliens in this fashion had not been lightly taken, for to many people they seemed a potential source of saboteurs and spies. Even in the early weeks of the War, before the internment of civilian enemy aliens had been completed, certain farmers had claimed that rick fires which had occurred in their area had been caused by clandestine action on the part of some of them.[3] In Norfolk, a few Dutch agriculturists, who had come over to this country before the War to teach local farmers to grow sugar beet, also came under suspicion once hostilities began. Despite the official neutrality of their homeland in the conflict, many villagers regarded all 'furriners' as possible spies.[4]

With such attitudes in mind, the Government proceeded cautiously when it came to using prisoners of war on the farms. Indeed, the first aliens to be suggested for large-scale agricultural employment were not Germans but Belgian refugees. These had been forced to leave their native country as the German armies advanced during the autumn of 1914. By early January in the following year about one hundred thousand of them had arrived in this country, and the occupations of almost a quarter of them had been classified.[5] Of these, a mere 654 had been engaged in agriculture in their own country, the vast majority being industrial workers. In these circumstances, British farmers were somewhat wary about taking them on, and those who did soon began to complain of their inefficiency or of their demands for higher wages. One Leicestershire man, for example, angrily described the case of a refugee who had refused to work because he was not paid 'Trade Union wages'. The farmer declared that he 'did not know what Trade Union wages were, but... if the Belgians were not prepared to work for a fair wage it would be better for the Trade Unions to keep them'.[6] On the Duke of Bedford's estate at Tavistock in Devon a number were taken on from January 1915 for work in the woodlands, but the overall total was small, with their monthly wages bill ranging between £30 in January, £15 2s. in October, and £17 in December of that year. The estate also spent £185 1s. 9d. on clothing for them.[7]

Other refugees found themselves in far remoter communities. One family of six arrived in the small Merioneth parish of Llanfair during the winter of 1914-15, the husband having previously been employed as a stevedore. They found great difficulty in getting any employment and for much of the time were supported by charitable gifts from the parishioners, supplemented by what the womenfolk could earn with their needle. They seem eventually to have returned to London during May 1916, thanks to the efforts of the Rector, who had been largely responsible for bringing them to Llanfair in the first place.[8] To people used to life in a bustling Belgian port the contrast between that and daily existence in a quiet corner of rural Wales must have been great indeed.

At this early stage in the War, therefore, when labour shortages were not severe, there was little enthusiasm in agricultural circles for the employment of inexperienced Belgians. Even the Duke of Bedford ceased to use them from 1917.[9] And as early as June 1915, branches of the agricultural workers' trade union were protesting against the 'employment of Aliens on the land', since that was undermining the bargaining position of their own members.

With the failure of this first initiative to mobilise foreign labour for British agriculture, several months elapsed before the next move came, in the spring of 1916. This time the proposal was to import workers from Denmark and, most surprising of all, from Schleswig-Holstein. For the latter now formed part of the German Empire, even though it had strong historical links with Denmark and there was evidence of Schleswig-Holsteiners deserting from the German army in order to enter that country as refugees, as the War progressed. Between three and five thousand ex-soldiers were thought to be in Denmark by December 1917.[10] From the British point of view, their main recommendation was that they were skilled agriculturists. Sir Auckland Geddes at the Ministry of National Service later called them 'some of the best farmers in Europe', and it was envisaged that both they and the Danes would be employed in Britain for at least twelve months. Their travelling expenses would be advanced by farmers who wished to engage them, on the understanding that such advances would be deducted from their wages once they began work. The men were to be young, mainly between eighteen and twenty-five years of age, single, and with practical farming experience, particularly of dairying, in their native land. When they reached this country they were to be boarded and lodged by their employers and were to be paid the appropriate local rate for skilled workers.[11] The plan remained under review for about six months but in the end little was achieved. As far as the Schleswig-Holsteiners were concerned, the lack of progress was attributable partly to objections from the Intelligence Department of the War Office, who feared that potential German spies might be imported among them, and partly to shortage of shipping space to carry them across the North Sea.[12] As regards the Danes, the poor rate of remuneration offered by British farmers, transport difficulties, and the objections of the Danish government, who took the view that they could not 'spare a single farmer', effectively torpedoed the arrangements. In the end only a few Danes were recruited.

Yet, despite this discouraging start, as the labour problems in British agriculture grew more severe during the autumn of 1917, under military recruitment pressures, the idea was revived. With the Government's campaign to increase the tillage area there was particular anxiety to secure additional skilled ploughmen, and by December 1917, secret negotiations were under way to bring in, as a first instalment, a thousand Danes and three hundred Schleswig-Holsteiners, but with the possible option of increasing the inflow of Danes to twenty thousand.[13] Ploughmen were the main priority, and the men were to be shipped into the country from ports in Sweden and Norway as well as Denmark itself. It was hoped to have the immigrants ready for work on the farms early in February, and in this context the Board of Agriculture regarded the 'Schleswig-Holstein farmer' as 'the first man to capture'. However, as in 1916, negotiations dragged on for many weeks without success, to the mounting impatience of the Ministry of National Service, which was spear-heading the recruitment drive. By late April 1918 all hope of bringing in the Schleswig-Holsteiners had been abandoned, and the proposed number of Danes to be recruited had been trimmed from a thousand to a mere two hundred.[14] Although Rowland Prothero reported that those Danes who were employed proved good workers, the Board of Agriculture warned that their numbers were too small for them to be made widely available.[15] From the point of view of the British farmer the venture had been little short of a fiasco. Nevertheless, the fact that on two occasions the Government had been prepared to contemplate the wholesale immigration of Schleswig-Holstein agriculturists at the height of the War throws an interesting light both on official attitudes towards the labour shortage on the land and the desperate measures considered to combat it.

It was in these circumstances, therefore, that during April 1916 the question of employing German combatant prisoners of war came under review. Hitherto few prisoners had been employed in Britain in any capacity, since they were normally either retained behind allied lines on the western front or were sent direct to detention in the dominions.[16] The proposal at this stage was for them to be used to help with timber supply work in order to substitute home-grown pit-props for imported ones. In the Cabinet discussion which followed, it was pointed out that Germans were already employed on various projects in France, and that a similar initiative might be taken here.[17] The plan was adopted and by early September 1916, out of 5,332 prisoners at work on different schemes in Great Britain, including quarrying, road building, and the extraction of gravel, over six hundred were employed at camps in England and Wales on timber cutting. However, at this stage one of the great problems was providing what was deemed an 'adequate' guard. In the case of one party of 135 prisoners, the local authority asked for, and obtained, a guard of seventy soldiers. Another difficulty was the potential hostility of the population at large towards the settlement of Germans in their midst, even with guards. To the War Office this was particularly important when considering the deployment of small parties of prisoners. As a memorandum of September 1916 put it: 'The atrocities in Belgium at the commencement of the war, submarine outrages, particularly the *Lusitania*, and Zeppelin raids have all acted against such employment'.[18] Nevertheless, the progress already made was considered sufficiently encouraging for consideration to be given to deploying prisoners on land reclamation and drainage work. From that it was but a short step to propose their employment in agriculture.

Already by the middle of November the Government was being pressed by MPs to use prisoners for farm work, and on 21 November, the Secretary for War, David Lloyd George, admitted that efforts were being made to discover the attitude of employers towards their recruitment for that purpose.[19] This was taken a stage further by James Hope, a Treasury minister, when he declared that a scheme was in hand under which small parties of men could be sent to individual holdings providing the employer would assume responsibility for their custody, housing and feeding.[20] But at that stage few agriculturists were willing to take on responsibilities which might prove both hazardous and costly, and so little progress was made.

Almost a month then elapsed before the Board of Agriculture brought forward a new plan, and on 16 January 1917, all

County War Agricultural Committees were circularised, advising them of the proposed developments. Under these, groups of seventy-five prisoners were to be made available to each county for use on farms, along with a guard of thirty-five soldiers. The men were to be lodged in a central depot and were to be allowed out each day in small parties of about five workers apiece, with their guard. Except under special circumstances they were to be kept within a three-mile radius of the camp, and farmers were to pay the authorities for their services at a rate which approximated to that paid to ordinary labourers in the area. In most cases this worked out at about 5d. or 5½d. an hour, of which the prisoners themselves received about 1d. or 1½d., the larger sum being paid to men who had some previous knowledge of agriculture.

Before any prisoners were allowed to move into an area, the County Agricultural Committee had to satisfy themselves that there was work for at least sixty-five of them for a minimum of two months, this employment to include not only the ordinary work of cultivation but the scouring and clearing of water-courses and ditches, and any other useful labour which would boost food production.[21] They were to be deployed only during the hours of labour customary for farm workers in the district, thereby reducing the temptation for farmers to use them as cheap labour to the detriment of their regular employees, and were not to work on Sundays except for 'the milking or tending of livestock, or attention to produce grown under glass'. Even then they were restricted to a maximum of two hours. As far as possible, efforts were to be made to include at least one prisoner in each of the working parties who had some knowledge of English, although no guarantees on this could be given. The military were to be responsible for their feeding and board, and if any were injured in the course of their work, the employer was exempt from payment of compensation under the Workmen's Compensation Act. The parties would consist primarily of ordinary private soldiers, since non-commissioned officers were not required to work unless they volunteered to do so, and officers were exempt from employment of all kinds.[22]

Alongside these plans for the creation of special agricultural camps, arrangements were made for a few men in appropriately located general prisoner of war camps to be employed on the land. These included Blandford and Dorchester in Dorset, and the records of one Dorset farmer show him receiving his first contingent of prisoners as early as 7 February 1917. The party comprised four workers, one cook, and their English guard, and they seem to have resided on the farm.[23] Prisoners were to be employed by this farmer for more than two years, the last group departing on 28 June 1919. But few of the large general camps had been formed with agricultural work in mind, and most were sited in or near industrial areas. Their use as sources of labour for the farms was thus strictly limited, and an inspection of thirty-five of them conducted in the autumn of 1918 showed that out of a total PoW population of 14,998 only 3,350 were employed in agriculture.[24] Even Blandford camp, despite its rural location, had only 200 men working on the land out of a total prisoner population of 407; of the remainder, 148 were engaged on Royal Engineering Services aviation projects. And at Dorchester, out of 1,030 prisoners a mere sixty were employed in agriculture, compared to almost 600 on Royal Engineering works and 233 employed by the Air Ministry.[25]

It was, then, in a hesitant and cautious manner that the Government introduced its scheme for the employment of PoWs in farming, and its initial proposals that 2,300 would be deployed by February 1917 proved hopelessly optimistic.[26] Even by 1 April, the total enemy alien workforce was only 830.[27] As the *Mark Lane Express* wryly observed, there was little sign that the plan would meet the most pressing needs of farmers.[28] For not only were the numbers sent to each county restricted and the radius of their deployment from each depot closely defined, but the shortage of prisoners within Britain as a whole made any more generous arrangements impossible. Ironically, it was the failure of the German spring offensive in 1918 which was eventually to boost the number of captives in allied hands.

Added to the scarcity problem was the pressure of competing demands for their employment, particularly on road and railway building, timber cutting, quarrying, engineering, and construction. There was, too, alarm in government circles that should any prisoners escape, there would be an immense hue and cry.[29] Sometimes, the hostility of villagers had to be taken into account, at a time when many of them had sons and husbands fighting and dying at the front. An Essex man recalled that when a prisoner of war camp was set up in his village there was grumbling about 'they bloody owd Germans livin' there in the lap of luxury, while our pore boys 'ev to suffer in France'. But no fault was found with their work, and gradually the hostility subsided. During one summer, when the strains of German songs could be heard in the still evening air, it had to be admitted that 'the perishers can certainly sing'.[30]

In Huntingdon, the first party of seventy men arrived during the third week of March 1917, while in Dorset, a major land-owner persuaded the authorities at the beginning of that year to allocate to him about thirty prisoners for his home farm of 1,200 acres. Most of the men selected had been land workers in their own country, and the venture quickly proved a success. In November 1917, *The Times* described the scheme in enthusiastic terms, seeing it as an example which others should follow:

> The plan involved the erection of no new buildings on the farm..., beyond the adaptation of three unoccupied cottages.... The cottages form one block, and communicating doors were made in the interior walls for the convenience of the prisoners, and the guard of three soldiers. The prisoners draw their rations from the camp at stated times, and one of them cooks for the draft... the dormitories and living rooms are neat and clean, and the area within the barbed wire fence is used for growing vegetables and breeding rabbits in wonderful abundance, the latter the progeny of a few given by the employer.
>
> In a few weeks the prisoners will have completed a year's work, and they have been tested in all kinds of labour... some of the men have driven horses in field operations, such as ploughing, harrowing, and drilling, others have done carting and others manual work. In all capacities they have shown equal aptitude and willingness to help. The standard of efficiency is high, and there has been no friction between the prisoners and the local workers. When I visited the farm the day's programme included the carting of mangolds from the field to the homestead... and only the armed guard and the tunics of the prisoners indicated the exceptional nature of the situation... the work on the farm is far more forward than is common in the district, and the additional 40 acres of corn grown this year as a direct result of the labour which has replaced that previously supplied by men at the front will next year be greatly increased... In addition to the work on

the home farm, whenever any of the farmers in the neighbourhood have been short of labour they have been assisted as far as possible with German labour.[31]

But elsewhere ill-feeling against the prisoners was more clearly manifest during the early days. Although the physical and verbal attacks feared by some government officials rarely materialised, there was reluctance on the part of many farmers to hire them, and among the labourers, to work alongside them. As late as March 1918, agricultural workers in one Cheshire village threatened to 'down tools' if Germans were sent to local farms — and this at a time when there were already more than three hundred prisoners at work in the county, either on the land or on related drainage projects.[32] Similarly in Leicestershire a reluctance to take Germans was noted: 'Some farmers object to employing them, and many of those who would do so are hindered by their employees, who object to working on the same farm with them'.[33] In Norfolk a conference of agricultural trade union delegates passed a resolution early in February 1917, angrily demanding that the PoWs should be used only in special gangs for land reclamation or drainage work '& under no circumstances should the Labourer be called upon to find Lodgings for such prisoners as has been suggested in certain quarters.'[34]

Even the Government itself had an equivocal attitude towards their deployment, in that it prohibited their use alongside Land Army women or near to the coast, and there were official warnings about the undesirability of their being allowed to work continuously in one place: 'Although they should be treated with such consideration as is consistent with the position they occupy, anything approaching friendly relations between themselves and our own labourers must be checked; and there is the risk that prisoners may ingratiate themselves with the farm hands, if they are working in close connection with them for any length of time'.[35]

The difficulties to which these attitudes gave rise were pinpointed in July 1917 by a camp commandant in Bedfordshire when he gloomily described his abortive efforts to encourage local farmers to employ the prisoners at his camp:[36]

Till the last few days [he declared] I have not had a single application, and now I have only been asked for about 20. I attended two potato-spraying meetings in order to inform the meetings that I would do all I could to provide the necessary labour. At one meeting I was informed by the chairman — the agent of a very large estate — that the farmers were prejudiced against them, and that their labourers would leave if German prisoners were employed. At the other village where I attended the meeting, the villagers, headed by the vicar, declined to avail themselves of German labour on any account, from prejudice.

As he sourly concluded: 'If other counties produce the same class of unpatriotic and narrow-minded inhabitants, the prisoners of war cannot be utilized to the extent they should be'. Even the *Mark Lane Express* involved itself in the issue. In a strongly worded article it pointed out that the prisoners had to be maintained in this country, and that meant growing food to feed them. 'Labour is wanted badly, and surely the prisoners captured in the war could not be more usefully employed than in assisting to produce the food required for their maintenance . . . no crop of corn will be any the worse because a German prisoner of war ploughs the land for growing, and no sentiment should prevent a farmer from employing this class of labour if it is offered to him'.[37]

Among some of the farmers, meanwhile, there is little doubt that the prejudice shown was not against the PoWs as such but because they were *substitute* workers who might take the place of their own sons, who could then be sent to the front. Added to this was the fact that on smaller farms there was often insufficient work for a party of four or five men. Lack of flexibility in the size of working parties was a particular difficulty in prisoner deployment in the early days. In December 1917, Rowland Prothero himself admitted that although the War Office had recently relaxed the conditions laid down for their use, 'they were still too stringent to allow of the farmers making the fullest use' of them.[38] There were also problems in providing guards for the smaller parties, and in the spring of 1918 one critic commented sourly on the waste of manpower this could involve: 'I have seen a soldier occupied all day in guarding two German prisoners at work on a 100-acre farm'.[39]

Not until January 1918 were the first concessions made to deal with this difficulty, when the War Office agreed that up to three prisoners might reside upon a farm without a guard. The employer had to assume responsibility for their safe custody and ensure that they were 'not interfered with by the inhabitants'. He was not to allow them to enter a public house or any other place of amusement, although they could attend 'British places of worship', if he or a responsible British male accompanied them and the relevant local authorities agreed. They were to be accommodated in 'healthy, comfortable and warmed premises' and to be provided with three meals a day. Their employer was responsible for supplying cooking utensils, crockery, lighting, and facilities for washing, as well as straw to fill their palliasses. For this, he paid the Government 25s. per man per week for their services, less 15s. a week for board and lodging. The prisoners themselves received from the military authorities the usual PoW agricultural rates of 2d. an hour for non-commissioned officers, and 1d. or 1½d. an hour for other ranks.[40]

Some of the camp commandants, however, appear to have interpreted the relaxation over the provision of guards more liberally than the Government intended. As early as March 1918, men were being sent out daily from Turvey Camp in Bedfordshire in groups of three or more to work on farms in neighbouring villages without any military escort. In one case it was noted that they were conveyed to their employer in a trap and then handed over to him; in another, 'The Farmer fetches them and brings them back'.[41]

Boosted by these concessions over deployment conditions, the demand for prisoner labour increased steadily over the following months. It was further encouraged by an easing of restrictions on the minimum size of camps. By June 1917 it had been established that for men engaged in drainage work, the batches of prisoners sent out could be reduced to forty men, with the guard also cut to one third of the number of prisoners. In January 1918 this was extended to agriculture itself, the main purpose being to make extra men available for the spring ploughing programme. The Government proposed to allocate one thousand extra men for this work alone.[42] Under the new arrangements groups of thirty to forty prisoners were to be sent to four or five selected places in each county to assist with tillage on farms within a radius of about five miles from the camp. They were to be housed in depots chosen by the Food Production Department of the Board of Agriculture and approved by the War Office. As far as possible, each was to be in or near a market town and with access to a railway station, while the military authorities would retain responsibility for the control, feeding, and clothing of the inmates.

Whilst they were within the depot, the prisoners were to be guarded, but during the day those working as ploughmen were to be sent out without armed escort in groups of four or five to work under the supervision of a soldier ploughman or a policeman ploughman, who would take part in the work and act as 'gang foreman'. Teams of horses and equipment might also be hired by farmers from the Food Production Department on piecework terms (for example, on light land the charge for a two-horse plough team was 20s. per acre; on very heavy land, a four-hourse team cost 35s. per acre).[43] Other rates charged included 5s. per acre for drilling and 3s. per acre for harrowing.[44] It was also possible for men to be despatched singly to help farmers who were short of ploughmen only. Prisoners sent to work in outlying districts were to be taken to their destination by wagonette, lorry, or train, as circumstances dictated. Both they and the gangs working nearer the depot were to be provided with rations for their mid-day meal by the military authorities.[45]

The large scale of this new operation inevitably caused teething problems, not least in securing suitable accommodation. Here disagreements arose between the Food Production Department and the War Office, with the former complaining of the latter's inconsistency. They pointed angrily to the fact that whereas at Spettisbury, Dorset, a barn had been considered suitable, at Shepton Mallet a disused hotel was rejected as not good enough. 'Two shops at Midhurst, Sussex, within a few yards of the Angel Hotel, were approved by the Eastern Command, while at Steyning in the same County, a house was rejected as it was close to a public house; this led to a delay of two months.' Security matters, too, entered into the debate, since there were restrictions on the employment of prisoners near to the coast or in the vicinity of munitions factories and aerodromes. Here, again, decisions differed, with the War Office approving the use of a house at Rainham in Essex, even though it was situated within a mile of a high explosives factory and of the estuary of the River Thames, yet rejecting the acquisition of Axbridge Workhouse in Somerset on the grounds of its proximity to the coast, although the building was fourteen miles from the Severn estuary.[46] Partly because of these administrative difficulties and partly because of a shortage of guards, by the end of the first week in February 1918, 4,713 of the prisoners allocated for agricultural duties were still not deployed.[47] By 20 May, that total had increased to 7,852, or about 44 per cent of all the PoWs specifically assigned to agriculture. Not until the following September did the number of men allocated but not yet employed at last fall below two thousand.[48]

In addition, significant regional differences occurred in the deployment of the prisoners. During the initial months, the highest proportion were to be found in the South-East, the South-West, and the Midlands, while Yorkshire and the Northern counties reported none at work, and Lincolnshire very few. Early in 1918, the West Midlands alone accounted for over a third of all PoWs working in agriculture within England and Wales, and the East Midlands for a further one-fifth.[49] All were areas with major outlets for civilian employment in manufacturing industry, and where the decline in the size of the agricultural labour force had been severe.[50] Worcestershire, with its market gardening preoccupations, was one important user of the PoWs, accounting for 875 of them in the spring of 1918. Warwickshire had 266 at around the same time, including one camp near Stratford-upon-Avon which was manned solely by non-commissioned officers. They had taken over a formerly derelict farm of 360 acres under the direction of the Warwickshire Agricultural Executive Committee and on 12 March the commandant reported that around one hundred acres of it had already been planted with spring beans and oats.[51]

In the country as a whole, meanwhile, forty-five agricultural camps had been set up by 9 February 1918, accommodating 4,279 prisoners. They ranged in size from Rothwell, with 214 inmates and South Ockendon in Essex, with 211, to Tutnall and Cobley, with thirty-five, and Woodham Ferrers, near Chelmsford, with thirty-seven.[52] Most were engaged in general farming duties, but 282 were allocated to market gardening and orchard work and 400 to various land reclamation and drainage schemes. By 20 May, the total had increased to 9,783 men in agricultural camps, plus 1,282 deployed from 'parent' general camps, making a combined total of 11,065 prisoners employed on the land. At the end of June this had risen again to 14,568, or almost one in three of all working prisoners in the country; they were housed either in one of the 190 camps now in existence or lodged upon farms.[53]

Over the following weeks the number at work continued to increase, as did the proportion of the total prisoner labour force engaged in agriculture. On 10 September 1918, when 25,213 men were at work on the land, they comprised 62 per cent of total prisoners employed.[54]

With such a large number of combatant PoWs deployed, the quality of their labour naturally varied in both effectiveness and efficiency. An inquiry instituted during the summer of 1918 concluded that although they worked methodically they were slow compared to their English civilian counterparts. Partly this was attributed to the fact that, as one official delicately put it, it was 'not to be expected that they should work with any particular zeal for the advantage of their enemies'.[55] Although, interestingly enough, only in a 'few' instances was it considered that they had actually sabotaged equipment.[56] Other factors were far more important in accounting for the relative slowness of their work. These included unfamiliarity with some of the tasks they were asked to perform, and variations in the calibre and zeal of their guards and camp commandants. Where these were lacking in vigour, the prisoners were likely to take advantage of the situation and reduce their output. Rider Haggard commented on the lethargic reaction of two Germans engaged in cutting weeds in the River Waveney near his Norfolk home: 'To me, and I looked at them for quite a long while, they seemed to do nothing except stare at the water while the armed guard walked up and down wearily and stared at them. I imagine that the British prisoners in Germany find it expedient and indeed necessary to work in a very different fashion.'[57]

The quality of the guards became a particular problem with the sharp increase in prisoner numbers during the final months of the War. By the summer of 1918 they included a mixture of civilian foremen, British non-commissioned officers, German non-commissioned officers, and members of the Royal Defence Corps, who were responsible for escorting the prisoners to their employment, overseeing them whilst at work, and ensuring that they carried out their tasks satisfactorily. But the real discipline was exercised by British non-commissioned officers, of whom there were only about one to every two hundred prisoners at that date.[58]

An Essex farmer who appeared before the Prisoners of War Employment Committee in June 1918 was particularly scathing on the subject of guards, declaring that if they had only displayed more energy in carrying out their duties, 'we would have got a good deal more done. I have noticed in going through the district that you never find the guards with the Germans. They are either at the back of the hedge or under a tree in the Summer, or somewhere tucked up in the winter. They simply leave the prisoners. They say they have really nothing to do with them, that they bring them to the farm, and it is for the farmer to see they work.'[59] He then added sourly: 'I never see the guard walk along the field . . . and when they are working the guard comes from the hedge. He never goes up and down when they are hoeing'. Equally, although the prisoners were supposed to be accompanied when they went upon a public highway, it was not uncommon to see a party of men marching along on their own as they moved from job to job. Occasionally this gave rise to protests from nervous civilians, but few PoWs tried to escape. In fact, in the country as a whole during the first three years of the War only one officer and two men actually succeeded in returning to Germany.[60]

The best workers, both as regards agricultural skills and general conduct, were the Saxons, Schleswig-Holsteiners, and Poles, while the Prussians were always regarded as more difficult to handle. One witness described them as 'brutal, unkind and uncouth'.[61]

Unfamiliarity with the work, poor supervision, and a lack of enthusiasm for their duties were, therefore, among the reasons for the relatively poor initial performance of many prisoners. But to a number of observers a still more significant factor was the poor quality of their diet. Often they were required to leave their camp at 6.30 or 7 in the morning to walk to work, and did not return until about 5 or 5.30 in the evening. Indeed, surviving time sheets for prisoners in Bedfordshire show men leaving the camp at 6 a.m. and not returning until 7 p.m., giving a total working day of 11½ hours, exclusive of meals.[62] To sustain them during their absence the men were normally provided with 4 oz. of broken biscuits of a piece of bread, and 1 oz. of cheese.[63] With the hard physical labour required of them, that proved totally inadequate, and many farmers began to supply them with extra food, even though this was illegal, unless the PoWs were resident on the farm. The problem was further exacerbated by the growing food shortages which occurred in the country at large during 1918. To nervous government officials it seemed that any concession made to prisoners was likely to lead to 'the most hostile reception by the public and in the press', which they naturally sought to avoid.[64] The question of prisoners' allowances was, indeed, repeatedly raised in Parliament, one MP asking the Under-Secretary of State for War whether he was aware that the 'inhabitants of Cheadle-Hume, Cheshire, . . . could only obtain 4 ozs. of meat' during one week in April, 'whereas the German prisoners at the Handforth internment camp, 1 mile distant, were supplied with 20 ozs. of meat'.[65] Even some Food Control Committees joined in the debate, following the introduction of rationing in the Home Counties early in 1918. From Sawbridgeworth came the angry complaint that whereas 'His Majesty's Loyal Subjects' were to be restricted to a weekly ration of 1 lb. of meat and 4 ozs. of margarine (or butter) each, the rations 'for enemy prisoners of War include 1 lb. 4oz. of meat and 7 oz. of margarine per week. This Committee hopes that the rations for enemy prisoners of war will be so reduced that His Majesty's enemies in England shall not be given more meat and margarine (or butter) than is allowed His Majesty's Loyal Subjects'.[66] Copies of the resolution were sent to the Prime Minister, the Food Controller, and the Secretary of State for War.

Under this pressure, the authorities decided to reduce prisoner rations further. From June it was agreed that instead of receiving 4 oz. of meat on five days a week, they were to be given meat on three days per week only, while all butter, margarine and milk were to be discontinued. On 12 July this was further revised, with jam now removed from the ration, and the daily quantity of cheese cut back to $\frac{4}{7}$ oz., though with an extra supply of rice and some margarine provided in lieu.[67]

Soon, however, the Ministry of Food came to the conclusion that the prisoners, with a daily calorie intake of approximately 2,700, were receiving 600 calories a day less than the minimum needed for hard manual labour. On their recommendation, changes were instituted, with commandants having to ensure that each man was supplied with at least 8 oz. of bread, 2 oz. of Chinese bacon, and 8 oz. of potatoes for his mid-day meal. Prisoners were also to be allowed to purchase 1 oz. of rice and 1 oz: of bread daily from the camp canteen to add to their basic supplies.[68] All other purchases were strictly limited, with the tobacco ration reduced to $\frac{3}{4}$ oz. a week during the summer of 1918, and prisoners forbidden to purchase anything beyond what was supplied by the camp canteen.[69] This could mean, as at Chepstow camp, that the men had so little to spend their money on that they resorted to gambling. As the commandant gloomily observed: 'if the canteen were provided with Horse-flesh and the prisoners allowed to buy it there would be less discontent and better work would be done'.[70]

Similar problems were encountered elsewhere, and it was not surprising that from time to time prisoners sought to circumvent the regulations by making illicit purchases from the civilian population. Despite the risks involved, a number of people did co-operate. A baker from Piddletown in Dorset, for example, sold two loaves and a bag of flour to a prisoner but was fined £50 for his pains when the transaction was discovered. And at Banbury, a youth who gave tins of cocoa to local prisoners was fined £5, with the magistrates expressing the hope that the punishment 'would be a warning to others'.[71] For those civilians who managed to escape detection, this surreptitious trading could be very profitable. The commandant of Dorchester camp reported one case in which a prisoner had purchased two tins of milk, two pots of jam, some flour and margarine for the high price of 25s. He had obtained them from 'a boy in the road', but as soon as the guard observed the transaction, the food was confiscated and the man punished, while the boy was reported to the local police.[72]

However, in practice it was the farmers who proved the biggest offenders when it came to supplying food to their prisoner employees. An Essex man openly admitted providing the PoWs working for him with boiled potatoes and coffee each day, pointing out that this only cost him about 2s. every three weeks, and that without the extra food they were virtually useless, especially during the afternoon session. Another witness from Huntingdonshire claimed that in his area the PoWs were given 'milk, coffee, boiled vegetables, & sometimes a boiled rabbit or something of that kind. We have found that they would eat their mid-day meal — that is the ration that they take out with them — before they get there [i.e. to the farm]'.[73]

Often, too, despite official warnings to the contrary, friendly relations grew up between the prisoners and their employer, his family, and his work force. The Essex farmer quoted above noted that when he first recruited Germans, his women workers were afraid to go into the same field with them. But that wore off within a month or two, and soon the women were quite ready to work alongside them. The two groups became quite friendly: 'in fact I have seen the women take them a jug of tea'. Similarly in Northamptonshire, when some of the prisoners were allowed to live outside the camps, local families were happy to accept them as lodgers.[74] But the childhood reminiscences of a Norfolk woman perhaps illustrate most clearly the warm relationship which could develop. The men here were engaged in drainage work on her uncle's farm, but their duties were not very arduous:

> [They] made us toys from wood in the hedges and we in turn took them bags of sweets... The British soldiers on guard told us we mustn't bring sweets, which to us children seemed un- kind (not knowing what a prisoner was really).
>
> The food the Germans had whilst working was a kind of broth,... heated in a huge cauldron over a wood fire in the field. One prisoner, an officer (a confectioner in Berlin in civilian life), when he came up to the farm for a supply of water asked to see Aunt Susan's oven in the wall. He also asked for eggs and the daily papers, speaking perfect English. These he would sit and read on the grass before returning to the meadow with a guard always with a fixed bayonet. The eggs, the German would quietly drop into the broth and when cooked take them out and eat them behind some bushes.[75]

She also recalled that the men wore navy uniforms with large red patches, these latter designed to make them easily iden- tifiable should they try to escape.

Another woman, who worked as a teenage maid on a farm at Great Canfield in Essex, likewise recalled supplying PoWs brought in from Great Dunmow depot with mashed potatoes, bread and tea for lunch each day, on her employer's instruction. 'I used to give out to them dessert spoons to eat with, they were *not* allowed knives. They used to smile and wink at me and seemed a jolly good lot of Chaps... It made me feel sad to see them in captivity'.[76]

So, as military recruitment in the countryside intensified during the last year of the War, the use of combatant prisoners in British agriculture became widely accepted. This was especially true during the hay and corn harvests of 1918, with demand for their services rapidly outstripping supply. On 12 August 1918, the Prisoners of War Employment Committee even had to reject an application for an additional 5,500 men for agricultural work because they had 'no prisoners available'.[77] This had happened despite the fact that the Board of Agriculture had laid down that all prisoners in agricultural camps and at least 50 per cent of those engaged on land reclamation work were to be released for the corn harvest. Other government departments employing prisoner labour were also to free as many of their men as they could for the same purpose. And once the labour needs of farms in the immediate vicinity of a camp had been met, the surplus workers were to be sent out in migratory gangs.

This use of gangs added valuable flexibility to the whole arrangement. They each included ten prisoners and two guards, with responsibility for their deployment left to the County War Agricultural Executive Committee. The only restrictions were the usual ones prohibiting their use near to aerodromes, munitions works, military and naval installations, and the coast, or areas served by a school-boy camp or ones containing women workers. The military were to provide the tents, stoves, bedding, and cooking utensils for the prisoners, and most of their food.

On the whole the combination of migratory gangs and fixed agricultural camps proved a success. In Oxfordshire, for example, where sixteen gangs were employed to assist with the corn harvest and with potato picking, only two instances were reported where the prisoners could not be employed, owing to 'prejudice on the part of farmers in the neighbourhood against their employment'. In both cases, the camps were quickly struck and the men removed to other parts of the county where this difficulty did not arise.[78] When the grain harvest had ended, some of the migratory gangs were retained for threshing work, under the same working conditions.

By the autumn of 1918, therefore, the number of prisoners at work had increased sharply. Three hundred and thirty depots had been set up in various parts of the country from which men were sent out daily for farm work. Each contained thirty or more prisoners. Even the Armistice did not halt the rise in the numbers deployed, as they helped to compensate for the withdrawal of alternative forms of substitute labour, such as British soldiers. In December 1918, the total at work reached 30,405, and this had climbed to 30,679 a month later.[79] The only change was that care was now taken to point out to Agricultural Executive Committees that prisoner labour should not be used where civilian workers were available. In addition, payments for accommodation, fuel and lighting, and any expenses involved in conveying the equipment and rations of the prisoners were to be met by the Executive Committee, who then deducted these expenses from the moneys received from farmers for the men's services. In no case was a sum greater than 1d. per head per night to be paid for accommodation, while farmers were apparently expected to pay for wear and tear to the men's boots. A surviving account submitted by Bedfordshire Agricultural Executive Committee in the spring of 1919 shows the substantial charge of 4d. per man per day levied for this particular item.[80]

Further slight modifications to the scheme came in February 1919, when it was agreed that farmers who were responsible for guarding prisoners during working hours might reduce the amount paid for the men's services by 4d. per prisoner per day. A similar abatement could be allowed if the prisoners were fetched more than one mile by the farmer or soldiers from agricultural companies whom he was employing.

Throughout the spring and summer of 1919 PoW numbers remained substantial, and gradually an undercurrent of dissatisfaction began to surface, strengthened by the belief that farmers were taking advantage of what was a cheap, disciplined labour force to the detriment of British civilians. The matter was raised in Parliament on more than one occasion, with one MP maintaining that farmers in the Brailes and Cherington district of Warwickshire were employing Germans from Brailes camp even though there were civilian workers in the area unemployed.[81] Another Member spoke of the growing 'friction' between civilian and prisoner labourers and claimed that cases had arisen where civilian workers had been discharged by agriculturists able to rely upon PoW substitutes.[82] In view of the extreme farm labour shortage during much of 1919, this latter claim should be treated with reservation. But is is clear that some farmers did welcome the use of disciplined, tractable prisoners who would not answer back at a time when civilian labourers were demanding — and receiving — substantial improvements in wages and working conditions under the terms of the 1917 Corn Production Act. One of those interviewed by *Country Life* in May 1919 waspishly inveighed against British workers who had 'come back from the Army' affected by 'its dangers and excitements'. His main hope was that Germany would refuse to sign the Peace Treaty so that he could retain his PoWs indefinitely.[83]

In the event, the Treaty of Versailles was signed at the end of June 1919, but it was not until the beginning of September that a repatriation programme was finally agreed upon. At that stage ther were still 19,319 prisoners going out to work from 321 agricultural camps, plus a further 1,735 boarded out with farmers, 1,008 sent out from 'parent' camps, and 3,041 working in migratory gangs. The overall total was thus 25,103. The plan was for repatriation to take place at the rate of 400 prisoners a day, but the railway strike in the autumn of that year caused further delay. Not until the end of November was the Board of Agriculture able to report that all prisoners boarded out with farmers or working in migratory gangs or from parent camps had been repatriated, plus about 15,000 men working from agricultural camps. More than two hundred of the camps had now been closed. The remaining PoWs were being repatriated 'as rapidly as circumstances permitted', and by the end of the year the programme had been completed.[84]

Combatant prisoners thus provided by far the most important form of foreign labour used on the land during the First World War. They were supplemented by a small number of interned civilians (or, as they were officially called, civilian prisoners of war) who in private life had often been employed as waiters or tailors, and consequently knew nothing about agriculture. A farmer who was allocated four Hungarians under this scheme reported that before internment they had all lived in London and had been employed respectively as a jeweller, a tailor, a ladies' hairdresser, and a pastry confectioner. 'They were most polite . . . and that was the best thing about them. They raised their hats to him'. In the end he decided to retain them, as they might be useful 'for planting a few potatoes'.[85] In Monmouth, where fifty-four civilian prisoners were employed in the spring of

1918, there was some dissatisfaction among civilian workers because they were paid the customary minimum wage for the area, which by this time amounted to 25s. per week, and in some cases were securing free lodging as well.[86] But in general their contribution was slight. Rowland Prothero, writing after the war, was dismissive of their role, noting that although the Home Office had arranged for the employment of both interned aliens and conscientious objectors on the land: 'Local feeling was... too strong against both classes. The number of aliens employed was under 2,000, and that of conscientious objectors scarcely rose above 200'.[87] It was, therefore, to combatant PoWs that the Government was forced to turn in order to ease its agricultural labour problems. The fact that, at a time of major conflict, so many people were prepared to accept the prisoners, even though their own sons might be away fighting at the front, was an indication that bridges could be built between peoples even in the most unpromising of circumstances.

But perhaps the most significant tribute to the prisoners came from the Board of Agriculture in December 1919, when the repatriation programme had been completed. 'Every kind of agricultural work was undertaken by the Germans,' it declared, 'including skilled market gardening by selected men, the preparation of land for trees, tree planting, the cleansing of water courses and the repair of river banks. There are cases on record in which crops would have been lost but for the assistance given from prison camps, and it may be stated that the conduct and behaviour of the prisoners gave general satisfaction... the fact that they were available during the 1919 harvest did much to meet the difficulties which arose in many counties owing to the withdrawal of the men in agricultural companies'.[88] In this case at least swords had been successfully beaten into plough shares, to the great satisfaction of all concerned.

Chapter 8

The Role of the Children

'The Board of Education had no powers to override the law with regard to school attendance in the employment of children, and the local authority was under no obligation to take proceedings for non-attendance if they were satisfied that a reasonable excuse had been given. The farmers who controlled the Rural Education Committees stretched this elastic "reasonable excuse" to cover in some districts children of twelve and even eleven years of age whom they wanted to employ.... Nothing is meaner in our war annals than this exploitation of childhood'. F.E. Green, *A History of the English Agricultural Labourer*, London 1920, 235.

'As regards the labour of boys of school age in agricultural districts it seems probable that they will be used nearly as much as during the past two seasons, in spite of the various representations which have been made'. *Times Educational Supplement*, 25 January 1917.

When War broke out in August 1914, among the earliest groups to be affected were, rather surprisingly, country children. Not only was home life disrupted by fathers joining the armed services and, in some cases, mothers being encouraged to work on the land or in the munitions industries, but they themselves were pressed into lending a hand on the farms or into staying at home to look after younger brothers and sisters whilst their mother went out. Significantly, as early as 1 September 1914, the Board of Education was informing the Soke of Peterborough education authority in Northamptonshire that although it had 'no power to give any general directions overriding the ordinary law with regard to school attendance and the employment of children ... [a] Local Education Authority is under no obligation to take proceedings in respect of the non-attendance of a child at school if they are satisfied that there is a reasonable excuse for non-attendance'.[1] Given that education committees in rural areas were frequently dominated by the farming interest, this attitude was interpreted by growing numbers of them as an open invitation to ignore by-law restrictions on child employment. At least five other authorities had received similar letters before the end of the year. In addition, there were cases, as in Somerset, where the authority was reminded that under its existing by-laws, youngsters could obtain partial exemption from attendance at the age of eleven. 'There is a further provision for total exemption at 12 in the case of children who have passed a certain standard, which is, in some parts of the county, as low as the fifth', Somerset was informed.[2]

Often, too, in both town and country this lax approach to attendance was reinforced by modifications to the school curriculum to take account of the new spirit of patriotism and self-sacrifice. Already in 1914-15, the Board of Education drew attention to the rolls of honour of former pupils which were appearing in many schools, as well as the special lessons which were being arranged and the 'collection of money and making of comforts for the soldiers and sailors at the front', which formed part of the daily routine. In the Board's view there was 'everywhere reacting upon school-life and school-training a quickened consciousness of personal and national ties, a keener sense of common sacrifice and common duty'.[3] This applied to villages like Wyke Regis in Dorset, where in October 1914 the school authorities proudly proclaimed that they had a 'roll of honour' of seventy-four former scholars and teachers who were 'doing their duty to their King and country . . . Now is the time for old scholars of eligible age and good health to fall in without delay . . . and swell the Roll of Honour to a hundred names'.[4] Elsewhere letters sent from the front by old boys to the head teacher were read out to the assembled pupils, or lessons were given by wounded ex-scholars to the older children.

In some places geography and history lessons were slanted to cover war topics. At Ivinghoe in Buckinghamshire the headmaster noted in his log book that he was 'struck at the information the class had of the "Great War" . . . Am devoting the time given to the History Lesson (or partly) on the newspaper reports, & am careful of the "cuttings", . . . they are instructive'.[5] Enthusiasm here was perhaps encouraged by the fact that the Chilterns were used extensively for military training in the initial stages of the War, and that included the Beacon Hill, which rises just behind Ivinghoe. The increasing activity inevitably had its effect on school attendance, too, as on 8 December 1914, when the master noted that the village was 'filled with recruits' from Lord Kitchener's volunteer army: 'cannons were placed on the Beacon and fired; as only thirty-three [pupils] turned up in the afternoon it was considered advisable to close the school for the afternoon'.[6]

Much the same sense of excitement and stir was created at Fletching in Sussex, with soldiers passing and repassing along the normally peaceful village lanes. Robert Saunders, the headmaster, commented on the effect this had upon classroom life:

> Big Room doing an exam, suddenly wild stampede heard in Infant Room, shouts in playground, Master looks out window, sees Governess, Teacher and Infants trekking to the gate to cheer a regiment of infantry followed by Red Cross vans. Settle down again when a trampling of horses, a regiment of cavalry; a rest then a rumbling of wheels, a long column of ammunition waggons; later big guns each with 4 horses. Teacher Kath generally manages to be in the playground when the RFA [Royal Field Artillery] go by on their horses and it seems to be the usual thing now as they reach the playground coming from Piltdown for every man to "eyes left" to see if Teacher is looking. One day as I came along there were some field guns outside school with a crowd of children round watching the men eating their dinner. The bell rang for school, the children rushed to join and some of the Tommies pretended to be children and ran too.[7]

Fresh impetus was given to celebrations like Trafalgar Day (23 October) and Empire Day (24 May). At Wigginton, Hertfordshire, Trafalgar Day in 1914 was marked by the children receiving an address from Colonel Kitchener, brother of the Secretary of State for War. He spoke to them on 'Determination, Energy and Pluck': 'Following this the Union Jack was saluted, and the children joined in the singing of the National Anthems of the Allies'.[8] Similarly at Llanychllwydog in north Pembrokeshire, Trafalgar Day celebrations in 1916 included a lesson on 'Nelson's achievements, and those of navy of today... rudimentary principles of naval warfare made manifest'.[9] Many other schools followed the same patriotic line.

But of all the changes introduced by the War, it was the use of child labour which was to prove the most controversial, not least because it represented a clear reversal of the pre-war trend towards eliminating the premature employment of young people. Admittedly some youngsters even before 1914 had continued to work on a seasonal basis, with boys in Lincolnshire widely engaged alongside women between March and May each year in setting potatoes, or helping to weed the crops. Later they were used for fruit and potato picking. In the fruit growing districts of the Tamar Valley in Devon and Cornwall and in parts of Kent, children were also widely employed as pickers during the appropriate seasons, while in hop-growing areas they regularly worked alongside adults as part of a family team.[10] Haymaking and harvest, too, provided some temporary employment for youngsters, although the growing use of self-binders removed a number of the tasks children had traditionally performed at harvest time. The decline in the corn acreage in the years before 1914 reinforced that trend. Nevertheless, Jim Priest, who was born at Parndon, Essex, at the beginning of the twentieth century, recalled the routine followed by a number of his friends. It was one which was typical of many country children:

> By the time you were 10 or 11 (and sometimes younger) you could do a stint of bird-scaring before and after school and on Saturdays. Crows and several other species could be particularly voracious at the latter end of the winter on fields of autumn-drilled corn, and February and March — often cold and frosty and wet — were special times for bird-scaring, as were some later months when the spring crops were being drilled . . . For a couple of hours morning and evening, and a full day (daylight to dark) on Saturday, a boy might earn threepence or fourpence . . . and even sixpence . . . for diligent bird-scaring . . . Bird-scaring gave a boy a footing on the farm, and, if he behaved himself, he might graduate to odd jobs around the farm-house and yard such as chopping sticks, filling coal scuttles, carrying milk buckets, collecting eggs and mucking out the hen-houses. It was never the slightest use complaining about any job you were given; if you didn't like it or just couldn't do it, then you were soon told to "clear orf" and somebody else took your place.

> Another wearisome task on the farm for small boys — and one in which they were sometimes joined by girls and women — was picking stones from land which was lying fallow for a season. This was a job which was usually done in the Easter holiday, and often it was piecework, the rate being a half-penny . . . a bushel. . . . Then, if Whitsuntide fell at the end of

May or early June — there was always a week's school holiday any way — some boys might be taken on for chopping out thistles from fields of spring-drilled corn. . . .

It was harvest time, however, which provided boys with their best opportunity. In the early years of this century, the summer holiday at Parndon School was always called the "harvest" holiday, and normally it started on the last Friday of July or the first Friday of August. But . . . [it] was sometimes subject to last-minute adjustment if the corn was ripening later than usual. Several boys in the 12 to 14 age group would proudly announce that they were going to do a "full harvest" on so-and-so's farm, and others of 10 or 11 upwards would report that they were going to have a horse-leading job when the corn-carting started . . . After a field had been cleared of the sheaves, a boy who was deemed fairly responsible might be given the job of driving a horse-rake to pull into neat swathes the loose ears which had somehow missed the reaper-binder.[11]

Yet, arduous though these tasks were, they were of limited duration only and were largely completed out of school hours. The broad aim of the authorities in stressing the importance of school attendance was generally accepted in most rural communities by the outbreak of War.

Nonetheless, many farmers continued to look with an unfriendly eye upon the improved instruction which was becoming available to their labourers' children. 'Too much education' was blamed for the alleged restlessness of young people in country areas and their increasing reluctance to accept the low wages and limited prospects which were still associated with farm work. They preferred instead to migrate to the towns or even overseas to Australasia and North America. One correspondent to the *Farmer and Stockbreeder* firmly declared that 'the number of years' a boy spent at school would 'never educate him', while the continual raising of the school leaving age was creating labour shortages: 'At twelve years of age I could take a pair of horses and plough myself. I received 4s. per week. At thirteen I could manage to take two horses and a wagon load of grain to the mill nine miles away, and during harvest I and another lad of fourteen regularly worked three horses on the fallow and milked twenty-two cows at night. For this I received 5s. per week'.[12]

With these attitudes it is not surprising that when War came and labour difficulties began to emerge in some places, farmers responded by demanding a relaxation of local by-laws to permit the greater use of children. Requests along these lines were formulated in the autumn of 1914, and at a meeting of the Yorkshire Farmers' Union in Doncaster at the beginning of October, one of those present suggested that where schools had been taken over as temporary billets by the military, the best arrangement would be 'for all the lads to go on the farms and for all the teachers to go to the front'.[13] A colleague agreed that it would be a great advantage 'if they could get boys between twelve and fourteen years of age, some of whom could plough nicely'. Shortly afterwards a meeting of the Nottinghamshire Farmers' Union pressed for the age of exemption to be cut still further, one man declaring that boys of ten were sometimes 'better and more helpful to a farmer than others who were thirteen years old'.[14] Significantly, on 26 January 1915 that county's school attendance sub-committee decided to allow youngsters 'between 12 and 13 years of age ... to leave school temporarily' to help in farm work when no other labour could be recruited. They also agreed that where youngsters were entitled to partial exemption certificates for the summer months under existing by-laws they could be allowed to anticipate the date from which these normally became available, namely 1 June.[15]

In Parliament, too, the question came under increasing debate. Already on 28 August, the Prime Minister, H.H. Asquith, had indicated that education authorities might use their discretion in releasing boys between 11 and 14 years from attendance so that they could assist in farming operations during the autumn and winter.[16] Just over five months later, Mr Peto, MP for Devizes, returned to the subject, asking that blanket exemption be given to all boys over the age of twelve who could obtain agricultural employment. Although the President of the Board of Education refused to agree to this, he did note approvingly that most authorities were not 'enforcing their ... by-laws ... harshly or inconsiderately'.[17] In other words they were not discouraging illegal child employment.

Faced with these pressures, local authorities began to waive their by-laws and to neglect to prosecute the parents or employers of those who were working under age. Typical of many was the resolution passed by the Lindsey, Lincolnshire, School Attendance Sub-Committee on 4 December 1914:

> The sub-committee considered the explanation of Mr. Johnson of Sturton cum Scawby, with regard to the employment of a boy of school age, and it appearing that the boy was employed to replace farm servants who had joined the Army RESOLVED that legal proceedings be not ordered in this case.[18]

Others took the view of Rowland Prothero, later to become President of the Board of Agriculture, when he asked rhetorically: 'in these days, what woman in the household would not consider the 4s. 6d. a week from her boy, whom she now has to feed at school, a perfect godsend to the home...? We ought to think twice before we cut her off from that'.[19]

So the regulations were bent, with 1,388 boys and 25 girls below the official leaving age given exemptions between 1 September 1914 and 31 January 1915, 54 of them under the age of twelve.[20] At that stage, thirty-four of the sixty-two local education authorities in England and Wales had granted at least some exemptions. Among the worst offenders was West Sussex, with 186 children excused. Already by 1 October 1914, this authority had agreed to give 'all possible facilities for boys over 12 years of age to leave school to work on farms provided that adequate wages are given'.[21] It did not define what 'adequate' meant in this context. Huntingdon, with 168 exemptions, Somerset, with 158, and Gloucestershire, with 125, were other counties heavily involved. Gloucestershire was, indeed, granting exemptions to eleven-year-olds, the secretary to its local education committee allegedly declaring: 'What good would the three or six months' schooling be to anyone if this country [were] to be starved and then beaten in the most tremendous war of all history. Young men and boys have gone to the fight from University and Public School, leaving their books for sterner work. May not the boy of the Elementary School be allowed to do his little bit...?'[22]

Not all education authorities, however, succumbed to the pressures during these early days. Hertfordshire, later to be a major offender, was one county which initially resisted, a committee member firmly stating that the farmers could get plenty of adult labour if they would pay for it.[23] In Worcestershire, Warwickshire, and Somerset exemptions were only granted when the County Council overrode the objections of its L.E.A. and gave authority instead to the district committees, on which farmers were normally influential.[24] In the case of Worcestershire, this led to clashes between the Council and its education authority, and to widespread exemptions being granted in certain of the market gardening districts, especially Pershore and Martley. A report by one of HM Inspectors of Schools during the summer of 1915 was bitterly critical of the position in the former area:

> In the Pershore District the situation is worse than in other parts of the County. There is no obvious reason for this discrepancy other than the apparent readiness of the District Committee to grant exemptions to all applicants. Not only does this district supply 156 of the 531 exemptions granted in the county, but it is responsible for 25 of the 33 instances of exemptions granted to children under 11 years of age.[25]

Despite these protests, the situation remained unchanged.

Meanwhile, to a growing body of observers it seemed that farmers were using the dislocations in the labour market as an excuse to recruit young, cheap workers rather than to pay satisfactory wages to adult males, or even to employ women. This was a view put forward by Sir Harry Verney, the Parliamentary Secretary to the Board of Agriculture, when he declared with surprising frankness: 'the real argument in the farmer's mind for the employment of boys... is that it is more convenient. You have your little boy on the spot; he is cheap'.[26] The Labour politician, Keir Hardie, likewise drew attention to a statement by a member of the Ashford branch of the Kent Farmers' Union that too much education would lead to labour shortages.[27] A third MP, Sir William Byles, complained that although the State had given children a charter of free, universal and compulsory education, in practice they were being deprived of it in 'this left-hand sort of way'.[28]

The farm workers' trade union joined in the debate, and at its Norfolk conference in February 1915, delegates protested emphatically against the employment of children of school age, declaring that shortages could easily be made good by employers offering 'an adequate wage'. A county conference held at Shrewsbury a month later went even further, pledging that if such youngsters were employed during school hours, members should 'at once withdraw all other labour from the farm or farms in question'.[29] But although the resolution was carried, it had little effect. With a membership fallen to about 4,000, the union was too weak to make such threats effective.

In fact it was during the spring of 1915 that the child labour lobby received its greatest boost when on 12 March, the Board of Education issued a circular for the first time explicitly authorising the employment of youngsters of school age 'as an exceptional measure permitted to meet a special emergency'. LEAs were warned against granting general exemptions and advised to give permission for a limited period only when no adult workers could be secured. The employment itself was to be 'of a light character and suitable to the capacity of the child'.[30]

With this discreet official backing, the numbers of children involved quickly mounted, as Table 1 shows:[31]

Table 1: Children granted exemptions for agricultural employment

Date	Aged 11-12 years	Aged 12-13 years	Aged 13-14 years	Total Boys	Total Girls	Number of authorities granting exemptions
1 September 1914- 31 January 1915	54	885	474	1388	25	34
1 February 1915- 30 April 1915*	51	2169	1084	3705	106	52
31 January 1916	144	4293	3589	7934	92	53
31 May 1916*	546	8018	5521	14441	1312	58
16 October 1916	420	7839	6656	13823	1092	57

*see note on page 182.

By 31 May 1916, when 15,753 exemptions had been granted throughout England and Wales, only four LEAs remained unaffected, namely the Isle of Wight, the Isles of Scilly, Carnarvon, and Denbigh, although Cardigan, with seven children exempted, had made little more than a token gesture.[32] By contrast, Huntingdonshire had 122 boys under twelve excused, out of a total of 588 children employed. Of this county it was said that the schools had been 'depleted' of boys between thirteen and fourteen years of age, and as early as July 1915, a confidential report by one of HM Inspectors had suggested that 50 per cent of the county's boys aged between twelve and fourteen had been granted exemptions. The whole system was so laxly administered that parents had gained the idea that boys could be withdrawn from school as soon as they could get a job, providing they had reached the age of twelve: 'The desire of parents to take advantage of the relaxation of the bye-laws in order that the children may earn money is, I think, the dominating circumstance in some parts of the county', he declared.[33] In Bedfordshire, at the same time, 33 per cent of boys aged between twelve and fourteen had been granted exemptions, in West Sussex, 23 per cent, and in Kent, 16 per cent. In some counties, too, the poor state of LEA documentation added to the difficulties. Of Somerset, it was reported that no central control was exercised: 'all was in hands of Distr. Com[ces.] . . . Hardly any records available'.[34]

However, apart from the under-estimating of child workers due to slack administration, there were other 'unofficial' absences to be taken into account. In Dorset, during the ten months up to June 1915, average attendances dropped to 88.6 per cent of those on the school registers, compared to a pre-war 91.9 per cent, with some children attending for two or three days per week only.[35] Elsewhere the War Workers' Emergency Sub-Committee reported cases where the regulations were brazenly flouted. They included that of a Norfolk boy, aged twelve, from Alby with Thwaite, who was employed in 1915 by a local farmer and contractor named Walpole. According to the subsequent report of HM Inspector, the man was a 'notorious' offender who had already been prosecuted several times: 'Walpole [is] an ignorant, money-making, unscrupulous fellow. He owns 3 or 4 farms, . . . enquiries show with him it appears to be entirely a matter of cheap labour; he openly says so, if accounts given are correct'.[36] In view of the fact that fines rarely amounted to more than a few shillings, he clearly considered it more economical to employ a boy at 3s. 6d. or 4s. per week, and risk that penalty, than to employ an adult. A second case involved an eleven-year-old from Chitterne, Wiltshire, who was described as 'no bigger than a whippet'. He worked ten hours a day for a wage of 4s. a week, and in academic terms had not progressed beyond the lowest level of the school code — Standard I. In his case, neglect by the local attendance officer was blamed, the man concerned having recently been imprisoned for contempt of court on a charge involving trust deeds. His successor had been appointed, but he was merely a 'war appointment', not the 'energetic man' whom the LEA would have wished to engage.[37]

Faced with this kind of evidence, the Government's anxieties began to grow. On 29 February 1916, in an attempt to prevent the situation deteriorating further during the busy spring season, the Board of Education issued a circular expressing alarm at the large number of exemptions being granted. An added worry was that certain authorities were now passing resolutions designed to allow children to be excused under twelve years of age. As the Board sternly commented, it was doubtful whether youngsters of that age who were excused for agricultural employment would ever return to school, 'at any rate for an effective period', and the interruption or discontinuation of education at that age, 'whether regarded from the point of view of the children themselves or of the general interests of the country or of the interests of agriculture [was] entirely lamentable'.[38] Unfortunately, the fact that the Government had previously taken no effective action against those authorities which had earlier permitted under-twelves to work inevitably weakened its influence and encouraged the more recalcitrant LEAs to pursue their own course.

A further problem was that many of the youngsters were given pathetically small wages, often of less than 1s. a day, for their labours. In Somerset, payments of 3s. 6d. a week were common, while in Norfolk the rate ranged between 3s. and 7s. a week.[39] Elsewhere, as in Cambridge, the amount might vary from 3s. to 6s. 6d. for a working week of between sixty and seventy hours. In this county the youngsters were expected to drive horses, weed, look after cattle, and carry out general farm work.[40] In the light of this information, the Board recommended in its February circular that unless the labour of a boy of school age was worth at least 6s. a week to the farmer 'the benefit derived from [his] employment is not sufficient to compensate for the loss involved by the interruption of [his] education'.[41] As a result of this initiative, the wages of some child workers were increased, although in Bedfordshire even five months later a few youngsters were still receiving only 3s. 6d. a week. However, the average for the county in July 1916 was 6s. 6d. per week, compared to 4s. 10d. a year earlier.[42]

But efforts to restrict the scale of child recruitment proved less successful, and, as Table 1 shows, by the end of May 1916 the total had mounted very considerably. In these circumstances, it was decided to institute a further enquiry, with major offenders like Bedfordshire, Huntingdonshire, Hertfordshire, Worcestershire and Gloucestershire under particular scrutiny. Huntingdonshire, described as one of the worst counties, now had 44 per cent of its boys aged between eleven and fourteen excused. Worcestershire, too, was causing anxiety, with the Board of Education emphasising the authority's statutory duty to enforce the attendance regulations. The county responded defiantly, declaring that they 'entirely refused to allow the casual employment of children on the land to cease even in the case of children under 12'. They also stated their confidence that Parliament and the general public would support their stance, 'and that the High Court would be most unwilling to grant a mandamus against the Authority to carry out peace regulations in time of war'.[43] Confronted by this refusal of co-operation, the Board felt powerless to act. One course of action considered was a policy of administrative harassment, perhaps by calling for special returns, but this was felt to be unwise in the case of Worcestershire. As a Board of Education official ruefully observed: 'we should probably be met by ... a statement that it was impossible in the depleted state of the county staff to carry out the work. At best, the preparation of such a return would be a very lengthy matter and it is doubtful whether, in the result, we should get any very definite evidence on laxity. Nothing is easier than to present a good paper case for excusing a child'. Even the holding of a public inquiry was considered inappropriate because of the difficulty in collecting the relevant data and calling witnesses: 'No doubt the teachers in the schools would be reluctant to give evidence which would damage their own authority and the Board have no power to compel the attendance of witnesses'.[44]

In part, its weak position stemmed from the knowledge that by authorising a system of exemptions in its March 1915 circular it had itself adopted a policy without legal sanction. If it now sought to amend the regulations or to introduce fresh legislation, critics could argue that what it was seeking was not 'to stop illegality but to prevent Authorities from committing any other illegality than the precise illegality which the Board were prepared to sanction'.[45] In such circumstances, it was easiest to do nothing. After some heart searching, that was precisely what the Board decided to do, the only exception being a decision to arrange another survey of the numbers at work. The selected date was 16 October 1916, after the peak of the harvest season had passed. The President of the Board, the Marquis of Crewe, in concurring in this inactivity, weakly noted that any attempt to pressurise local authorities would lead to their receiving 'a large measure of popular sympathy'.[46] Caught between LEA determination to grant exemptions at all costs, and the central government's reluctance to intervene effectively, the employment of country children continued virtually unabated. Among the 14,915 under-age children at work on 16 October were 567 boys and 78 girls in Huntingdonshire, and 681 boys and 89 girls in Hertfordshire, both of which had received special attention from the Board and its inspectors. In each case the figures were higher than those for May. Worcestershire, too, remained unrepentant. The 544 boys and 110 girls exempted on 16 October were slightly up on the respective figures of 516 boys and 133 girls exempted in May.[47]

Faced with this evidence, on 26 November 1916, the Marquis of Crewe expressed the defeatist view that since between November and February there was little work for children on farms, efforts should be made to concentrate school work in that period.[48] With such an abdication of responsibility at the highest level, it is not surprising that in April 1917 a fresh circular issued by the new President of the Board, H.A.L. Fisher, announced that schools might receive their full financial grant if they were open for a mere 320 sessions a year instead of the 400 hitherto demanded.[49] A shorter school year thus became a further device to increase the opportunity for children to be used on the land. Interestingly enough, in his diary the new President, a former vice-chancellor of Sheffield University, admitted his ignorance of rural educational questions and noted that he was accepting coaching on the subject from the former director of Rothamsted Experimental Station, A.D. Hall, who was now at the Board of Agriculture.[50]

In some schools, too, the hours of attendance were adjusted to fit in with the children's work plans. During July 1918, Durham LEA agreed to alter the hours at twelve schools in the county so that pupils could work on the land outside class hours. And at

Little Brickhill, Buckinghamshire, in the spring of 1916 the school day commenced at 8 a.m., with a 'luncheon' break taken between 10.20 and 11.30 a.m. Lessons finally ended at 1.40 p.m., with the children then free for the rest of the day to work on local farms.

Elsewhere the timing and duration of holidays were altered to meet agricultural needs. In Staffordshire, managers of rural schools were requested by the LEA to divide the six weeks' summer holiday, where necessary, to cover hay-making and potato-picking activities, 'children, from former experience being little use in the corn harvest'.[51] Similar action was taken in Lindsey, Lincolnshire.

Meanwhile, the general policy of granting exemptions continued, despite these extra concessions. Although no national figures were published after 16 October 1916, a few county statistics have survived and they indicate a broad upward trend in child employment during 1917:[52]

Table 2: Children employed in agriculture in certain counties with certificates of exemption

	16 October 1916			Late 1917		
	Boys	Girls	Total	Boys	Girls	Total
Leicester	313	3	316	727	—	727
Lincoln (Holland)	120	59	179	576	324*	900*
Hereford	134	9	143	284	23	307
Rutland	42	5	47	37	4	41
Worcestershire	544	110	654	544	110	654
			1,339			2,629

*This included 118 girls exempted from attendance for varying periods for the purpose of looking after the home and the younger children whilst their mothers worked. This was described as 'quite a new departure' for the LEA in 1917.

Figures for 1918 are even more scanty, although in Kent it was reported that 3,980 special exemptions had been granted in the course of that year (3,188 to boys and 892 to girls).[53] This compares with 1,148 boys and 520 girls exempted in that county on 31 May 1916. The demand for labour was, of course, highly seasonal here, and as late as 1920, following the passage of the 1918 Education Act, the LEA made it known that it would not take action against employers for infringements of the law in connection with hop-picking. Most schools arranged special holidays to take account of the requirements of the hop harvest.[54] During the War these arrangements were even easier to make. By contrast in Warwickshire, only 250 children were said to be specially exempted on 31 May 1918, compared with 499 two years before.[55] With such limited evidence, generalisations are impossible, although one writer has recently suggested a tentative figure of 50,000 children working in agriculture under the exemptions scheme in 1918; he does not, however, show how that figure is calculated.[56] More to the point, perhaps, is the statement made on 10 August 1917, by the President of the Board, H.A.L. Fisher, when he claimed that during the first three years of war some 600,000 children had been withdrawn prematurely from school for employment. 'They are working on munitions, in the fields, and in the mines'.[57] He did not amplify that statistic but when it is appreciated that in 1914 there were only about 587,000 children aged between twelve and thirteen at school, the scale of the exemptions becomes apparent, as does the spread of the age range which must have been involved. And since agriculture was the major user of child labour — according to two American writers perhaps nine-tenths of the exemptions were for agricultural work — the size of the problem is obvious.[58]

However, during the final months of the war, it is likely that numbers stabilised, thanks to the effects of the shortening of the school year, the rearrangement of holidays to fit in with farmers' work plans, and the availability of other forms of substitute labour. Possibly, too, the criticisms which were increasingly voiced on the child labour question had some effect in moderating employment, at any rate for labourers' children. The offspring of the smaller farmers were probably still as heavily engaged as before.[59] Indeed, the *Schoolmaster* reported with evident satisfaction the prosecution and conviction of a Cornish farmer who had employed his eleven-year-old son on the farm instead of sending him to school. The action was regarded as a salutary warning to all who were engaged 'in the most odious kind of "profiteering" that the Education Acts are neither repealed nor suspended "for the duration" '.[60]

The Medical Officer of the Board of Education likewise expressed concern at the way in which children were carrying out heavy manual work. He recommended that no child under fourteen years of age should be exempted from education either half-time or whole-time, 'for purposes of employment for profit'.[61] And despite the opposition of farmers and their supporters, this was incorporated in the 1918 Education Act. Unfortunately that measure did not come into operation until the War had ended.[62]

The educational press, too, joined in the attack. The *Times Educational Supplement* condemned as 'premature and unwise' the practice of releasing twelve-year-old boys for employment, and claimed that the wages they received, of around $1\frac{1}{2}$d. per hour, were not worth the sacrifices involved.[63] The *Schoolmaster* took a similar view, castigating the casual way in which LEAs accepted exemption arguments. 'Is "Education Committee" to be a misnomer altogether in such areas? And are farmers... to be still the dull and dulling masters of the rural future, as they have been the dull and dulling stewards there of the past?'[64]

The two American observers mentioned earlier, writing in 1918, were even more forthright in their condemnation, considering that an increase 'nothing short of appalling' had taken place in the number of working children aged between eleven and fourteen who, 'prior to the war, would have been protected by child labour and compulsory school laws'. They pointed to Wiltshire, where boys who had attained the age of eleven and had reached the fourth standard, were not required to attend school at all, and where only those below that grade, who were specially excused, appeared in the official lists. In some cases schools were closed at noon or altogether at times of special pressure, 'and in others headmasters were directed to let children of eleven and over leave without record when needed for farm work'.[65] With such policies, the true number of children working under age was likely to be far higher than official statistics indicated.

The effect on the children themselves is recalled by an Oxfordshire man who left school at the age of twelve in 1917: 'I and my school mate Fred Walker... went to work on farms run by two brothers. . . . We two boys had to load all hay and corn from the fields that year, feed the pigs and cows, and all other jobs on the farm'.[66] On leaving he was given a certificate which stated that he was to return to school if the war ended before he was fourteen, but in practice he never went back. Most other boys in his position followed that example.

Elsewhere critics commented adversely on the growing unruliness and discourtesy to be found among many young people.[67] Even pupils who stayed at school became restless when they saw their friends becoming wage-earners. The fact that a large number of fathers and older brothers were away from home also added to discipline problems, since mothers on their own found it difficult to control their older and more boisterous offspring.

Even the ending of the War did not bring about an immediate change in the attitude towards child labour, for it was not until March 1919 that the Board of Education at last issued a circular requiring LEAs to apply school attendance regulations once more.[68] As commentators were quick to point out, this was very different from France, where even during the difficult days of war the Minister of Education had insisted that the education and welfare of children should be carefully attended to.[69]

The unfairness of the situation was further underlined by the fact that public and secondary school children, who normally came from better-off homes and were bigger and stronger than their elementary counterparts, were only expected to lend a hand during their vacations. This included the sons of landowners and the larger farmers, who would usually help on the family holding during the holidays. But on a *general* basis, even that contribution was not organised until 1916, when special agricultural 'camps' began to be established for secondary school pupils. During the 1917 harvest, about four and a half thousand boy volunteers were engaged, accommodated either in large central camps of fifty or so, or in smaller squads billeted in barns and other buildings near a farm.[70] Significantly the minimum age for these youngsters was sixteen, although 'exceptionally strong' boys of fifteen could be accepted, and they were expected to work for only three weeks at a time during the peak harvest months of August and September, and a fortnight at other periods.[71] It was very different from the position of the young elementary school workers, and it was hardly surprising that a report of October

1917 should comment on the astonishment of farmers at the superior physique of the public school boys. They must, indeed, have presented a sharp contrast with the eleven and twelve-year-olds normally recruited.[72]

By the harvest of 1918, their numbers had increased to around 15,000, with some used to gather special wartime labour-intensive crops such as flax. As early as 1916, a sixty-strong party of boys from Bristol grammar school was employed on this task in the Yeovil area. Their camp, like most of the larger secondary school establishments, was run along officer training corps lines, with the boys rising at 6.45 a.m. to the sound of a bugle, and leaving for work at 9 a.m.[73] Although most of the volunteers here and at other camps worked hard, the programme inevitably had a holiday atmosphere very different from the remorseless daily grind endured by their elementary counterparts engaged in the ordinary farming round. One Eton boy who served a two-week stint on a farm in Essex later described it as the most perfect holiday he and his friends had ever spent.[74] The farmers also paid a higher rate of 5d. or 6d. an hour, or 3s. a day, for the services of these boys, compared with the 6s. a week suggested by the Board of Education for elementary scholars.

Boy scouts, too, joined in the campaign. One master who escorted a group of eighteen from London on a flax weeding expedition during May 1918 recalled the astonishment of his boys when they were told by young country lads that they regularly worked on the farms for nine hours a day. The scouts were exhausted after working a daily stint of six hours.[75] Significantly, in November 1918, the very month of the Armistice, it was decided to discontinue the special use of volunteer secondary school boy labour, although, as we have seen, the exemptions for elementary scholars were not withdrawn until several months later.[76]

Astonishingly, too, in his reminiscences of the food campaign of 1916-18, the President of the Board of Agriculture referred only to the aid given by secondary school pupils when discussing the contribution of juvenile labour to the war effort. The role of the elementary scholars was ignored.[77]

However, work on the farms was not the only way in which village children promoted the war effort. One early campaign involved their participation in a 'National Egg Collection' for wounded soldiers and sailors. Still more widespread were the

arrangements made from August 1917, in co-operation with the
Food Controller, for pupils to collect horse chestnuts, acorns,
and blackberries during school hours. The chestnuts and acorns
were used for animal fodder, and the blackberries sent to central
depots to be made into jam for the armed forces. Entries in the
log book for Lower Heyford school in Oxfordshire show con-
signments of blackberries despatched to Hartley's and Pink's
jam factories in London, and also that of J. Keiller. The children
were paid 3d. per lb. for their labours and this was handed to
them when the relevant cheque arrived.[78] The horse chestnuts
were also used to replace grain in certain munitions processes.
Considerable quantities were collected and it was pointed out
that for every ton of horse chestnuts gathered, half a ton of grain
could be saved for human consumption. Berkshire children
collected over 50 tons of horse chestnuts during 1917 alone,
while a year later, with the schemes still in full operation, their
Buckinghamshire counterparts gathered about 130 tons of
blackberries.[79] This compared with 70 tons in the previous year.
In Dorset, 91 tons of blackberries were gathered in 1918; in
Norfolk, 75 tons; and in Gloucestershire the formidable total of
313 tons.

A further way in which the youngsters assisted in food production was by cultivating special school vegetable gardens, the
so-called 'Victory' plots. The Board of Education declared its
desire early in 1917 that children should be 'made to feel that
they are doing national work by growing vegetables for the
nation's needs'. For 'in time to come they will like to think that,
young as they were, they did their part in the Great War'.[80]
Potato growing was particularly recommended, but a circular
issued to teachers in rural schools also advised the adoption of
poultry keeping, the rearing of rabbits, and bee-keeping, while
the girls were to be instructed in jam making and fruit bottling.[81]

At school level the daily routine was inevitably affected by
these initiatives. At Pitstone, Buckinghamshire, the mistress
noted that an extra plot of land had been secured for the boys at
her small school and this they were cultivating with the aid of
gardening tools borrowed from neighbouring Ivinghoe. When
the War had ended she proudly listed her school's 'Record of
National Service'. It neatly summarises some of the ways in
which rural children were expected to assist the war effort, apart
from their direct contribution through work on the farms:

1917

Victory Potato Plot

 Poles of ground — 5 nearly.

 Yield — 12 bushels.

Collection of chestnuts — 5 bushels.

Collection of acorns — 1 bushel.

Collection of eggs for wounded — 65

Garments made for soldiers, i.e. day socks, mufflers, bed socks, mittens — over 100.

1918

Proceeds of Children's Concert given for

 Pitstone Boys at the Front — £9 6s. 6d.

Entertainment on Empire Day — £1 0s. 6d.

30 knitted garments sent to the Red Cross.

Victory Potato Plot yielded 17 bushels.[82]

Elsewhere schools made their contribution to the war savings movement. In Cardiganshire, the local War Savings Committee commented that in the year ending September 1917, £219,183, out of a total of £233,337 subscribed in the county to the 1917 War Loan, had been invested through associations formed in the rural parts of the county in connection with schools. According to the Board of Education, the sums thus invested amounted to about £2,100 per school. In England and Wales as a whole by 1918 approximately 14,000 schools in both urban and rural areas had become engaged in War Savings work.[83]

In all of these ways, therefore, country children contributed to the war effort. Sadly it was often at the expense of their own schooling. But while some observers, like F.E. Green, could deplore this 'exploitation of childhood', others took a different stance. The *Mark Lane Express*, a mouthpiece of the National Farmers' Union, was quite unrepentant when it declared firmly: 'we believe in the lads who, in the ordinary course of events, will get their living on the land being educated; but let it be an education that will fit them for the life's work they will have to do, and a part of it should be practical instruction in those manual operations which the boy performs when he is exempted from the school desk to assist in the production of food'.[84]

Once the Armistice came village children shared in the re-joicing as enthusiastically as their elders. At Fletching, the headmaster noted that when the news reached his school just before noon, 'the Union Jack was at once hoisted and the children cheered loud enough to be heard all over the parish. When I came home to dinner every one was out putting up Flags & colours, and. . . a scratch team started to ring the Bells. . . . The children were not very keen on Lessons in the afternoon so I gave an address on the War & the Armistice after which we sang Patriotic Songs. . . the children formed a long procession & marched up & down the street singing till it was time to go home'.[85] Only later was the toll exacted from the youngsters in the form of a disrupted education and a disturbed home life to be fully calculated.

Note to Table 1 on page 170:
    The discrepancies in the age breakdown totals and the overall totals for 1 February 1915-30 April 1914 and 31 May 1916 are accounted for by Kent, which submitted aggregate figures only, without any breakdown for age, for these two periods.

9. Soldier helping woman farm hand to gather crops

R H. BROCK

Plough Girl. "MABEL, DO GO AND ASK THE FARMER IF WE CAN HAVE A SMALLER HORSE. THIS ONE'S TOO TALL FOR THE SHAFTS."

10. Woman land workers were the subject of scepticism

11. Village woman harvesting

12. School boy helping
with milking

Chapter 9

The Rural Community and its Leaders at the end of The Great War

'Amusements and pleasures were practically non-existent. One farmed, one made money, but war conditions made it impossible to enjoy it, so one carried on, as did every other class, hoping and longing for the finish of the war, and a return to normal conditions.... There was no planning for future years — the future of all England seemed very dark and uncertain — but there was always more necessary work in front of us each morning than could possibly be done in the day. So we did what we could, day by day, and left the future to Providence'. A.G. Street, *Farmer's Glory*, London 1959 edn, 194.

'The effect of war time (fourth year) is apparently deadening to the outward religious life of the agricultural labourer. In spite of the minimum wage, the war has not brought him any vision or new hopes — only a growing discontent with his present position, & with the Church which has acquiesced in it.... The war is dimly felt to be an exposure of the hollowness of our Christianity. Farmers & labourers alike are full of questions as to the value & utility of the Church... people are more ready to see through shams, & more anxious to be rid of "bunkum" than before.... The *heart* of the country people is sound. There is much kindness and goodness ever ready to break out, & plenty of response to what is called here "practical Christianity".' Comment by the incumbent of Horley with Hornton, Oxfordshire, March 1918, in Clergy Visitation Returns, Oxford Archdeaconry, MS Oxf. Dioc.*c.*380 at the Bodleian Library, Oxford.

During the final two years of the War more and more people, in countryside and town alike, began to suffer from the debilitating effect of the prolonged strains which it imposed. Although the will to win was still there, it was overlaid by a growing weariness and a general pessimism. People were prepared to help one another in times of difficulty, but for many the daily routine became a dulling round of hard work and stoic endurance in the face of adversity. This was especially true where families had lost sons or fathers at the front, and where the whole predictable framework of their lives and religious faith had been under-mined. As a perusal of clergy visitation returns for the Oxford diocese will confirm, by the spring of 1918 in countless villages almost all the young people had moved away — into the armed forces, the munitions factories, or to some other area of war pro-duction. Typical of many was Childrey in Berkshire, where out of a total population of about five hundred people, seventy young men had departed, or Tingewick in Buckinghamshire, where 120 men had joined up, something like 18 per cent of the total inhabitants.[1] And from Mollington in Oxfordshire came the terse observation: 'Owing to the War all our young men and women have left the Parish'.

For parents and friends left behind there was a constant nagging anxiety and a perpetual waiting for news, or for the arrival of the dreaded telegram from the front which would inform them of their loved one's death. Later a formal letter or card would be received giving further details, and many families would place that in their cottage window as a memorial.[2] It was a grim reminder to all of the threat which hung over them.

The incumbent of Cranborne in Berkshire was one who noted some of the deep-seated changes in village life which had been wrought by 1918:

> Many of the big houses are empty or have temporary tenants & many of the people occupying the cottages have gone away.... As to the poorer people & uneducated the shock of losing their relations has caused some unsettlement of belief.... "I will never pray again", said one woman who lost her husband. "I prayed for my boy morning & night, & now he is killed, what was the use of my praying," said a mother.[3]

It was to revive the religious belief of the doubters and to strengthen that of the faithful that in 1916 the Church of England embarked upon a National Mission of Repentance and Hope.[4] But in country areas at least, it seems that the people were too preoccupied with other matters or too disillusioned for it to succeed.

Even in the upper ranks of rural society, although the heavy losses of the first years of war were not repeated in 1917 and 1918, there was a steady and inexorable toll exacted. During that period six peers and sixty-five peers' sons died as a result of the hostilities — twenty-four of them aged twenty-five or less.

They included the nineteen-year-old 7th Earl of Shannon, and at least five others who were only nineteen or twenty when they were killed.

But the war did more than denude the countryside of so many of its young men. It also created a shortage of skilled labour, as craft workers joined up or migrated to more remunerative employment. This inevitably affected the carrying out of maintenance and repair work, particularly on the farms. Already by October 1917, a survey had revealed that in twenty-six counties, the shops of 515 blacksmiths and 216 wheelwrights were closed, and those of a further 706 blacksmiths and 428 wheelwrights were understaffed.[5] About ten months later, Rider Haggard in Norfolk observed gloomily that the local blacksmith at Ditchingham was being called for a medical examination: 'if he is taken I know not who is to shoe the horses or to do other necessary jobs'.[6] Often, too, the effects of labour losses and raw material shortages made it almost impossible for those tradespeople who remained to conduct their businesses efficiently. In March 1918, the Rector of Stondon Massey in Essex noted the plight of a local builder who had not only lost his son at the front but had seen his labour force pruned from a pre-war twenty-two to six: 'he has recently received notice that these last six might be more "beneficially employed". The Government's control of lead is very strict, and its hold upon iron and timber makes the use of these commodities almost prohibitive'.[7] Elsewhere the makers of agricultural implements and of fertilisers were diverted from their peacetime pursuits into producing munitions. Ransomes of Ipswich were soon involved in the manufacture of shell and fuse components, mines, trench howitzers, and other weapons, while from 1916 they began to produce aeroplanes. Under pressure from these military contracts, the firm had little opportunity to create a much-needed tractor division or to meet other demands from its agricultural customers.[8] Likewise farm machinery production at Garretts of Leiston was curtailed when they switched over to making shell cases, carts, and horse-drawn general service waggons for the Army, as well as steam power plants to supply power-house requirements at the larger military camps, and aircraft. Indeed, as early as 1914 they had decided to discontinue their remaining trade in seed-drills, horse-hoes, and manure distributors. The stock, drawings, records and goodwill were sold to the Rayne

Foundry Company in Essex.[9] This ended a farming connection which went back to about the 1820s.

Where army camps or aerodromes were established, the disruptive influences of the War became still more obvious, as former labourers were hired at enhanced wages to work at them, or as new businesses sprang up to meet the needs of the large numbers of young men attached to them. At Milton in Berkshire it was the appearance of a large military depot which had disturbed life in that small community. Not only was higher pay offered but employment opportunities were increased. 'Many families who before the war were earning about 14/- a week, . . . began to earn as a family £2 to £4 a week (if not more)', wrote one critic. 'Moreover in nearly every house lodgers are now taken in and this has seriously affected the religious life of the parish . . . the effect of having so many soldiers in the place has induced many who used to attend church to go for walks etc. instead . . . there is certainly a tendency in many "to make hay while the sun shines".'[10]

A.G. Street described these developments still more graphically in his novel, *The Gentleman of the Party*, which was based upon personal observations of life in Wiltshire during the Great War. In his fictional village of Sutton Evias, which by 1918 had become home to about eighteen thousand troops, those older farm labourers who had continued to work on the land felt themselves strangers in their own community. Wherever a site could be secured, timber-built shops had been erected by enterprising villagers for the sale of every conceivable item wanted by men of military age, and soon the parish even boasted a makeshift cinema. The once peaceful valley was turned into a bad imitation of the Strand, and all the while the troops came and went in growing numbers. 'The strains of "Colonel Bogey" played by a military band told people for miles round that yet another draft was *en route* for overseas. . . . By this time the road to Salisbury was in good repair, and ramshackle cars of all kinds began to earn their owners enormous incomes. Silas Meade, who had been earning big money at camp work, now that this was slackening off, bought a car. . . . In wet weather or fine, in daylight or dark, Silas took the troops into Salisbury when they were sober, and fetched them home again when they were drunk. . . . The older men might criticise the changes which war-time conditions had brought about in their villages, in their one-time workmates, in their wives, and in their children; but no-one took any notice of them. England was at war, and war was the business of youth, youth of both sexes. Strange young girls in khaki drove military cars all over the place; land girls, stranger still because of their breeches and man-like swagger, were to be found on most farms. . . . Down in the "Bell and Shoulder" the conversation was all of war and of women, and the remarks of ancient oracles like Eli Noakes and old Fred Delicate fell on deaf ears.'[11] The greater prosperity secured by the camp workers and village entrepreneurs was thus counterbalanced by an erosion of many of the traditional rural values, with their complex mixture of integrity and narrowness of vision.

Often, too, especially on the fringes of London, what one contemporary impolitely labelled the 'air-raid funkers' moved out into the villages and added to the pressure on housing accommodation. At Ascot-under-Wychwood in Oxfordshire, Kathleen Ashby remembered a number of Londoners settling in, including a young writer and publisher who took one of the farmhouses. The Ashbys themselves gave shelter to a refugee child as well as to a number of weary relatives from the towns.[12] It was another aspect of that relentless fusing of town and country which the War was bringing about and which had as its further manifestation the mounting number of industrial enterprises which were being established in rural districts. Both trends were to continue and intensify in the post-war world.

But perhaps one of the saddest features of the War's disruption of normal relationships was the sense of alienation it engendered between the men at the front and their families at home. This had been present even in the early days but grew more severe as the years of bitter warfare dragged on. Aubrey Moore, a Leicestershire Rector's son, who joined up in 1914 when he was twenty-one, spoke for many when he wrote angrily: 'We were thrown into the whirlpool of war when little more than boys, returning, those who were lucky enough to do so when war had ended, "old" in everything but years, with the background of experiences and responsibilities unknown to older generations, while in previous peacetime we would hardly have been regarded as sufficiently senior to balance the cash book or to operate a lathe!'[13] Another veteran of the trenches similarly observed: 'The newspapers, to keep up morale at home, would describe the moment of attack in dramatic, inspiring words. . . . It wasn't quite like that with our exhausted, dejected men. All of us, I knew, had one despairing hope in mind: that we should be lucky enough to be wounded, not fatally, but severely enough to take us out of this loathsome ordeal and get us home.'[14]

It was during precious leaves snatched from the stress of the battlefield that these feelings of mutual incomprehension showed themselves most painfully. People in England, relying for information on a highly selective account of events published in the popular press, had little understanding of the misery of trench life, with its hours of boredom and squalor relieved by moments of sheer terror. Consequently, even the most casual remark could rub the edge of nerves already raw. Ernest Kingsbury, a private in the Devonshire Regiment, remembered such encounters in his Somerset village when he was on leave: 'It was when one would meet an old . . . friend and over a shake of hands the first words would hit you like a seven pounds sledge hammer, i.e. "Hello Ern, you on leave, when are you going back?" It is the last five words that were to cause a near cleavage of a long friendship. Later when others went on leave home, we were to hear repeatedly how they met up with those hated words and what the words implied. It ran so very close to the flappers of that same period who thought it the thing to do to pin a white feather on some poor devil that had been glad to put his uniform aside and once again feel civilian clothing around his body'. Then he added bitterly: 'I found my real rest amid the fields alone around the village outskirts . . . I could not discuss the war as I knew it with my relations or with old civilian friends'.[15]

To many other desperate spirits, the unchanging serenity of nature also offered a balm which human contacts could not provide. Thus that relentless opponent of the war, D.H. Lawrence, wrote from his Cornish refuge in the autumn of 1916: 'I hate humanity so much, I can only think with friendliness of the dead . . . Here . . . there is great space, great hollow reverberating silent space, the beauty of all the universe — nothing more'.[16] Although Ernest Kingsbury and his comrades would probably have expressed it more prosaically it was this need for solitude which they shared.

Siegfried Sassoon, visiting relatives and friends in the

Cotswolds, likewise lamented the barrier which had grown up between the men at the front and their uncomprehending fellows at home:

> How had Uncle Hamo and Mr. Horniman managed, I wondered, to make the war seem so different from what it really was? It wasn't possible to imagine oneself even hinting to them, that the Somme Battle was — to put it mildly — an inhuman and beastly business. One had to behave nicely about it to them, keeping up a polite pretence that to have taken part in it was a glorious and acceptable adventure. . . . I had felt that no explanation of mine could ever reach my elders — that they weren't capable of wanting to know the truth.[17]

These sentiments were reinforced among many of the troops by the belief that people at home were continuing to prosper whilst they were suffering miserably on the battlefield. Among soldiers from town and country alike there was the conviction that munitions workers, in particular, were pampered and pandered to, though the wants of the front line fighting man were ignored.[18]

Even after the war these bitter mental scars were slow to fade. Equally persistent was the physical toll exacted in terms of injured limbs, and bodies weakened by the discomforts of trench life. Many returned home only to die shortly afterwards from tuberculosis or the effects of gas poisoning. Others were never again able to do a full day's work. The Rector of Stondon Massey was not alone in remarking upon the young fit men who had joined up in category A1 of the military health code and had returned at the end of hostilities as B2. Indeed, in the annual reports of the Registrar General for Scotland, war-related deaths were recorded for every year between 1919 and 1939.[19] Unfortunately his counterpart in England and Wales did not follow a similar practice, but there is no doubt that after the Armistice countless returned soldiers suffered for years from the effects of wounds and deprivation.[20] It added yet another layer to that invisible wall which had grown up between those who had served in the war and those who had not, and which made it more difficult for ex-military men to slip back into civilian life.

Meanwhile, during the last months of hostilities tensions also developed within the home community between families who had relatives in the armed forces and those, particularly the sons of farmers, who had escaped. At Piddington, Oxfordshire, the incumbent reported on the way in which 'the desire to escape military service' had 'in some cases led to much trickery and falsehood. One family has gained considerable notoriety in this way, the result of which has been much talk & excitement, which have largely counteracted any good spiritual effect the war might otherwise have had'.[21] These uneasy relationships were carried through into the post-war world. At Islip, another Oxfordshire village, Robert Graves witnessed the acrimonious debates which took place at parish council meetings over the subject of a recreation ground or the building of new cottages to accommodate returned ex-soldiers who wanted to marry but had nowhere to live with their wives. 'Nasty innuendoes were then aimed at farmers who had stayed at home and made their pile, while the labourers fought and bled. The chairman calmed the antagonists'.[22]

The sharp rise in food prices, especially before the imposition of government controls, coupled with the general shortages, added further to farmers' unpopularity in the later war years. It was widely felt that as producers they were not only making huge profits at the expense of their poorer compatriots but were able to obtain as much food as they wanted for themselves. They were also accused — largely without evidence — of hoarding supplies in order to make prices rise still higher. According to one MP, by the spring of 1917 'there [was] no more unpopular class than the tenant farmers of England ... wherever you go you hear nothing but bitter complaints against the ... farmers ... as to their want of patriotism in keeping their sons back and sending their labourers to get killed, [and] the enormous prices they are charging for foodstuffs'.[23]

Within many rural parishes, feelings ran high when local tradespeople were suspected of favouring the well-to-do at the expense of less prosperous families. In *Akenfield*, Ronald Blythe recorded the bitter recollections of a Suffolk wheelwright and blacksmith over the unfairness of food distribution in his area. This applied even when rationing was introduced in 1918: 'I can remember being really hungry ... Rations! That was a joke. We never saw sugar at all. We used to have golden syrup in our tea and if we couldn't get that we had black treacle ... The farmers' houses were full of food, dairy butter, sweet cakes, meats —

everything. They got it off the shop-keepers. They had some kind of mutual arrangement'.[24] Similar memories are retained by the son of a farm worker from Standlake in west Oxfordshire. On one occasion when his father came home there was no bread in the house: 'Our baker would go round the village and deliver to the farmers and the well offs and if he had any left you may be lucky.' His father rode over to the next village and managed to obtain a loaf from the baker there, but the injustice of it rankled with the family for years. Again, despite the introduction of compulsory sugar rationing from January 1918, at ½ lb. per head per week, labouring households often found it impossible to get supplies in Standlake. 'I can remember... when we were in the haymaking field... wives and mothers took the tea [to the workers] and the farmer's family had white sugar on their raspberries and father and the other men had none for their tea'.[25]

In order to remove some of the worst abuses, in February 1918, the compulsory rationing of meat, butter, and margarine was introduced over a large part of southern England, and this was converted to a national scheme by the middle of July. Even the *Mark Lane Express,* the newspaper of the National Farmers' Union, recognised the belated justice of this, especially as regards meat. For supplies of that had become chaotic early in 1918, principally because of a change in the Government's maximum pricing policy which, by foreshadowing lower prices for the early months of 1918, had caused most farmers to dispose of their fatstock during the previous autumn — to the detriment of consumers in urban and rural areas alike. On 8 April 1918, in an article welcoming the introduction of meat rationing, the *Express* pointed to the problems which had arisen in many country districts where families relied for their supplies upon the visit of a butcher's cart: 'When meat became scarce the cart stopped, the labourer's supply of meat was cut off, and, being a long way from butchers' shops and meat queues, very little flesh has been eaten in many cottage homes for several months... we welcome... a scheme of rationing that will enable men on the land and their families to get a share of the reduced supply of meat in the country'.

But shortages were not the rural worker's only problem. High prices, too, inhibited him from purchasing even those items to which he was entitled, as the cost of living jumped in four years to just double its July 1914 level.[26] In May 1918, even, the Food

Control Committee in Midhurst, Sussex, appealed for an increase in labourers' wages in that area to enable them to purchase the special supplementary rations offered to manual workers, to which they were entitled: 'The Divisional Commissioner should ... be informed that a large proportion of the applicants in this district although granted Supplementary rations had not taken up their cards as they were unable to afford to purchase the ration'.[27]

These difficulties were confirmed by a national survey undertaken for the Agricultural Wages Board during April and May 1918, which stressed that many households were unable to purchase the meat or the fats permitted for their ration: 'in families where there were children and little or no earnings supplementary to those of the father, some of the meat and bacon coupons were unused'.[28] The survey showed that, on average, families were eating only about four-fifths of the meat they had consumed in 1912, less than half the cheese, and about three-quarters of the fats.

After the War, rationing was retained briefly, surviving for meat until November 1919, for butter until early 1920, and for sugar until November 1920.

A particular problem for labouring families was that, as we saw in chapter 3, throughout the first three years of hostilities average agricultural wage rates lagged seriously behind the rise in food prices. Inevitably real living standards suffered. Only where a member of the household was able to secure employment outside agriculture did this not apply, and relative prosperity was enjoyed. As early as February 1917, a conference of Norfolk delegates of the National Agricultural Labourers and Rural Workers' Union demanded a national minimum wage of 30s. under the new regulatory machinery proposed by the Corn Production Bill.[29] In the event that proved over ambitious. The figure imposed in the summer of 1917 was only 25s., a sum already too low to meet war-time inflation but one which helped to raise earnings in some of the worst-paid areas. Thereafter, as the district wages boards were appointed, minimum rates were established for each of the counties. The first to be approved by the Central Wages Board was for Norfolk, where the rate was fixed at 30s. for a working week of fifty-four hours in summer and forty-eight in winter; overtime was to be paid at 8½d. an hour for weekdays and 10d. an hour for Sundays. A half-holiday was also granted on Saturdays. The award came into operation in May 1918, save for the half-holiday, which was held over until March 1919. Other counties followed suit, many getting 30s. per week, some 31s. or 32s.; and a few several shillings more. Thus in Lancashire, Kent, and Surrey, 33s. was awarded, in Middlesex and Lincolnshire, 34s., and Cheshire, 35s. A year later, the Norfolk minimum was raised to 36s. 6d., but in Northumberland and Durham at the same date it had reached 42s. 6d., while in Middlesex and Lincolnshire it was 40s. 6d. and in Cheshire 38s.[30] In arriving at these figures, district wages boards had to take into account both existing pay levels and the general earnings position in the area.

As a result of these changes, living standards slowly moved upwards, although even at the end of hostilities they had not quite recovered their 1914 level. On the favourable side, however, there had been some much-needed equalisation of wage rates. Wiltshire, for example, had ceased to be the extremely low pay area it had been in 1914.[31] The process was continued in the immediate post-war years, and in May 1920 the low wage areas of England and Wales were finally brought up to a minimum rate of £2 2s. a week, while the national basic summer hours to which these rates applied were reduced from fifty-four to fifty. The farm workers' trade union, meanwhile, demanded a national minimum of £3 per week. It also insisted that farmers should be responsible for providing all the tools necessary for carrying out the work of a holding, instead of expecting workers to find some of their own hand implements, and for supplying a protective suit of oilskins where men were required to work in the rain.[32] But these requests, modest though they might appear, were rejected by farmers who were only too well aware how far existing changes had increased unit labour costs. So, agricultural workers' average earnings continued to be well below those of their urban counterparts, even though their living costs, like those of the town worker, were continuing to rise. At their peak in November 1920, food prices were almost three times the level of July 1914.[33] And food still absorbed a major share of the farm labourer's weekly budget.

Apart from these important economic influences, however, the creation of the wages machinery had significant industrial relations implications as well. Farmers who had refused to acknowledge the existence of the agricultural trade union movement in 1914 now had to meet representatives of the two major organisations as colleagues on the wage negotiating committees. Although many farmers welcomed the greater uniformity of pay rates which resulted from these arrangements, a considerable minority disliked on principle the fact that their representatives were sitting down on terms of equality with those of the workers. Some, like A.G. Street, mocked the bureaucratic character of the new committees and complained that the 'friendly intimate' relationship which had hitherto existed between master and man was being destroyed.[34] Such a view conveniently ignored the fact that in the early stages of the war, farmers had failed to raise workers' wages in line with increasing prices or their own advancing profits.

But the new bodies were not solely concerned with regulating minimum wages and enforcing overtime payments on every farm in the land. Through the county agricultural committees, representatives of the workers were taking part in decisions as to whether a farm was over-staffed and could spare a man to the army, or whether it conformed to current manning levels. At the same time, the growing scarcity of workers had turned the bargaining power in the labour market against employers, so that for the first time in living memory a threat to give notice became an effective sanction against those farmers who could not get on with their men. To some agriculturists, this reversal of the pre-war power structure within their industry was intolerable.[35] Yet however much they might dislike it, they had little choice but to accept the new situation. Those who ignored the minimum wage provisions could be fined, and whether they agreed with it or not, the negotiating machinery was destined to remain in operation as long as there were guaranteed prices. Even farmers like the dairy and market garden producers of Lancashire and Cheshire, or the sheep men of Cumbria, who derived little benefit from the guaranteed prices on wheat and oats because they grew such small quantities of these crops, still had to pay the minimum wages assigned to their area. In Westmorland, as late as June 1918, less than 0.3 per cent of the county's 242,103 acres of cultivated land was under wheat, and only just over 11 per cent was under oats; almost 80 per cent remained under permanent pasture. And the rugged character of the terrain made any significant departure from that situation unlikely. In Lancashire, too, over 60 per cent of the cultivated area remained under permanent grass in 1918, while wheat accounted for under 6 per cent of the acreage and oats for 14 per cent.[36]

The changing economic and social balance to which these developments gave rise inevitably affected relationships upon individual farmsteads. Among tenants and owner-occupiers alike there was a growing recognition of the need to work together if they were to achieve the best position for their industry. Membership of the National Farmers' Union in England and Wales rose sharply to reach around 50,000 at the end of 1918, before moving up again. There was also a promotion of co-operative schemes for the marketing of produce or the purchase of supplies. This was a trend encouraged by the Board of Agriculture as well as by the independent Agricultural Organisation Society, which had been set up in 1901 for that very purpose. As a consequence, societies for the co-operative purchase of machinery appeared in places as far apart as Hayling Island in Hampshire, the Isle of Wight, and Knutsford in Cheshire, while in Anglesey co-operative cheese factories were established for the first time in the county's history.[37] The Isle of Wight society was formed by twelve farmers, who each took up two hundred £1 shares; on these they paid up 1s. per share, and an overdraft from the bank provided the rest of the capital. Their first purchase was a steam plough to carry out work previously performed by hand and horse labour.

But it was in the sphere of employer/worker relations that the greatest differences could be discerned. Not only was membership of the labourers' unions vastly increased, as we saw in chapter 3, but there was a greater feeling of self-confidence among the men. From Glamorgan by the spring of 1918 there were complaints of growing distrust and hostility between employers and workers, with the former claiming that the men were 'taking undue advantage of the shortage of labour to advance new and unjustifiable wage claims and other demands'. There were also widespread allegations that labourers were displaying a 'decided tendency to "slack" work'.[38]

These problems affected the larger landed estates, too, as the erstwhile leaders of rural society found their authority no longer accepted with the ready acquiescence which had applied before 1914. On the Ward family's Chilton estate in Berkshire, the agent sadly informed his employer that not only were labour shortages eroding standards of maintenance, but the men themselves had become 'most independent; it is practically impossible to fill up gaps'. Significantly, when the estate clerk of works threatened to resign because of disagreements with his assistant, Sir John Ward impressed upon his agent the need to make concessions in order to keep the man on, warning that they would never get anyone else 'that would not be a continual source of bother & worry. Give him a rise of wages, and if it is his cottage that is wrong, tell him we will add to it after the war'.[39] In the end the necessary arrangements were made and the clerk of works agreed to stay, with an assistant of his own choosing. Such anxiety to retain a single employee was very different from pre-war practice, when the ability to hire and fire had been accepted as the normal prerogative of the estate owner. It was a situation landowners were forced to accept with as much grace as they could muster, though that did not make the experience any more palatable. This was shown in Rider Haggard's bitter complaints about the poor performance of men employed on his home farm in Norfolk:

> In all my farming experience of about thirty years, I have never known the men work so badly.... Although their harvest money is very large, about £11 a head, and their labours are very light, as even the barley is cut with reapers and binders, they are slower and less efficient than they have ever been. Indeed it exasperates one to watch them dawdling about their business.... Both Mr. Simpson, my agent, and Longrigg, my steward, say that the fact is that the more money the East Anglian labourer makes, the less will he do... what will happen after the war in all the labour troubles ahead, I am sure I do not know.[40]

In the months following the Armistice these accusations of idleness and incompetence continued to be heard. Thus Castell Wrey, the Brassey family's irascible land agent, who managed 2,700 acres in Northamptonshire, complained in the summer of 1919 of the 'wilful' deterioration in the standard of work carried out:

> I had a case only last week when I started thrashing oats direct from the farm. Two of my men wanted to go off to play in a cricket match, [it was a Saturday afternoon] and they

went. They gave me no notice, and I had to stop, and the whole of my gang was upset ... And also when they were at work, with the exception of a few old honest men, I can prove from my wages sheets that the amount of work is not done that was done formerly.[41]

Some of this falling away he attributed to the influence of the agricultural unions, especially where the branch officials were not farm labourers but worked on the railways or in other trades. That was the case in his particular locality.[42] The rest he saw as the inevitable outcome of the changing spirit of the age and the willingness to question old values. The effect of the wages board machinery, with its careful definition of what constituted a working week and what counted as overtime, was also blamed by many.[43]

Allegations of poor workmanship are, of course, as old as farming itself but there is little doubt that the men did feel a greater sense of their own importance than had applied before 1914. This showed itself even in their political attitudes. For the first time in the General Election of December 1918, the Labour Party fought a number of rural constituencies, and although it lacked funds and organisation, as well as transport to convey electors to the polls, a respectable number of votes was secured in most divisions. At Kings Lynn in Norfolk, the General Secretary of the National Union, R.B. Walker, was all but elected, securing 9,780 votes to the 10,146 obtained by the Coalition candidate. And at a bye-election held in 1920, the Union's founding father, George Edwards, freed from his old allegiance to the Liberal Party, was returned as Labour MP for the South Norfolk constituency. It was a seat in which the rural vote was very important.

In the closing stages of the War, therefore, landowners and farmers both had to come to terms not only with labour shortages and the use of substitute workers like land girls or German prisoners of war, but with the fact that their former authority over their workers had been eroded, at any rate temporarily. It was a bitter pill, made still more unpleasant by the bad weather and prolonged harvest that plagued farmers, in particular, during 1918; the harvest on that occasion lasted about half as long again as in an average year.[44] In the end its successful ingathering was made the subject of a congratulatory *Punch* cartoon.

But if these were all matters of serious concern to farmers, they were not their only problems. As the columns of the agricultural press make clear, another cause for growing apprehension, at any rate for tenants, was the upsurge in estate sales which became apparent from the end of 1917. Landowners had been restrained by public opinion and the provisions of the Corn Production Act from increasing farm rentals, even at a time when their tenants' incomes were rising sharply. Indeed, on 1 February 1917, eleven of the largest of them had signed a letter to *The Times,* expressing their determination not to raise rentals on their estates during the 'continuance of the War' and calling on other owners to follow that example. Yet, whilst they observed this restraint, both their tax burden and their expend- iture on wages, repairs, and maintenance had increased. Income tax, for example, which had taken barely 4 per cent of gross rents on the Wilton and Savernake estates before 1914, was taking over a quarter by 1919, and the burden of all direct taxes together, namely land tax, rates, and income tax, had risen from 9 to 30 per cent of the rental.[45] Similarly, on a 4,200 acre estate in Cambridgeshire investigated by J.J. MacGregor, an increase in the gross income of about $6\frac{1}{4}$ per cent during the years 1915- 19, compared to the immediate pre-war position, was more than matched by an $8\frac{1}{2}$ per cent rise in gross expenditure. That increase was accounted for almost entirely by extra taxation, rates, etc., these public burdens advancing by more than 46 per cent compared to the pre-war situation. In this case, the modest improvement in gross income was accounted for by virtually one item — timber sales. Income from woodlands rose from a pre- war yearly average of £1,114 to £5,677 in the period 1915-19.[46]

Alongside that, there were memories of the long years of depression at the end of the nineteenth century, when land sales had been almost impossible to arrange, and of the pre-war threat of legislation hostile to the landed interest by the then Liberal Government. For the first time, too, landlords exper- ienced the realities of government interference and control through the activities of the County War Agricultural Executive Committees. And although many co-operated willingly with the directives to plough up land or to reduce their stocks of game, to others it seemed an unacceptable interference with their property rights. Agents were forced to appear before the committees to plead for a change of mind concerning orders which their employer found particularly objectionable. But if this proved ineffective, and an owner continued to ignore the directives, he might be prosecuted. At the end of May 1918, the Earl of Aylesford of Packington, Hall, Warwickshire, was fined £70, with £5 costs, at Coleshill Police Court for failing to comply with an order of the County Committee to cultivate a field on his estate, while a few weeks earlier, Lady Russell of Chorley Wood House, was fined £100 with costs at Watford Police Court for defying an order of the Hertfordshire Committee. These were not isolated incidents, and they were in marked contrast to the position of unquestioned authority occupied by most estate owners in the pre-war countryside.

It was under such circumstances that Henry Rider Haggard could comment gloomily in the spring of 1918: 'now-a-days the ownership of land is nothing but one constant worry and expense, especially if it be burdened and repairs are needed, while [the landlord] is loaded with abuse, pelted with "orders" and hunted by perpetual demands for money. Also he is threatened continually with all sorts of vague but oppressive legislation'. *Country Life*, too, joined in the argument, claiming that landlords had been badly treated, with rentals kept artificially low and the return on land amounting to a mere $2\frac{1}{2}$ per cent of its capital value: 'Our contention...is that the regulation forbidding the increase of rents... is discouraging the flow of landlords' capital into agriculture... if a man has no sport in a country, no profit and no nothing, except indeed it be taxation, of which there is more than enough, he has more inducement to sell his land than to improve it'. Where sons had been lost at the front or had been badly injured, these personal tragedies reinforced the sense of gloom which pervaded many country houses as the War moved towards its end.

So it was that as the demand for land began to improve in the last months of hostilities, many owners decided to sell. They included Rider Haggard himself. He calculated that by disposing of two farms at North Walsham and investing the proceeds he could raise the net income from that property by 60 per cent.[47] Castell Wrey, the Brassey family agent, made much the same point when he noted that with the capital realised, estate owners could secure a return of 4 or 5 per cent on the money, instead of the 2 or $2\frac{1}{2}$ per cent they had obtained from the land itself.[48] Elsewhere, astute owners seized the opportunity to clear past debts by disposing of outlying or distant properties; or consolidating scattered estates by selling peripheral land and purchasing more adjacent property. As Heather Clemenson comments, thanks to these moves 'a number of large estates were able to enter the inter-war decades cleared of indebtedness, more compact and in a healthier financial position than in the pre-war years'.[49]

In 1919 the economic incentives to sell were further reinforced by the Budget, which raised death duties on estates valued at £2m. or more to 40 per cent, in place of the 20 per cent maximum which had previously applied.[50] In addition, under the new arrangements land was to be valued at its current selling price, instead of the former valuation on the basis of existing rents. This encouraged the sale of land to pay the duties, since the sum on which the duty was levied was greater than the capitalised value of the existing rental income. If such sales were not made, then the death duty burden would be particularly heavy, as Lord Hugh Cecil angrily pointed out. For even at that date people (especially the *nouveaux riches*) were prepared to pay a higher price for landed properties because of the status attached to their ownership, than their commercial return alone would have warranted: 'a duty levied according to the selling price of land . . . is excessive when compared with the income derived out of the land, out of which the tax must be paid'.[51] But these protests were unavailing, and the new levels of duty were imposed.

However, alongside such economic preoccupations, there were important social considerations as well. To many old style leaders of rural society it seemed that their predominant position had been irrevocably undermined. They had been 'disheartened, not to say cowed, by the obloquy heaped upon them by agitators. They [had] got it into their heads that they [were] not popular with the majority'. Hence they had become 'as frightened as mice'.[52] Such was *Country Life's* assessment of the situation, and although exaggerated, it had more than a germ of truth in it. Many estate owners had grown uneasy, and were unwilling to hang on to property which appeared likely to prove both a wasting asset and a subject for public controversy. So they decided to sell.

To the tenant farmer, on the other hand, particularly the man on an annual contract, this large-scale disposal of land was a

new and disturbing development. Often the change of ownership meant that sitting tenants were given notice, or at best were
offered the chance of purchasing their holding. A number, em-
boldened by the prosperity of the War years and the guarantees
of the Corn Production Act, resolved to pursue the latter course,
often borrowing money for the purpose at high interest rates. If
they did not, they had to embark upon a frantic search for
another property to rent. The speeding up of this sales merry-go-
round was reflected in the rising price of land. The sale price per
acre increased from an average of £29 12s. in 1918 to £35 2s. in
1920, only to fall back sharply to £28 12s. in the recession year of
1921.

In the meantime, farmers, supported by the National
Farmers' Union, pressed for governmental action to give
security of tenure to those men who were cultivating their land
efficiently, at least for the duration of the War. Early in 1918,
Mr Nunneley, the NFU's new President, told a meeting of
Hertfordshire members that 'the most urgent question they had
to face was that of security of tenure... Hundreds of farmers
were having their farms sold over their heads, and were having
notice to quit.' A resolution was unanimously passed pressing for
County War Agricultural Committees to be empowered to veto
any notice to quit given to a farmer who was cultivating his land
satisfactorily, 'until a measure giving proper security of tenure
be passed into law'.[53] On 8 July the NFU's newspaper, the *Mark
Lane Express*, returned to the subject:

> It is only too manifest that the rush to sell agricultural land
> has become a menace to agriculture.... The practical
> stoppage of shooting, the forbidding of agricultural shows
> and other local gatherings, together with the 50 per cent rise
> in rural railway fares, and the withholding of petrol for
> motors have between them shifted 'amenity' from the
> country seat to the town hotel.
>
> At the same time, the rise in the rate of interest obtainable
> on gilt-edged securities has made the rent of agricultural
> land appear absolutely insufficient, except in cases where a
> genuine local attachment subsists... However these things
> may be, the advertised approaching sales of country pro-
> perties, 'with farms,' constitute a most formidable list; and it
> keeps on increasing....

The *Express* proposed the placing of a motion before Parliament demanding that no farmer, except on grounds of inefficiency, could be disturbed in his tenure 'till one clear year after the war'.

The *Farmer and Stockbreeder* also joined in the campaign, warning that a tenant who was under notice to quit could not concentrate his full attention upon the task in hand, so as to achieve maximum output: 'In truth, he may be likened to one farming with a rope round his neck. The more he does for the farm, the more will it command in the market;... Our suggestion — which is virtually the suggestion of most of the agricultural societies which have considered the subject — is that land sales need not be interrupted, but that for at least two years after the war the sitting tenant should be left in possession provided that the County War Agricultural Committees signify their approval of his method of farming... It is of little use appealing to men to farm well while they are sitting under notice to quit'.[54]

In the House of Lords, a pre-war President of the Board of Agriculture, the Marquis of Lincolnshire, responded to the clamour by introducing a private member's Bill proposing that during the war a notice to quit should not be served on any farmer save with the endorsement of the relevant Agricultural Committee.[55] But to many of his fellow peers this was an unacceptable extension of state interference into private property rights, and it was rejected. Equally, Rowland Prothero, the current President of the Board, firmly refused to act. He pointed out that 'however undesirable it was there should be any displacement of desirable tenants, changes of ownership could not well be prevented, and speculative purchase of farms to a certain extent followed'.[56]

So the sales continued unabated. On 4 November 1918, alone the *Mark Lane Express* listed the forthcoming auction of 8,810 acres of land by Messrs. Knight, Frank and Rutley. They included 2,500 acres on the Chadacre Estate in Suffolk, 1,735 acres on the Ratton Estate, near Eastbourne, and 1,200 acres on Lord Leigh's Little Leigh estate. In all, this firm disposed of 454,972 acres in 1918. *The Times,* in drawing attention to the way that the larger owners were divesting themselves of outlying portions of their property, noted that among the buyers were some who sought 'a channel for investment of war profits'. Purchases by sitting tenants had also occurred on a large scale, and 'where auctions have taken place the particulars have generally been well scored with entries to the effect that various farms were withdrawn, having been sold to them'.[57] After the War the process was accelerated, with more than a million acres estimated to have changed hands in 1919 and sales records broken again in 1920. Early in 1919, for example, over 7,000 acres of the western portion of the Duke of Westminster's Eaton estate was disposed of to tenants for £330,000, while in 1920, the Duke of Rutland sold 28,000 acres — or about half his Belvoir estate — for £1.5m. Urban estates were also broken up in this feverish upsurge of activity, with the Duke of Bedford selling £2m. worth of his Bloomsbury ground rents, and Lord Portman 7 acres of Marylebone, among others.[58] Small wonder that by May 1920, *The Times* could plaintively observe: 'England is changing hands. . . . Will a profiteer buy it? Will it be turned into a school or an institution? Has the mansion house electric light and modern drainage?' Or that the *Economist*, commenting on the 'remarkable change in the ownership of land', could add on 17 January in that year: 'Farming on a large scale by public companies and co-operative societies and land speculation by syndicates and private individuals are factors which have had considerable influence in raising prices'. So great had been the volume of transactions that 'many solicitors were compelled to refuse to undertake property transfers, giving as reason that they had in hand so much uncompleted business'.

Among the purchasers, however, was the new class of town businessmen mentioned by *The Times*, who had amassed comfortable fortunes during the hostilities and now wished to retire to enjoy the pleasures of rural life. Their aim, according to A.G. Street, was not so much to cultivate the land as to 'get a nice home, some good sport, and a background for their families'.[59] They were prepared to pay dearly to buy a property that they desired, and the price of holdings was consequently forced upwards.

Overall between 1918 and 1921 perhaps a quarter of the land of England changed hands in this unprecedented surge of activity, and whereas owner-occupiers had held around 11 per cent of the cultivated area in 1914, by 1927, when the boom had burst, that figure had risen to 36 per cent. A similar proportion of total holdings was also in the possession of owner-occupiers in 1927, compared to 11.3 per cent of holdings so owned in 1914.[60]

Yet although these changes reduced the role of the traditional noble and gentry families, they by no means disappeared. Indeed, almost half a century later such leading gentry houses as Loseley Park, Surrey; Felbrigg Hall, Norfolk; Capesthorne Hall, Cheshire; Burton Constable, Yorkshire; and Alscot Park, Warwickshire, were still maintained and lived in, mostly by descendants of the original builders.[61] Equally, representatives of the major landed families continued to take a lead in their counties, serving on local councils and acting as governors of schools and other institutions. But their position was far more circumscribed and restricted than had been the case even during the 'great depression' years at the end of the Victorian era.

Meanwhile, by 1920 some of the worst anxieties of farmers over the tenure issue had been met. Under the Agricultural Land Sales (Restriction of Notices to Quit) Act, 1919, any notice to quit issued whilst a holding was being offered for sale was automatically invalidated. The following year this was taken further by the Agriculture Act, which increased the security of tenure of both tenant farmers and their labourers. If the former were given notice, save for bad husbandry, they could now claim one, or in certain circumstances, two years' rent by way of compensation for disturbance, instead of the previous indeterminate allowance of the 'costs of disturbance'. Agricultural labourers who occupied tied cottages similarly gained by becoming entitled to two months' notice to give up possession, instead of the hitherto customary week.[62] It became the duty of the reconstructed agricultural sub-committees of the county councils, which in 1919 replaced the old war-time executive committees, to act as courts of appeal both for landowners wishing to turn out a tenant for bad husbandry (thereby escaping the payment of compensation), and for farmers seeking to gain possession of their cottages.[63]

During the last stages of the War, therefore, there were anxieties and uncertainties on many fronts within the rural community. But throughout the greatest fear of all related to the course of events on the battlefield itself. That struggle had dragged on for so many years and had claimed so many victims that some began to despair of its ever ending. Even when rumours of an Armistice began to circulate, few dared to believe them. And when, on 11 November, that longed for event at last took place, it seemed 'almost as if one heard a dead silence and then ... the whole nation gave a sigh of relief. A few moments later the people had gone mad'.[64] So wrote Mrs C.S. Peel, of her own recollections of that day. Siegfried Sassoon, on a brief visit to Oxfordshire, had much the same reaction:

> Walking in the water meadows by the river below Garsington on the quiet grey morning of November 11th, I listened to a sudden peal of bells from the village church and saw little flags being fluttered out from the windows of the thatched houses on the hill. Everyone had expected to hear that the Armistice was signed; but even now it wasn't easy to absorb the idea of the War being over. The sense of relief couldn't be expressed by any mental or physical gesture. I just stood still with a blank mind, listening to the bells which announced our deliverance.[65]

In the southern coastal counties of England the relief was especially profound, for there the war had been uncomfortably close. Many homes had echoed to the thunder of the great guns firing on the battlefield a few miles away across the channel, and the conflict had seemed an ever-present reality. During June 1918, the headmaster of Fletching school in Sussex had commented on the 'Thud & Throb of the guns, night & day in France ... yesterday I could even hear them in-doors. Aeroplanes are constantly going over & will soon be as common as Motors & attract as little attention'.[66] Five months later, the mood was very different. In a letter to his son in Canada, he described the village's reaction to the announcement of peace: 'I expect you are wondering how we all feel over the Armistice. The news reached Fletching about 11.45 a.m., and was soon brought down to School where the Union Jack was at once hoisted ... Ma & the girls couldn't sit still & kept rushing to the door to see what was going on ... After tea our Church Clock, which had been silent all through the War struck at 6 & has continued striking day & night. It may seem a little thing to you, but to all here it meant much, and sounded like the voice of an old friend returning from the grave'.[67] But he remembered, too, the darker side of the struggle, with the loss of thousands of young men on the battlefield and the serious maiming of many of those who had survived:

> I think most people feel that some time must elapse before we can properly celebrate peace, our feelings have been too

much harassed and our sympathies too often called forth, for the losses of our friends & neighbours. As I look back over the last 4½ years I can see so many tragedies in families I know well, & I can see so many of my old boys who are dead or wounded, or dying of consumption & recall them as boys at school where I used to urge on them the duty of patriotism, so that at present, it doesn't seem right that those who have escaped shall give themselves up to Joy days... there is an almost universal feeling throughout the country that Honour shall be rendered to the dead & sympathy shown to the bereaved...

Already, too, the dreaded influenza epidemic, which was eventually to claim 150,000 lives in England and Wales, was sweeping the country, bringing in its wake yet more grief.

Soon steps were being taken to construct permanent memorials to those who had fallen. As early as December 1918, in the Ongar area it had been decided to erect a cottage hospital for that purpose, and over the next few years in countless communities collections were organised for the building of village halls, or the erection of cenotaphs, to commemorate the dead. Or perhaps, in the smallest rural parishes, it would be merely a modest plaque erected in the local church.

Yet, if these were the long shadows cast by the War, for the survivors the gradual ending of restrictions and the widening of leisure opportunities led to an upsurge of pleasure seeking and a determined search for congenial companionship. At its simplest level it found expression in the growth of organisations like the Women's Institute or, from 1921, the British Legion. Both were non-political and non-sectarian and aimed to recruit members from all classes of society. 'This is the first organization I've been able to join in the village,' declared one early member of the Women's Institute, 'everything else is got up by the Church or the Conservatives and I am a Catholic and a Liberal'.[68] In the post-war years the Institutes provided country women with a valuable opportunity to run their own affairs, as well as to gain confidence in public speaking and in taking a lead in village life. They also led to the formation of choirs, drama groups, and folk dancing teams in villages where previously there had been no distinctive recreational activities for women. As the East Sussex Federation declared, in urging its members to revive folk dancing, they would find thereby a new interest in life: 'the "daily round and common task" will go all the better to the lilt of a Morris tune'.[69]

Among the better off sectors of rural society, meanwhile, there was a widespread desire to be out and about. *Country Life* captured the new mood on 7 December 1918, with articles on 'The Future of Fox Hunting', 'Shooting After the War', 'The Re-birth of Racing', and 'The Revival of Cricket'. A few months later, it was describing the general resurgence of gaiety. 'No day seems quite long enough . . . and it is something of a privilege for those who have passed their first youth to be surrounded and carried along by a crowd of young spirits who are bent upon . . . dining, dancing and theatre-going, with golf and . . . hunting thrown in'.[70]

A.G. Street described in detail his own response to the coming of peace, and to the widespread belief that this had been a war to end all wars, and that the future must inevitably be brighter than anything that had gone before. To him and his friends, the signing of the Armistice had been like the lifting of a heavy weight:

> All classes indulged in a feverish orgy of all those sports and pastimes which had been impossible for four long weary years.
>
> Rural communities were no exception. Hunting, shooting, fishing, and the like, suddenly reappeared in our midst. In the summer tennis parties became the order of the day. Farmer's Glory was going to be as splendid as of old, only more so. More so because we all had money to burn. I find this hard to write. It is not a pleasant thing to set down on paper what a tawdry life one lived in those few years . . . But the majority of farmers took no thought for the morrow, their only idea was to have a good time. Instead of living for one's farm, the only desire was to get away from it and pursue pleasure elsewhere.
>
> And I was as bad . . . as any one. I kept two hunters, one for myself and one for my wife; and glorious days we had together with the local pack. I went shooting at least two days a week during the winter. We went to tennis parties nearly every fine afternoon in the summer, and, in our turn, entertained up to as many as twenty guests on our tennis-court, and usually to supper afterwards. . . . In short, farmers swanked. It would not

have mattered so much if they had confined their swanking to their immediate surroundings, . . . but it was the motor car which made a lot of this swanking possible. . . .

Prior to its arrival in country districts, the radius of a farmer's social activities was restricted by the capacity of his horse and trap as a means of transport, but the car infinitely extended the possibilities. Farmers now went away from home for frequent holidays, to seaside resorts and to London. They discarded the breeches and gaiters of their ancestors for plus-fours of immaculate cut, incredible design, and magnificent bagginess, in which garb they were to be found on every golf course . . . Personally, I started golf in 1919, and in 1921 I was the proud possessor of a handicap of eight, which statement tells only too plainly the amount of time I must have spent at the game.[71]

The sales catalogues for landed estates during the early 1920s reflected these sporting preoccupations. Like their Edwardian predecessors they laid great stress upon the first-rate shooting facilities offered, or the unrivalled opportunities for hunting, fishing, boating or golf. '[This] Residential Property, which is enclosed within its own ring fence, . . . possesses well placed woods and plantations giving excellent cover for a large head of game', trumpeted one advertisement for a property of 1,300 acres in West Cornwall.[72] 'Excellent Salmon and Trout Fishing in the Rivers Lune, Wenning and Greta', proclaimed another, for an estate on the Lancashire/Westmorland border, 'and there are Trout in the Beck running through the Park. The County is Hunted by the Lunesdale Harriers and the Oxenholme Staghounds, while there is also a Pack of Otter Hounds'.[73]

But the easy times were not destined to linger. Soon the clouds of economic recession began to gather, as the onset of agricultural and industrial depression and the bitter post-war struggles between capital and labour manifested themselves. In considering these events, pride of place is usually given to the plight of the hard-hit urban centres and the areas of manufacturing production. But the people of the countryside, too, suffered, after the sudden and devastating collapse of agricultural prices during 1921/22. That uncertainty was to persist for the remainder of the inter-war years and was to colour every aspect of rural life.

Chapter 10

Epilogue: The Inter-War Years

'British agriculture is not a cheerful topic; on the contrary, it is gloomy and depressing... Corn growing is on the rocks; its S.O.S. signals are flying in all directions; no life-boats are as yet in sight... Our home market for agricultural produce, which should be the best and most stable in the world, is... the profitable plaything of foreign producers'. Lord Ernle, *The Land and Its People,* London n.d. (*c.* 1925), 216. (As Rowland Prothero, Lord Ernle had been President of the Board of Agriculture from 1916 to 1919).

'The depressed condition of agriculture inevitably had repercussions on other rural occupations, with the result that migration of labour was not confined to workers on the land. Thus village craftsmen such as blacksmiths, saddlers, carpenters and wheelwrights also felt the wave of depression... many of the younger men, who in former days would have traditionally followed in their fathers' footsteps, answered the call of the city or of the factory or obtained contractor's work in the countryside. Even many of those employed in the ancillary occupations of rural life — assistants in village shops, rural road workers and railwaymen — wherever possible "bettered" themselves by getting a job in the town. Even in the County Constabulary a move to a town was looked upon as a "promotion".' *Report of the Committee on Land Utilisation in Rural Areas,* Parliamentary Papers 1941-42, Vol. IV, 16.

Despite the substantial increase in food production which had occurred under government influence during the final years of the War, by 1918 agriculture had already ceased to be a major force in British economic and social life. In the two decades of depression which followed, the industry was to undergo a further sharp decline, its share of national income falling from over 6 per cent in the War years, to an estimated 4.2 per cent in 1924 and 3.9 per cent eleven years later.[1] That slide was symptomatic of the diminished role of the industry itself.

For many farmers and landowners it was the speed of the post-war changes which was to prove so bewildering, as the value of agricultural output dropped by perhaps 50 per cent in the course of a decade. (See Appendix 2). Within two years, from 1920 to 1922, the price of barley and oats had halved and that of wheat dropped by a third. The system of guaranteed prices, carefully constructed in 1917 and confirmed in the 1920 Agriculture Act, was swept aside in 1921 just when it was needed most. Small wonder that MPs like F.D. Acland, former Parliamentary Secretary for Agriculture, spoke of the event as evoking a sense of shame. He then added despondently: 'No farmer will want to see a representative of the Ministry on his farm because of that breach of faith'.[2] Nor did the process of decline end there. After a period of relative stability in the mid-1920s, further disastrous price falls set in from 1929. For wheat the lowest price on record was only reached in 1933, when it dropped to 5s. 2d. per cwt. At least one authority has suggested that this was probably its lowest level since the sixteenth century.[3] A year earlier, the Cereals Committee of the National Farmers' Union had referred to the 'tragic financial position' of British cereal growers, and had pointed to their desperate situation, hampered as they were by low prices and unfavourable climatic conditions, which had made the 1931 wheat harvest the smallest ever recorded.[4]

But the main cause of Britain's difficulties undoubtedly lay in the world surplus of food. Already by the mid-1920s, home-grown wheat accounted for little more than one-fifth of the available supply, compared to nearly one-quarter before 1914.[5] And in the world crisis of 1929-33, when other European markets became increasingly protectionist, Britain was the object of large-scale dumping, with the volume of food imports in October 1931 estimated to be 35 per cent above normal.[6] Not until the passage of the 1932 Wheat Act did the government at last revert to its war-time policy of price guarantees for that product, at a time when it was finally casting aside the free trade ideals which had served as conventional wisdom since the repeal of the Corn Laws in 1846. Similar guarantees for oats and barley had to wait until 1937 and only came into operation in 1939.

During the 1920s, however, the Ministry of Agriculture (converted from a Board in 1920) had been unreceptive to proposals for economic relief through subsidies. And the view of Lord Ernle, former President of the war-time Board, appeared to confirm that among the industry's friends there was little hope of assistance from any official source. 'Nothing seems to me more certain in politics', he wrote, 'than that British agriculture will be neither subsidised nor protected'.[7] The only exceptions to that *laissez-faire* philosophy were the introduction in 1925 of a modest subsidy designed to encourage the growth of sugar beet in this country, and the implementation of a series of measures to reduce the burden of rates on agricultural land and buildings. This culminated in 1929 in their total derating.[8] The sugar beet subsidy proved of particular benefit to farmers in the hard-hit Eastern Counties, as men from Kent to Yorkshire grew beet rather than the traditional fodder crops of swedes and turnips, utilising the beet tops and pulp as fodder instead. But with a total acreage at the end of the 1930s of less than 350,000, sugar beet remained of limited importance as a cash crop to most farmers in England and Wales. Indeed, because low transport costs were essential for the achievement of profitability, most growers were to be found within twenty-five miles of a beet factory.[9] Wheat and sugar beet subsidies together accounted for four-fifths of the £104 millions paid out in price subsidies during the inter-war period, and by the end of the 1920s eighteen sugar beet factories were in operation.[10] All save four of them were in the Eastern Counties.

But if the arable men had been most seriously affected by the pressures of overseas competition, they were not alone in their difficulties. Meat and dairy producers, despite their access to inexpensive foreign animal fodder, faced the problem of cheap imports, too, while production of hay was in most years far below the war-time peak of 8.8m. tons.[11] Meat producers suffered particularly from the greater importation of chilled beef from Argentina and of bacon from Denmark. Even the offering of a fat cattle subsidy in 1934 proved insufficient to make good the losses of producers.[12] A similar move to assist pig farmers came four years later, after the abandonment of an abortive attempt to raise prices by controlling imports. The nation's butter consumption likewise became a major preserve of the foreigner, while cheese imports remained high, and fruit and vegetables were facing competition on a scale unknown before the War, with much fruit brought in from North America. However, changing dietary habits ensured a growing demand for market garden produce, and employment in this sector increased. (See Appendix 1). By the mid-1920s a Ministry of Agriculture survey indicated the high degree of foreign penetration of the British home market, and this trend was confirmed by later surveys.

Table 1(a): Percentage of home-produced food in total supplies

	Pre-war: 1905-9 average	1924-7 average	1936-9 average
	Great Britain	Great Britain	United Kingdom
Wheat	24.8	21.0	22.7
Barley	59.8	57.3	46.2
Oats	73.8	85.1	94.3
Sugar	—	6.2	17.9
Potatoes	92.0	88.0	95.9
Beef and veal	52.6	43.2	49.1
Mutton and lamb	51.5	44.2	35.9
Pig meat, including lard	35.8	32.1	n.a.*
Butter	13.0	13.4	8.9
Cheese	24.2	23.1	24.1
Shell eggs and egg products	32.4	44.6	61.2

*In 1936-39, 77.7 per cent of pork was home produced but only 29.3 per cent of bacon and ham.
From *A Century of Agricultural Statistics* (HMSO 1968), 48, 56 and 58.

From 1931 attempts were made to curb the growing imports of horticultural products by the imposition of tariffs, and import quotas were later adopted for a number of other products, to the disapproval of *The Economist*, which referred to the 'near-sighted fallacies of protectionist dogma'. But as Table 1(b) shows, their effects were limited. They were in any case undermined by the adoption of imperial preference through the Ottawa Agreements of 1932, since the cutback secured in the foreign supplies of certain products was more than matched by an increase in imports from the Empire. The main purpose of the Agreements had been to seek a freer market for British manufactured exports, and, in return, concessions had to be made in respect of those imports which formed the bulk of the trade of the Dominions, namely agricultural products.[13]

Table 1(b): Index numbers of the volume of food imports
into the United Kingdom

1927-29 average = 100

		Wheat and Flour	Meat including Bacon	Dairy Products	Eggs	Fruit	Vegetables	All Food
1930		99	106	109	107	99	101	105
1931		110	117	123	104	120	156	117
1932		96	112	127	84	118	142	111
1933		103	101	133	76	107	87	107
1934		95	94	142	81	88	81	104
1937		89	95	136	103	85	86	103
1938:								
	Total	92	95	138	114	107	79	106
	Empire	129	142	158	63	217	130	143
	Foreign	59	71	119	125	61	66	83

From Michael Tracy, *Agriculture in Western Europe (after 1880)*,
London 1964,168.

Only in the case of poultry and eggs was the level of
dependence on overseas supplies substantially reduced in the
inter-war years (see Table 1(a) for the position regarding eggs),
while liquid milk sales and, to a lesser degree, potatoes,
remained in the hands of home producers. Milk output was,
indeed, rising sharply, increasing by 13 per cent between 1925
and 1930-31 alone. But even that trend was not without its pit-
falls. For as more farmers turned to dairying as a way of
salvaging something from the wreckage of their agricultural
operations, prices were driven down. Markets dissolved into
chaos in the early 1930s, reinforced by the fact that growing
imports of dairy produce from 1929 were pushing down the
prices offered for milk by the creameries. More men turned to
the liquid market, which by 1930-31 already absorbed 75 per
cent of total output, and thereby forced prices lower still. Those
in remote areas, like the hill farmers of Wales, who could not
easily reach retail outlets, were compelled to feed milk to calves
and pigs, since home-produced butter, upon which they had
formerly depended, had now become virtually unsaleable. And

in Somerset, more than half a century later, memories remain of normally phlegmatic dairy farmers breaking down in tears as they saw their life's work swept away into bankruptcy. Not until the establishment in 1933 of the Milk Marketing Board, with its powers to regulate supplies and markets, was order gradually restored. Significantly, farmers from Somerset were particularly prominent in promoting that organisation.[14]

'The "milk" kept West Cumberland farmers out of the bankruptcy court', was a comment heard in that district as late as 1950, and it was a view shared by countless farmers elsewhere during the 1930s.[15] The following summaries extracted from the accounts of a pastoral farmer from Queniborough, Leicestershire, confirm just how great the dependence upon liquid milk and poultry sales could be. They also show how seasonal factors affected overall profitability, as, for example, during the dry spring and summer of 1938 when fodder prices rose sharply.[16]

Table 2: Income and expenditure of a farmer from
Queniborough, Leicestershire, 1933-38

	1933-34	1934-35	1935-36	1936-37	1937-38
	£ s. d.	£ s. d.	£ s. d.	£ s. d.	£ s. d.
ANNUAL INCOME From Milk, Livestock and Wool — year ending 29 September	653 6 3	805 13 6	554 9 4	625 10 7	591 1 10
Of which *Milk*	504 0 3	505 13 6	409 16 10	451 8 7	442 12 8
From Poultry and Eggs — year ending 31 October	394 8 9	361 11 5	358 9 6	303 2 11	303 0 6
ANNUAL EXPENSES From Milk, Livestock and Wool enterprise — year ending 29 September	424 0 3	518 6 8	422 19 0	370 3 3	502 12 0
Of which *Rent*	175 0 0	175 0 0	175 0 0	175 0 0	175 0 0
Fodder	94 11 3	139 10 8	79 18 0	68 15 0	129 19 3
*Labour**	125 0 0	129 16 0	125 3 0	121 18 3	119 0 0
From Poultry and Eggs enterprise — year ending 31 October**	171 3 8	126 8 11	138 14 4	133 7 8	159 13 6
Profit on Milk etc.	228 9 0	287 6 10	132 0 4	255 7 4	188 9 10
Profit on Poultry etc.	223 5 1	235 2 6	219 15 4	169 15 3	143 7 0

*One full-time labourer only employed.
**Includes only feeding stuffs, pens, etc. Rent and labour charged to Milk etc. Account.

13. Boy scouts acting as despatch riders

14. German prisoners of war bagging potatoes

15. German prisoners of war at leisure

16. Blacksmith and his wife at work

The principle applied to milk of organised marketing through producer-elected boards was also extended to potatoes, hops, and, less successfully, to pigs and bacon during the 1930s. But there is little doubt that, as in the late nineteenth century, the agriculturists best able to survive were those who could turn to vegetable and fruit growing, poultry rearing, or liquid milk sales. Poultry keeping ceased to be the pin money of the farmer's wife, as the Queniborough example demonstrates, and became an important part of the whole farming enterprise. Indeed, a number of specialist producers began to appear, particularly on the fringes of the larger towns, where they had easy access to markets for their products. Elsewhere, as in Wiltshire, Dorset, Hampshire, and parts of the Eastern Counties, the increase was concentrated on mixed farms, where it helped to compensate for the problems encountered by the arable sector.[17]

But those arable men who were unable or unwilling to make such changes faced a severe buffeting from the depression. Already by 1922 an investigation carried out for *The Times* disclosed losses of £5 per acre in Norfolk, and of £8,000 upon 600 acres in Bedfordshire, while the overall condition of agriculture in the North of England was succinctly described as 'far worse than that of forty years ago'. Farmers in the southern counties were equally 'on the verge of bankruptcy'. They included the Wiltshire agriculturist, A.G. Street, who claimed to have seen an income of £2,000 per annum earned at the end of the war dwindle to almost nothing by late 1921. In desperation he turned to dairying, building up a milk round in nearby Salisbury. His labour force was sharply reduced and he also cut back on the size of holding he rented. In this fashion he managed to carry on, although, as he later admitted, during that period he and his wife must have subsisted on less than two hundred pounds a year.[18]

Part of Street's difficulty lay in the fact that in 1918, following the death of his father, he had taken on the family farm at a rental almost twice that paid by the old man. As a consequence of the high prices then ruling and the underlying security seemingly offered by the price guarantee system, he had agreed to this after being told that the estate was not going to bargain with him and that they could 'in all probability obtain an even higher rent in the open market'.[19] In the end, as we have seen, by modifying his farming methods he survived. Others were less fortunate. Any newcomer who had purchased stock and implements during the inflationary conditions of 1920 found by 1927 that similar items could be obtained for 40 per cent less outlay. Especially hard hit were those ex-soldiers who had moved into farming after the War, perhaps on government promoted smallholdings schemes, and had not enjoyed the cushion of substantial war-time profits. Their capital simply melted away.

By the late 1920s, Street was commenting on the financial failure of men hitherto considered comparatively wealthy. Farm bankruptcies reached a national peak of 600 in 1932, compared to a total of 497 in 1931 and 428 in 1933. But throughout the period 1922-33 they remained above the 1911-13 annual average of 322.[20] And many of those who escaped that dire fate were still forced to give up their holdings because of shortage of cash. The total of farmers and graziers recorded in the Censuses dropped from 264,093 (male and female) in 1921 to 248,246 a decade later — a reduction of 6 per cent. The number of individual holdings also fell back, sometimes because land was taken in hand by its owners and elsewhere because properties were merged to form larger units, or land usage was changed through industrial and housing development. In remote areas of the country, such as parts of Wales and Cumbria, isolated farmhouses and cottages were abandoned or were used solely as barns and byres.[21]

Still more significant for the industry's future was the growing trend for farmers to encourage their sons and daughters to move into jobs unconnected with agriculture when they left school. This is confirmed by the sharp fall in the number of relatives recorded in the Censuses as helping on the land (see Appendix 1). 'A bank or Government appointment was looked at as a safe haven for life', wrote Street. 'It became preferable to let one's son do anything or even to do nothing, rather than to finance him in any farming venture'.[22] Only in those districts where family farming was customary and community ties strong did this not apply. In Wales, in 1931 farmers and their relatives still accounted for more than 60 per cent of all persons engaged in agriculture, many of them operating on little more than a subsistence basis. In the county of Cardigan alone the 3,806 male and female farmers were assisted by 1,035 male and 223 female relatives; male employees numbered 2,468 and female employees 210. Sons and daughters worked for little more than their keep, although when a son married his father would normally expect to set him up in a farm of his own. This was 'consciously regarded as compensation for the services he had rendered the family during his youth'.[23]

In Westmorland, Cumberland, and Cornwall in England, the proportion of employees to farmers and relatives working on the land was similarly low.[24] Here, too, kinship ties within the farming community remained strong. Yet many, even there, were attracted by the broader prospects offered by industrial and commercial developments in other parts of the country, despite the overall economic depression. It is one of the paradoxes of the rural scene that although traditional links to the land remained strong in these areas yet the number of people living within their borders continued to decline. During the 1920s *all* the Welsh counties, *except* for Carmarthen, Flint and Denbigh, and the English counties of Westmorland, Cumberland, Rutland, Herefordshire, and West Suffolk experienced an absolute decline in their population.[25] Virtually all were heavily agricultural in character, and most were characterised by family farms.

The net result of these varying pressures on the agricultural community was that, as in the 1880s and 1890s, so in the 1920s and 1930s, there was a sharp reduction in the arable acreage of England and Wales, as land was allowed to tumble down to rough grazing or to go out of cultivation altogether. The 10.2m. acres of tillage in England and Wales in 1918 had dwindled to 8m. by 1925 and to around 7m. a decade later. It reached its lowest point in 1937 at 6.7m. acres, compared to the pre-war low, of around 8.5m. acres recorded in 1913.[26] Rough grazing (both in sole occupation and in common) had increased by about 1m. acres over the same period (1918-1937/38).

The move away from arable production was particularly noticeable within the traditional pastoral areas. In Wales, arable acreage dropped by 21 per cent between 1921 and 1929, and by a further 16 per cent between 1929 and 1939. In the southern and south midland districts of England, too, the fall was over 22 per cent in the former period and 17 per cent and 18 per cent, respectively, in the latter. In the northern region, a 14 per cent decline between 1921 and 1929 was followed by almost 10 per cent more in the following decade.[27] Compared to the immediate pre-war period, farmers near Tyneside, the northern textile towns, and the Welsh coalfields were, of course, adversely affected in their marketing opportunities by the mass unemployment in these localities. In the North as a whole, less fertile and more distant fields reverted to rough pasture and bracken. Elsewhere sheep raising and dairying were increased, with milk sold in the nearby industrial towns.

In East Anglia, by contrast, the dry climate mitigated the drift away from arable, and over the period 1921-1939 the arable acreage only dropped by 14.5 per cent, compared to 34.3 per cent in Wales and 36.5 per cent in the south midlands. Nevertheless much land was allowed to go out of cultivation. Large tracts on the sandy breckland on the Norfolk/Suffolk border reverted to gorse, bracken, and rabbits, since the low crop yields did not make cultivation worthwhile. One man farming at Orwell in East Suffolk abandoned almost a thousand acres of heathland to a sheep walk, so as to conserve his capital for land that would yield some profit.[28] Similarly on the fens and marshes of the coast, less land was ploughed and weeds and grasses were allowed to flourish unrestrained. By November 1931, Lord Hastings, a major landowner and farmer in Norfolk, could describe the immediate prospects of his county as 'the blackest winter that arable agriculture has ever known...thousands of acres of arable land for which it is impossible to obtain any tenants, and from which it has been necessary to discharge the whole of the labour'.[29] Unemployment, although generally lower in agriculture during the inter-war years than in most other industries, rose sharply in the early 1930s in the Eastern counties of Cambridgeshire, the Isle of Ely, Essex, Norfolk and Suffolk. And since farm workers were excluded from the benefits of unemployment insurance until 1936, this meant that they had to rely on the vagaries of poor relief for their subsistence. Expenditure on this doubled within these five counties between 1931 and 1932, and doubled again in the financial year ending March 1933.[30]

In Essex and Suffolk, too, thousands of acres of water logged marshes, which up to 1920 had produced wheat, beef, and milk, were allowed to become derelict, as livestock was sold to pay off debts and was not replaced. Winter gales breached the sea walls, which then remained unrepaired, and dykes were no longer cleared out. Only the wild fowlers and shooting parties gained from the changes.

With such conditions, the countryside itself assumed a desolate and abandoned appearance in many places, and a brooding spirit of pessimism permeated the outlook of a considerable proportion of its inhabitants:

> the number of derelict fields, rank with coarse, matted grass, thistles, weeds and brambles, multiplied; ditches became choked and no longer served as effective drains, hedges became overgrown and straggled over the edges of the fields, gates and fences fell into disrepair; farm roads were left unmade. Signs of decay were to be seen also in many of the buildings. Barns and sheds were not put in order; farmhouses were allowed to deteriorate; agricultural cottages went from bad to worse.[31]

There was an increasing tendency, born of necessity, to farm for quick cash returns rather than to consider the maintenance of the long-term fertility of the soil. Improvements in plant breeding and a slow increase in the use of artificial fertilisers raised crop yields slightly, but for livestock little advance could be discerned.

Meanwhile, tenant farmers looked for, and received, rent rebates and reductions from their landlords, who were then unable to afford much-needed capital improvements and renovations to their properties. Buildings remained unrepaired, drains were not relaid, and farm roads were not mended. It was in recognition of these difficulties that in 1925 an abated rate of estate duty was introduced for agricultural land, although, as a corollary, by 1939 the maximum rate of estate duty had risen to 60 per cent. Especially fortunate were those tenants whose landlords had non-agricultural earnings to cover the cost of cottage improvements, or the reconditioning of cowsheds and dairies to meet the new health regulations — though even these external revenues were reduced by the depression in manufacturing and mining. Overall, an official estimate suggested that whereas rentals in England and Wales in 1925 had averaged 31s. an acre, by the early 1930s this had dropped to 28s. an acre, albeit with wide variations around that figure according to soil, size of holding, and location. As much as 50s. an acre might be paid for rich fen soils and market gardens near towns, while hill land or exceptionally light or heavy soils fetched mere shillings.[32] In the Eastern division of England alone the estimated gross rental value of agricultural land fell by 23 per cent between 1925 and 1931, and in the North-East by 21 per cent.

In the years that followed, farms in East Anglia were being offered at nominal rents, or even rent free, by owners desperate to avoid further deterioration of the soil or the expense of having to take land in hand. At least one large landowner paid people to farm his land for him, while those families who were forced to sell part of their estates considered themselves fortunate to get a rock-bottom price for it. Early in 1932 it was reported that almost 8,000 acres in Lincolnshire had already been let rent free for two or three years, and more was expected to join it.[33] Inevitably in districts like the Yorkshire Wolds and Holderness, where large arable holdings predominated, the departure of even one tenant became a matter of concern for the landlord and his agent, and the disappearance of two or three tenants together presented a formidable problem, as efforts were made to find replacements. On the Burton Constable estate in Holderness, untenanted land increased from 2,000 acres in 1929 to 4,000 in 1933, leaving a bare 6,000 acres still yielding rent.[34] In other cases, substantial rent arrears were allowed to accumulate. On the Sledmere estate in East Yorkshire out of a nominal rental income of £20,000 in 1933, £5,000 was outstanding in arrears, and the sum owing in this fashion was rarely much below £2,000 in any year between 1934 and 1939. Similar arrears were built up on Lord Hotham's estate in the same county. On average, landlords' outgoings, which before the War had been around 35 per cent of gross rental, amounted in the early 1930s to perhaps 50 to 60 per cent of that figure.[35]

As more and more properties fell into disrepair, some commentators began to press the need for public ownership of the land. They included Viscount Astor and B. Seebohm Rowntree, who pointed out that the state was already undertaking certain functions formerly carried out by landlords, such as giving grants for experimentation and research, or the improvement of livestock, and providing subsidies for fertilisers and drainage work. Ownership was only a step farther along the same road. 'As a practical policy it would seem best to concentrate on taking over land where capital investment was most urgently required. A scheme could be devised whereby parcels of land could be transferred to public ownership from time to time'.[36] But such a departure from conventional politics was unacceptable to the National governments of the day, which had many other calls upon their resources, and it was left to the Socialists to make state ownership of the soil one of their policy objectives.

Even at the beginning of the 1940s the average rental of all holdings in England and Wales was only about 27s. per acre, although, as before, there were wide variations around that figure according to the location of the holding. Whilst 14 per cent of the cultivated area in the productive Holland division of Lincolnshire was let at 80s. per acre or more, in the the remote Welsh counties of Cardigan and Merioneth, with their large sheep farms, 16 per cent and 13 per cent, respectively, of the total cultivated area paid only 10s. an acre rental. A mere 1 per cent and 3 per cent, respectively, paid 60s. to 80s. an acre, and none paid over 80s.[37]

But worst placed of all in the depression years were those former tenants who had purchased farms in the great land sales boom of 1918-21, when perhaps 6m. to 8m. acres changed hands. In that optimistic market, a new generation of yeomen farmers was born, with about 20 per cent of the land of England and Wales in 1921 owned by those who occupied it. In 1914, that figure had been only 11 per cent and in the early 1940s, after some fluctuations due to the depression, it had reached 33 per cent.[38] With the onset of recession in 1921/22, these new owners were rapidly plunged into crisis, without any landlord to shield them. In many cases their difficulties were exacerbated by the fact that they were burdened by large debts incurred in the purchase of their holding, which they were unable to repay, and the interest upon which became a crippling drain upon already depleted resources. In the 1930s it was commonly observed that the 'banks virtually owned half Norfolk, and that the new owner-occupiers had fared the worst of any section of the agricultural community since 1920'.[39]

Another difficulty was that, as landowners, they were required to pay tithe rentcharge, which was still imposed by both ecclesiastical and lay owners and which had originally been levied to provide for the upkeep of the Church. Tithes had been reorganised in 1925 on a financial basis totally out of line with the low prices ruling in the early 1930s, and to many hard-pressed farmers it seemed an unacceptable and unnecessary impost on their already inadequate incomes. Many argued that the upkeep of the national Church should be a national responsibility and should not fall so heavily upon one sector of the community only. During the early 1930s in the most heavily burdened areas of the south and east of England, there were widespread refusals to pay. Associations of Tithepayers were formed in Suffolk, Norfolk, Essex, Cambridgeshire, Hampshire, Devon, Cornwall, Kent, Sussex, Oxfordshire, Berkshire and Wiltshire, for the purposes of pressing for a reform of the system.[40] The Essex Association, for example, took a stall at the County Agricultural Show in June 1932 in order to explain its position. Even the National Farmers' Union formed a Tithe Committee, although many of its members were, as tenants, not directly affected by the tithe dispute. Often, in order to recover the sums owing, County Court bailiffs were called in by the tithe owners to distrain on corn stacks, cattle, pigs, and other property, with an effect on church/farmer relationships only too easy to imagine. One Norfolk man, the owner of about 200 acres, expressed the view of many when he declared: 'I have been church warden for nearly 20 years and did what I could in the parish. . . . I have had to work from daylight to dark, and make my family do the same, to try and keep the cart on the wheels. The tithe is about half my rental value, and I reckon since 1931 has been paid out of capital. I feel the Parson is taking too much out of me and my family, and I cannot go to Church, it does me more harm than good'.[41]

In many parishes, skirmishes took place between the bailiffs and local people, as attempts were made to block roads to prevent the distrained goods being taken away. Relations between farmers and the police also deteriorated when the county constabulary was called in to maintain law and order whilst forced auctions were in progress, or to protect bailiffs carrying away stock and agricultural implements. At Wallingford on the Oxfordshire/Berkshire border an auctioneer's car was tarred and feathered, whilst he was attempting to conduct a sale of property on a local farm. Elsewhere bells were rung to call up help from neighbouring villages, and meetings were organised to publicise the farmers' cause. One East Anglian poster bitterly proclaimed: 'It's "dearly beloved brethern" on Sunday. It's confiscation of corn stacks! on Monday'. However, for the clergy concerned, not only did the 'tithe war' create unpleasant social relationships between themselves and their parishioners but it deprived them of part of their income. As the incumbent of Hermitage, Berkshire, declared in 1933: 'My greatest trouble & anxiety at the moment is that I am owed £150 approximately on account of Tithe. My chief tithe payer has not paid anything for 2½ years.... This is a serious matter with 3 children to educate'.[42]

Eventually the issue was investigated by a Royal Commission in 1934/35, and in 1936 fresh legislation provided for the ultimate extinguishment of the tithe rent-charge system, as well as giving some short-term relief to the farmers. Under the new arrangements the Government paid the Church £53m. and lay titheowners, such as the Oxford and Cambridge Colleges, £17m. in compensation for abolishing the tithes, but sought to recover the money from the farmers over a sixty-year period. If any farmer defaulted on his annual payments, the amount could be recovered directly from his bank account, or by intercepting his milk cheque, rather than by distraining on his property. This made the collection of tithe a much quieter but more effective affair, and robbed farmers of the propaganda value which the forced sales and the distraints had previously offered.[43]

Alongside these problems was the fact that labour costs were higher, being, according to one estimate, in 1929 double what they had been in 1914. Wages, despite economies in the use of labour and some increased deployment of machinery, still accounted for almost one-third of the arable man's outgoings in the late 1920s (at 31.2 per cent), compared to 29.2 per cent spent on feeding-stuffs, seeds and manures, 10 per cent on livestock, and 14.8 per cent on rent and rates, where the farmer was a tenant. A further 14.8 per cent of outgoings was spent on miscellaneous items.[44] During the next decade determined efforts were made to prune labour, both by the use of machinery and by reducing husbandry standards. On larger farms, tractors, milking machines, and even a few combine harvesters were employed, with perhaps 38,500 wheeled tractors in use in England and Wales in 1938. On one 750 acre farm in the Yorkshire wolds, where eighteen men and about forty horses had been at work in the 1920s, only five men were working a decade later, using tractors and combine harvesters. Cropping and livestock policy had been changed, and no horses were kept at all.[45] But most farmers could not afford the heavy capital outlay that this involved, and preferred the less expensive alternative of the horse. Despite mechanisation and the decline in the arable acreage which required their services, there were still 563,000 horses used for agricultural purposes in England and Wales in 1935-9, compared to 799,000 in 1920-24.[46] Up to the Second World War they provided the main draught power on most farms, and Gosforth in West Cumberland was certainly not the only parish still without a tractor at the end of the 1930s.[47]

For many agriculturists, therefore, the means of survival were found in changing methods, adopting lower husbandry standards, working longer hours, and reducing their labour force. Often, too, among the smaller men, the old custom of lending machinery or labour to one another continued to apply. Perhaps a man would send his son to help with the hay harvest of a neighbour and would then receive in exchange the loan of that larger farmer's mowing machine for his own fields. Or a small-holder who grew no corn might give a day's work at threshing time and receive a bag of corn for his poultry or a bull's service for his cows in recompense.[48] In Cumbria those few cultivators who did not need to borrow equipment or refused to lend it were regarded with disfavour as 'a poor mak o' farmer'. Stories, often untrue, were told of their husbandry deficiencies, and they were accused of allowing dykes to fall into ruin, or sheep to stray off their land in the winter months, 'all of which are considered to be particularly offensive charges by farmers in Gosforth'.[49] Certain of the worst off even had to fall back on the practice of 'halving'. That is, they borrowed their livestock from a dealer and were then entitled to a half share of the proceeds for maintaining them. A variation on this practised in Gosforth was the acceptance of cattle and sheep from dealers for the payment of a small weekly sum to cover maintenance: 'undercutting in the price of winterage, in an attempt to gain this welcome source of income, was fairly common'.[50]

Some men combined agriculture with another job. About one-quarter of all farmers were reported to have a subsidiary employment by the end of the 1930s. This included running a milk round, hiring out machinery to fellow farmers, under-taking outside haulage and contracting work, acting as auctioneers and valuers, or perhaps taking on an occupation far removed from farming, such as looking after a shop or a public house.[51] Trade directories show a sprinkling even took on an insurance agency. The diaries of a farmer cultivating over 150 acres at Maidwell in Northamptonshire show the kind of casual haulage jobs which were carried out:[52]

1922

7th February: 15½ cwts. coal — Mrs Castle (4/6).

10th February: Piano for Castle — Station (7/- + 1/8)

10th March: Grant's furniture to N'ton [Northampton]

1st July: Carted coal — Rector.

Often these tasks were undertaken at relatively slack periods of the farming year and provided a useful way of earning cash with horses which would otherwise have been idle.

In the holiday-making districts, summer visitors were taken on almost all the farms that could accommodate them, and, as at Gosforth, 'the money derived from this practice undoubtedly saved many farmers from bankruptcy'.[53]

However, if the break up of so many landed estates had caused problems for the new owner-occupiers more severe than those faced by their tenant counterparts, it had other economic and social repercussions as well. No longer were landowners available to provide the cohesive cement of village life in the way they had often done in the past, or to give a lead in organising entertainment and charitable help for cottagers. Even where properties were retained, a harder-headed, more commercial approach was frequently applied, as outgoings were kept to a minimum. In some cases private estate companies were created as a way of tax avoidance, until the benefits to be derived from this were curtailed by the 1940 Finance Act. And everywhere the status of landed families was diminished, while many of their political and cultural ideas were subjected to increasingly bitter attack. Little scope remained for the exercise of effective political power, and even sporting rights were often let to wealthy businessmen or foreigners. By the 1930s game preservation as a whole had become less significant.

Large domestic and garden staffs ceased to be engaged to care for the house and grounds of country manors, as landlords pared their personal expenditure. The advent of the motor-car ensured that the dozen or so grooms and helpers formerly employed in the stables of the larger properties were replaced by perhaps two chauffeurs. Often the big house itself was sold, or in a few desperate cases, demolished, as the former owner moved into a smaller property elsewhere on the estate, or as the estate itself was broken up. As early as May 1920, *The Times* was lamenting that many houses were being turned into schools or institutions. And it was in these circumstances that the Duke of Portland, writing in the mid-1930s, gloomily compared the pre- and post-war countryside. 'When I first lived at Welbeck', he declared, 'the great neighbouring houses, such as Clumber, Thoresby and Rufford were all inhabited by their owners, who ... employed large staffs. ... Now not one ... is so occupied, except for a few days in the year, and the shooting attached to them is either let or abandoned'. However, he did admit that some things were done better in the 1930s than in earlier decades. His selection was dentists' equipment and motor transport![54]

The clergy, another group of former community leaders, were unable to take over the role of the landowners on any scale. They were hit by the falling value of their stipends and by the fact that in a society where religious values were increasingly questioned, by Anglicans and non-Anglicans alike, after the cataclysm of war, their standing had diminished. The attitude of many of the critics was summed up by a Suffolk labourer, when he sourly observed of the local parson: 'I shouldn't mind his job. He don't do only one day's work a week, and the rest of the time watches other people workin'.'[55] In West Cumberland the limited respect accorded the Church was clearly reflected in the dismissive comment: 'If he won't mak a farmer, mak him a parson'.[56]

Meanwhile, the weakening of the bonds which had linked landowners and their tenant farmers had its counterpart in the changing relationship between farmers and workers. Many of the latter, impatient with the low wages and poor prospects offered by agricultural labour, or made restless by their years of military or munitions work experience, left the land. As a Norfolk labourer put it: 'the war had changed the men who had been in the army. They were better educated. ... They had a different feeling when they come back: they were not going to do the same things or put up with as much as they'd done afore they went out'.[57] Over the period 1921-24 the total of male and female agricultural workers (including those who were part-timers) averaged about 816,000, but by 1938 that had declined by more than 25 per cent to 593,000. The number of regular male labourers in the same period fell from around 587,000 to 472,000, a drop of nearly 20 per cent.

In some cases, the decline was due to the 'push' effect of farmers seeking to reduce their labour costs, but often there was the 'pull' exerted on the workers by the greater amenities and prospects of town life or industrial employment. Few labourers could hope to rise in the world by amassing sufficient funds to enable them to take a farm or smallholding of their own. Instead they faced the daunting prospect, particularly on stock farms, of working seven days a week for relatively little reward. Their feelings were summarised by an ex-farm worker from Buckinghamshire who left the land in 1928: 'I was a regular milker until I was eighteen and then I began to get annoyed when my mates were all dressed up on Sunday afternoons, so I left the farm'.[58] The better wages he and others like him were able to earn in their new posts helped to promote a modest prosperity within village families, enabling them to acquire some of the cheaper consumer goods which were now coming on to the market. These included household appliances, cycles, motor-cycles, more fashionable clothing, and a greater variety of foodstuffs. They also enjoyed a regular Saturday half-holiday and a free Sunday — something upon which many farm workers could not count. Indeed, in the matter of leisure time their relative inferiority was underlined by the fact that even when the Holidays with Pay Act was passed in 1938 they were marked out for special treatment. Not only was the maximum holiday allowed for agricultural labourers limited to seven days — exclusive of public holidays — but not more than three days could be taken consecutively. This meant that every man had to take his one week's vacation in three separate instalments. Not until 1947 was that particular anomaly removed.

The drift from agriculture was especially noticeable amongst the younger generation. For men under 21, the decline was nearly 44 per cent between 1921-24 and 1938, compared to a drop of 19 per cent for those over 21.[59] The existence of cheap newspapers and the wireless spread an awareness of conditions in the world outside, while the greater availability of bicycles and the introduction of motor buses made it easier for men and women to reside in villages but to travel into nearby towns for both entertainment and employment. Adrian Bell, for one, noted how the dress of film devotees in his Suffolk parish was influenced by their regular visits to the cinema.[60]

Some people also moved away because town employment was thought to have a higher status than that in the country, or because they were ambitious for their children, and often the village school did not offer adequate preparation for the vital scholarship examination for entry to a grammar school.[61] Other forms of secondary education were also scarce in many rural counties. The position in Surrey, where rate income from new housing estates was growing rapidly, and where by March 1937, over two-thirds of all pupils over the age of eleven had secondary-type education in central schools, may be compared with Oxfordshire, where rate revenue was low and where even in 1938 there were still forty-three all-age schools in the county.[62] In other cases, in the more remote communities, distance and family poverty prevented even those who had won scholarships from taking them up. Only a few authorities, like Buckinghamshire, offered bicycles to some of their scholarship winners to ease travelling problems. Cambridgeshire's pioneering efforts to create village colleges, which would act both as senior schools and as educational centres for the whole parish, likewise had little influence outside its own borders.

But of the many factors contributing to the growing discontent with farm work, there is little doubt that poor pay and unsatisfactory living accommodation were the most important. The earnings difficulty was agravated by the dismantling of the war-time minimum wage machinery under the 1921 Corn Production (Repeal) Act. As a result of this, membership of the agricultural workers' trade unions fell rapidly, that of the National Union dropping from perhaps 93,448 in 1920 to 22,085 by 1924, and remaining below the 30,000 level until 1937.[63] The Workers' Union suffered even more severely. By 1924 its agricultural membership had slumped to only about one-fifth of its post-war peak, and at the end of the 1920s it was reported that numbers had dropped to a mere five thousand. Not until 1937/38 did support for either Union significantly increase, as the large pool of unemployed labour, and the depressed conditions in agriculture generally, inhibited any earlier upturn in membership levels. In the meantime, efforts to replace the statutory district wages boards with voluntary joint councils of employers and workers, as proposed in the 1921 Act, proved of little interest to the farmers. The whole scheme was a complete failure, as many MPs had predicted in the bitter debates which had attended the passage of that legislation.[64]

Shortly before its demise the Agricultural Wages Board itself had reduced the national minimum wage from 46s. to 42s. a week. But by the spring of 1922, many men were earning only 32s. per week, and rapid falls followed thereafter. Longer hours were also being required, and by the end of 1922 it was estimated that an ordinary farm worker without special responsibilities might be earning a mere 28s. a week, an increase of perhaps 50 to 60 per cent over the pre-war average, while the cost of living was about 75 per cent above the pre-war position.[65] Further cuts followed until in February 1923, Norfolk employers proposed the introduction of a basic wage of 24s. 9d. for a fifty-four hour week, and with deductions for 'wet time' when men were unable to work on account of bad weather. This could reduce earnings to 18s. per week or less, and the National Union, pushed beyond endurance, decided to call a strike. Soon the dispute spread to Workers' Union members in Cambridgeshire and West Suffolk. Eventually a settlement was reached, providing for a guaranteed week of fifty hours for a wage of 25s. and with further hours up to fifty-four to be paid at the rate of 6d. per hour. Beyond fifty-four, special overtime rates were to apply.[66] For the Union, the main gain was the retention of the guaranteed week, at least in Norfolk. As Howard Newby comments, ' There was to be no return to the pre-1917 horrors of casualization', with deductions from basic rates regularly taking place when no work was possible.

These benefits were made more secure in June 1924, when the Labour Minister of Agriculture, Noel Buxton, introduced fresh legislation to reinstate the Wages Board machinery. He gave as his reason for so doing, the low pay which was still earned within the industry. According to official estimates around 68 per cent of total male labourers were living in counties where the normal weekly rate was under 30s. 'The proportion of those who get only 25s. is 23 per cent ... The irony of it all is, that you have these people producing meat and producing butter, and they have none for themselves or their children'.[67] After the 1924 initiative, earnings in agriculture still remained relatively low — even at the end of the 1930s average wages were only about 56 per cent of those in industry — and there were sharp regional differences. In addition, thanks to a Liberal Party amendment during the Committee stage of the legislation, the Central Wages Board was deprived of its power to amend the wage rates and hours proposed by the county committees, and thereby to mitigate some of the earnings disparities between areas. But at least the minimum wage arrangements provided a safety net for basic pay.[68] As under the war-time legislation, farmers who failed to pay the relevant amounts could be prosecuted, and in 1926 fifteen inspectors were appointed to ascertain whether the established rates and hours were being properly applied. During the first year of operations they carried out test inspections on 150 farms, employing 915 workers. Of that total, 206 were found to be underpaid. In subsequent years it was discovered that about 18 per cent of the cases investigated showed workers were underpaid. In an industry where men were employed in relatively small units, scattered over a wide area, it was a constant battle for government officials and union representatives to ensure that they received their just deserts. But at least after 1924 both workers and employers knew just what those deserts should be.

Of equal significance in raising the living standards of labouring families was the sharp drop in consumer prices, especially during the early 1930s, with the cost of living falling by about 13.5 per cent from July 1929 to July 1932. Between 1924 and 1936 it has been estimated that real wages rose by twenty per cent. [69] The smaller size of families, as contraceptive techniques became more widely known, reinforced this general improvement. Diets became more plentiful and varied than before the war, and clothing was of a better quality. The dire poverty experienced in a number of rural households during the Edwardian era had largely disappeared, and a budgetary survey undertaken in 1937-38 by the Ministry of Labour revealed, for example, how much more meat was now being eaten. Over a quarter of the average weekly expenditure on food was spent on this item alone. Butter, too, was more likely to be purchased than the cheaper alternatives of margarine or lard, and there was more fresh milk sold. Eggs featured prominently in most diets, many of them produced by a family's own hens. Bread and cereals, once the great standby of rural meals, now took only about one-tenth of total weekly expenditure.[70]

Between 12 and 13 per cent of the households surveyed received an allowance of potatoes from the employer, but elsewhere vegetables were grown in gardens and allotments, and convenience foods like jellies and custard powder made their appearance on working-class tables.

As before the War, basic earnings might be supplemented by the opportunity to rent a cheap cottage or to obtain free or low-priced produce of one kind or another from the employer. But, as at that time, by no means all men enjoyed such benefits. Only 18 per cent of the Ministry of Labour households received a regular milk allowance, for instance.

The standard of accommodation in many cottages likewise remained poor. In fact Astor and Rowntree, writing at the end of the 1930s, considered rural housing to have been 'one of the most neglected features of our rehousing campaign since the war'. And when the unsatisfactory condition of many urban slums is considered, that was a severe indictment indeed. By 1939 at least half a million new or improved dwellings were still required to cover the official programme of slum clearance and decrowding. There was also the difficulty that for agricultural workers living in tied accommodation, the loss of employment meant the loss of a home, too. Efforts were made to promote housebuilding in rural areas through the provision of special government subsidies, as under the terms of the 1924 Wheatley Act. This offered a subsidy to local authorities of £9 per house per annum for forty years in urban areas, but £12 10s. in rural parishes. Nevertheless, twelve years later, Sir Kingsley Wood, the Minister of Health, was still stressing the need for rural district councils to take advantage of aid to provide better houses in country areas.[71] But the fact that a financial contribution to the building programme had to be made from the rates made most rural councillors reluctant to embark upon a major programme to provide cheap rented accommodation.

Another disadvantage for those living in the countryside was the inadequate provision of services like piped water, electricity, and main drainage, which were already widely available in the towns. Cooking had often to be carried out on the kitchen range or in a wall oven. One woman who was brought up at Great Moulton, Norfolk, in the 1930s ruefully recalled how often the oven fire died down at the crucial moment, 'causing the pastry bowl to be left in order that more fuel could be collected'.[72] Even many farms were without basic services — those vital prerequisites for a comfortable life. A National Farm Survey undertaken at the beginning of the 1940s revealed that only 47 per cent of farmhouses in England and Wales had a piped water supply, while a further 45 per cent relied on a well as their principal source of supply; among the remaining 8 per cent, a number had to obtain their water off the farm premises altogether. The position was particularly serious in Norfolk, where a mere 19 per cent of farmhouses had piped water, and in East and West Suffolk, where the proportion was 16 and 18 per cent, respectively. Likewise in Wales, only 32 per cent of holdings enjoyed this amenity.[73] A woman who grew up on a farm near Stokenchurch in Buckinghamshire remembered that they had to rely upon a pond to provide drinking water for their cattle, and upon three underground fresh water tanks, collecting water from the roof of the house and buildings, for domestic use. But these supplies proved inadequate. During the very dry summer of 1921, all the ponds dried up and the water for the livestock had to be fetched by water barrel from a source five miles away: 'This meant continuous shifts of water-cart day and night. The water was "bucketed" out of a small lake . . . My mother had to drive about four miles to get drinking water from a spring'.[74] Similar problems existed for cottagers, while the use of polluted water continued to give rise to periodic outbreaks of typhoid in many rural communities. Improvements there had been by the end of the 1930s, especially in the South-East and the Midlands, but much still remained to be done.

Electricity, too, was found in few villages outside the favoured Midlands and South-East. By the early 1940s about 27 per cent of all farm holdings had electrical power in England and Wales, with Wales, East Anglia, the South-West and the far North again coming off worst. Indeed, in Radnor a derisory 1 per cent of farmsteads had electricity, and in Anglesey, 3 per cent. But the English counties of Devon and Hereford, with 14 per cent, and East Suffolk, with 19 per cent, were scarcely well placed. Although a determined effort was made to rectify these weaknesses through the construction of a national grid system during the 1930s, as the statistics show, progress was slow. The need to provide small sub-stations capable of handling the peak load on individual farmsteads kept costs relatively high in more remote areas, and further discouraged installation.

Yet, despite these difficulties, the very real progress made in improving the quality of rural life should not be ignored. Already by the mid-1930s that acute Yorkshire observer of the social scene, Winifred Holtby, could note the changing conditions in her home parish of Rudston, compared to the position before 1914:

> I remember a village with no artificial light, no telephone, no telegraph, no health insurance system, no means of transport except our own pony-trap and the weekly carrier's cart, with its slow horse which took an hour and a half to get to the nearest shops. I remember the alarms of sickness at night, the long painful hours of waiting for the doctor, the babies that died unnecessarily, and the rigid class divisions. I remember my father... opposing the Saturday half-day for his farm labourers. I remember the village idiots too; in my childhood they were a recognised feature of every countryside. And then I think of today's raised wages, the improved housing, health services, buses, women's institutes, the regulated hours of work, the wireless, the young farmers' clubs, the playing-fields, the well-run homes for mentally defective children, the rural community councils...[75]

Many, too, valued the friendship and the sense of 'belonging' which village life could still offer through its traditional network of kinship and neighbourliness. Dances, football and cricket matches, drama societies, flower shows, and village feasts were organised in most communities, often using the local school or village playing field as their focus. The seasonality of agricultural activity was reflected in the way that many entertainments were arranged for the slack months of the farming year. In Montgomeryshire, for example, May and late October were the months for fairs in the market towns, while social events held in the summer, such as preaching-meetings, singing festivals, Sunday School tea-parties, and sports were as far as possible fitted into the months of May and June when agricultural activities were below their peak.[76]

One other aspect of country life remains to be examined, and that is the position of the rural trades and industries. By 1914 the spread of industrialisation and the improvement in transport facilities, following the building of the railways, had already undermined many of the old crafts. The work of the miller had dwindled with the decline in English wheat production during the late nineteenth century, while the village tailor, dressmaker, and shoemaker had seen their work fall away in the face of cheaper factory-made goods. In the inter-war years these trends intensified, as small local industries collapsed in the face of foreign competition or changes in manufacturing methods. They included the slate mines of Carnarvon and Merioneth, the Welsh flannel mills, 'basket-making in the Kennet valley in Berkshire, the wattle and turnery trades along the Chilterns which used the coppice and timber of the beech woods', and inshore fishing in Devon, Cornwall, and the Eastern counties. [77] At Blisworth in Northamptonshire, the ironstone works closed when it became no longer economical to extract the ore by pick and shovel. [78] At the same time, new factories were erected in formerly rural or semi-rural towns like Oxford, Dunstable, and Slough, and in them were established consumer-orientated industries, like motor vehicles or electrical engineering. Many younger workers, dissatisfied with employment in the villages, seized their opportunity to move into them. This applied not only to agricultural labourers but to craftworkers and trades-men, who were often dismissive of their elders' reverence for established skills and what they considered outmoded traditions. There was, in any case, a reduced demand for their services in country parishes. Wheelwrights and harnessmakers, in particular, were affected by the advent of the motor vehicle and the decline in the number of farm horses, and they dwindled rapidly, as Table 3 shows. It was small wonder that the Farnham wheelwright, George Sturt, should comment gloomily on the way in which orders for standard woodwork had dropped in his shop. No longer was there a call for basic items like carts, wheels, barrows, and similar products, which had once been the mainstay of his business. [79] Blacksmiths, too, had ceased to be makers of machinery and implements, and had moved over instead to repair work and farriery, while a few converted themselves into motor mechanics and petrol salesmen. Small

N.B. The decline in the number of wheelwrights was particularly sharp in the 1920s — by 80 per cent in the case of Cumberland, and by over 50 per cent in the cases of Devon, Dorset, Norfolk and Caernarvon. The *increase* in the number of carpenters during the decade in many counties was probably a product of the expansion in housebuilding during these years.

Table 3:
Some rural trades in twelve specimen counties: 1911-31
(From Census Reports)

Administrative County (excluding County Boroughs)	Year	No. of Carpenters	No. of Blacksmiths and Forge Workers	No. of Saddlers and Harness-makers	No. of Wheel-wrights and Cartwrights
Buckinghamshire	1911	1,605	774	160	264
	1921	1,776	645	83	198
	1931	2,312	512	57	108
Cambridgeshire	1911*	1,359	654	158	225
(excluding	1921	844	279	55	112
Isle of Ely)	1931	1,108	245	39	60
Cumberland	1911	1,856	1,238	137	22
	1921	1,252	906	61	26
	1931	1,221	668	52	6
Devon	1911	4,183**	1,806	335	n.a.***
	1921	3,127	1,234	190	517
	1931	4,337	977	130	255
Dorset	1911	2,024	832	159	210
	1921	1,680	575	84	178
	1931	2,171	424	65	79
Huntingdon	1911	374	226	54	66
	1921	370	170	28	65
	1931	384	135	31	38
Norfolk	1911	2,565**	1,758	333	n.a.***
	1921	2,081	1,217	197	388
	1931	2,388	946	151	190
Rutland	1911	132	83	24	42
	1921	103	56	14	27
	1931	113	49	12	22
Westmorland	1911	612	234	46	18
	1921	471	156	17	14
	1931	495	141	9	8
Cardigan	1911	601	272	45	21
	1921	399	187	33	38
	1931	427	160	19	21
Caernarvon	1911	920	545	47	39
	1921	843	434	33	33
	1931	929	353	20	14
Radnor	1911	220	107	14	35
	1921	141	67	8	29
	1931	149	52	9	24

*Included Ely in the 1911 Census.
**Includes labourers also in these counties.
***Figures are not available for the administrative county without associated county boroughs. For these combined areas, the number of wheelwrights was 737 in Devon and 595 in Norfolk, in 1911.

businesses did not disappear from villages, but they changed in character and kind. Instead of *making goods,* most of their proprietors became sellers of services or of goods made elsewhere, which they merely retailed. Even at remote Llanfihangel in Montgomershire, Alwyn Rees reported at the beginning of the 1940s that hardly anything was manufactured locally. There were 'no tailors, shoe-makers, furniture-makers or even dress-makers. An occasional cart is still made, but generally speaking the function of the wheelwright and the smith has changed from making implements to repairing the products of factories — even horseshoes are imported ready-made'.[80] The village shops, although ostensibly concerned with groceries, in practice offered a wide range of goods, including patent medicines, brushes, twine, rope, nails, lamp-wicks and paraffin, meal and chicken feed, clothing and stationery. One Llanfihangel shopkeeper also dealt in butter and eggs, taking a selection of his shop's contents around the farms by motor vehicle twice a week. Money was only used to settle the difference in value between the items purchased from the mobile shop and the farm produce collected. This latter was then sold at a nearby town on market days to dealers from farther afield. A second shopman ran a bus and hackney carriage business as a side line.[81]

Elsewhere similar trends could be discerned, and it was on grounds such as these that a contemporary claimed in the late 1920s that 'almost the entire rural population' consisted 'of farmers, farm workers and village merchant-tradesmen'. She then added gloomily:

> As things are now the village boy has no choice but to become a farm-worker or an unskilled labourer or to leave the district. . . . The craftsman was an important and respected personality in the village. His independent position and his dealings with the farmers showed him a different side of the farmer's character than that which the less educated labourers see. He was proud of the apprenticeship he had served, of the long tradition behind him, and of whatever skill he possessed. He brought to local affairs an outlook somewhat different from that of the farmer, and all this was to the good in rural society.[82]

So it was that the Great War and its aftermath speeded up changes already signalled before 1914, and led ultimately to an overturning of the established social and economic order. To A.G. Street, the years after 1918 saw a 'waning of the glory', a casting aside of the old ways, and a tentative and cautious adoption of fresh ideas. For agriculturists such as he, these included greater mechanisation and the acceptance of growing government intervention through production quotas, marketing schemes, subsidies, and import controls on a wide range of products. Farming itself became more an industry and less a way of life, as agriculturists sought for new ways to improve profitability. There was, in particular, a noticeable curtailment in the use of casual labour, except in the market gardening and fruit growing areas. '[It] has occurred to me', declared Street, 'that one farms better in a settled rut of some kind or other. The war unsettled a good many one-time stable things, and in farming it is the change over from one rut to another which has been so painful and expensive. The chief difficulty has been to find another rut or system that will pay'.[83]

For craftsmen, too, it was a time when skills hitherto cherished became increasingly irrelevant, and when workers who had prided themselves on their ability as makers of goods had to settle down as mere repairers or vendors of those produced elsewhere. Cottage industries like lacemaking, straw plaiting, and glove making, which had once provided major employment outlets for village women in the areas in which they were found, and which were already under severe pressure before 1914, disappeared during the inter-war years. Most women found little work in country districts outside the ranks of domestic service, laundry work, and, to a very limited degree, agriculture. But in this latter there was a sharp decline in the female contribution during the 1920s and 1930s. The role of the milkmaid was taken over by milking machines, and the drop in farm butter and cheese making lessened the demand for women to work in the dairy. Only in the market gardening and fruit growing districts was there still a significant demand for casual female labour. A few women were able also to move into the factories which were springing up in some erstwhile rural communities, or to get work in local shops or offices, travelling to work each day by bus or train. But most country women had no employment of any kind outside their home, and for the younger girls who had to make their way in the world there was little alternative but to leave home to seek a post, probably as a domestic servant in a town household. In 1921, out of 3,115,608 females over the age of twelve recorded as residing in rural districts, only 755,865, or less than one-quarter, had a separate occupation — a smaller proportion than in 1911. On the other hand, social opportunities were widening, especially with the spread of the Women's Institute movement (there were nearly 3,500 of these in 1925) and the increased availability of buses for travel to nearby market towns. Equally, the expanded provision of district nursing, midwifery, and medical services, often under the aegis of the local authorities, helped to remove some of the anxieties of illness and disease. Under the Midwives Act of 1936, all authorities were at last required to provide trained midwives — something of considerable importance to prospective mothers in remote rural areas, out of easy reach of hospital and sometimes even of G.Ps.

Improvements in education and the increased availability of books and newspapers widened the mental horizons of villagers, too. The wireless played its part in this, although not always in the way expected. One Buckinghamshire clergyman even attributed his smaller Sunday congregations to its influence. As he disconsolately told his Bishop, when they were asked why they did not attend Church they replied: 'We likes the wireless. You get nice singing, and sometimes a nice sermon; and if you gets a bishop or an 'ighbrow you switch 'im off: and you can't do that in Church, you see'.[84]

A final change remains to be noted, namely the spread of suburban development and the effect this had upon the rural community. Long before 1914 the growth of commuter traffic had been discernible in many country areas situated around the major conurbations, especially London. But after 1920 that process was speeded up, and numerous villages were transformed within a few years into dormitories for middle-class urban workers. Landscapes were blighted by a proliferation of housing developments, as well as by intrusive advertisement hoardings and petrol depots. From 1926 the Council for the Preservation of Rural England sought to restrain these excesses by a judicious propaganda campaign, and its efforts were bolstered in 1932 by the passage of a new Town and Country Planning Act. This, despite some weaknesses, underlined the importance of preserving a decent physical environment, if necessary through the exercise of restrictive powers by planning authorities. Yet the building of more houses continued apace, to meet the growing middle-class demand.

Inevitably the relationship between the 'incomers' and established villagers was sometimes fraught. The latter often resented the lack of understanding displayed by their new neighbours for the well-tried values of country life, while the former frequently regarded local inhabitants with amused contempt as mere 'country bumpkins'.[85] Their greater affluence and wider leisure opportunities were also causes for envious comment among their rural neighbours, as were their often well-meaning attempts to take over the running of parish clubs and social events.

Nevertheless, despite the friction which could occur between the two groups, these alterations in the character of so many rural parishes did not presage their disintegration, but rather their gradual restructuring upon fresh lines. 'A healthy village community', wrote Astor and Rowntree at the end of the 1930s, 'will not be one composed of a mass of low-paid labourers looking to those above them for initiative and leadership. It will be one composed of persons engaged in a wide variety of occupations, who are prepared to take an increasing share in the life of their district'.[86]

In the event, the consolidation of this changed social order was not to be accomplished before the waging of yet another World War, which served to blur still further the old distinctions between town and country, and to impose its own requirements upon the countryside by way of munitions factories, aerodromes, and army camps. The Second World War, like the First, demanded a major response from agriculture, and in order to ensure that this was forthcoming there was a still more elaborate apparatus of control and direction introduced. As a consequence, Britain 'developed the most highly mechanized agriculture in the world, and by the end of the war nearly half of the nation's total consumption of foodstuffs were being produced within the national boundaries.'[87] But the way in which that was achieved is another story!

Appendices

Appendix 1

Agricultural employment in England and Wales 1901-31

Source: *The Census Reports*

	1901	1911	1921	1931
MALES				
Farmers/Graziers	202,751	208,761	244,653	230,879
Farmers' sons and relatives	89,165	97,689	80,257	72,593
Farm bailiffs/foremen	22,623	22,141	22,462	16,588
Shepherds	25,354	20,838	11,240	10,298
Agricultural labourers and farm servants:				
in charge of cattle	81,302	69,094	59,382	62,342
in charge of horses	154,377	128,122	113,616	69,754
not otherwise distinguished	348,072	425,063	376,331	334,590
Woodmen and foresters, and their labourers	12,034	12,301	11,443	12,401
Nurserymen, Seedsmen, Florists, Market gardeners, etc	123,125	140,103	220,716	266,659
Agricultural machine proprietors and attendants	6,480	7,286	11,078	8,172
Gamekeepers	16,677	17,148	9,367	10,706

	1901	1911	1921	1931
FEMALES				
Farmers/Graziers	21,548	20,027	19,440	17,367
Farmers' daughters and relatives	18,818*	56,856	15,384	8,189
Farm bailiffs/foremen	39	25	217	114
Shepherds	12	6	42	25
Agricultural labourers and farm servants	11,951	13,214	32,265	17,744
Nursery workers, Florists, Market gardeners, etc.	5,104	4,202	10,500	7,923
Agricultural machine proprietors and attendants	65	60	100	58

*The Report on the 1901 Census stated that 'the female relatives of farmers returned as assisting in farm work were not completely shown'; hence the relatively low figure for this year.

N.B. The number of women tending cattle, dairying, etc. fell from 10,603 in 1921 to 6,461 in 1931, thanks in part to the greater use of milking machines and to the decline in the farm production of butter and cheese.

Appendix 2

Estimated Value of Gross and Net Output of Agriculture in the United Kingdom, by groups of years

Current Prices

1894-1903 to 1935-39

	1894-1903	1904-10*	1911-13*	1920-22	1924-29	1930-34	1935-39
Value of	£m.	£m.	£m.	£m.	£m.	£m.	£m.
Crop output	49.77	50.68	56.23	126.97	72.06	59.93	n.a.
Livestock output	133.01	150.07	165.89	363.00	207.61	176.54	n.a.
Value of gross output	182.78	200.75	222.12	489.97	279.67	236.47	279.00
Less							
Feeding-stuffs	34.86	38.27	44.39	81.00	67.78	53.32	70.00
Livestock	5.75	5.58	5.39	11.21	16.62	14.50	14.50
Seeds	3.37	3.44	3.80	8.36	4.62	3.75	4.00
Fertilisers	4.82	5.74	7.09	18.47	10.12	8.42	9.97
Machinery expenses	1.35	1.58	1.89	12.43	8.67	6.81	11.00
Other expenses	9.57	11.10	12.48	25.53	14.52	10.10	11.00
Total	59.72	65.72	75.03	157.00	122.33	96.90	120.53
Value of net output	123.06	135.03	147.09	332.97	157.34	139.57	158.53

*The discrepancy in the totals for costs for 1904-10 and 1911-13 compared to the detailed items probably arises from a rounding off of the decimal figures.

N.B. The United Kingdom does not include Éire after 1922.

'Gross output' represents the value of production sold off the national farm (agricultural holdings only) or consumed in farm houses. Subsidies are excluded, except for the portion of the sugar subsidy received by farmers.

'Other expenses' *excludes* land tax, rates, and depreciation

The value of gross output in 1894-1903 at £182.78m. compares with a figure of £247.18m. in 1870-76, before the onset of the agricultural depression. The value of *net* output of £123.06m. in 1894-1903 compares with £183.05m. at the earlier date, i.e. 1894-1903 proved the low point for the period after 1867, when the collection of reliable statistics began.

Source: E.M. Ojala, *Agriculture and Economic Progress*, London: OUP, 1952, 61.

Appendix 3

Village Life in Essex 1916-19

Extracts from a journal kept by the Reverend E.H.C. Reeve, Rector of Stondon Massey, at Essex Record Office, T/P.188/3. In 1911, Stondon's population was 240.

1916
7th February: Feb[ruary] 10th had been appointed as the day on which the new Military Service Act will come into operation and on March 1st (three weeks later) all but those specially exempted between the ages of 18 and 41 years will be held to have been enrolled...
26th February: The single men have been coming forward in good numbers during the month of February, and there will be few left after March but those who are engaged on the land or in the milking trade, or those who are held indispensable to the keeping of stock. Women are being advertised for to undertake employment in the field; domestic servants, both men & women, are to be regarded as unnecessary; pleasure gardens and hot-houses are to be looked upon as luxuries only to be open in war-time to the few...
25th March: Probably the cream of the youth of the country has now been enlisted, and those who are now being swept in under the Military Service Act will be largely men who have no taste whatever for military enterprise. A lad who has done some useful work in the Rectory garden has now left as a recruit in the 3rd Essex Reg$^{t.}$ for drill at Chatham. He is stated to have said that he felt he owed a greater duty to his mother at home than to King George; for his mother had done much for him, whereas the King, so far as he knew, had not rendered him any service! One must pardon the rather narrow minded view of King & Country under the somewhat trying circumstances. There is little doubt that a few months experience of military life &

companionship will add breadth to his shoulders and his outlook also!

27th March: A battery of Garrison Artillerymen passed through High Ongar Street on this day on the way from Epping to Ingatestone. They were 250 strong, and had with them a 'Long Tom' gun drawn by eight horses. Many trains have been passing through Brentwood during the past week, laden with troops, there being some idea of an early raid by the enemy on the East Coast.

3rd April: An air-craft raid took place on the night of April 2, and from the Rectory we could plainly hear the engines of a Zeppelin airship, and the frequent discharges of the machine gun at Kelvedon Hatch, responded to by others posted at different points in the surrounding country. It was strange to hear the miniature corncrake rattling forth in the quiet night, and the rooks and other birds disturbed in their slumbers calling out in protest.

1st August: Arthur Roast, lately employed at the Rectory, is now in France, and writes home cheerful letters to his mother, as all the men do, bidding her not worry about him. Roast was always a "good shot", few birds escaping him even as a boy when out with stones or catipult (*sic*). The neighbours believe that as a bomb thrower into the enemy's trenches his fame will be sure to establish itself!

8th September: The Great guns in France were clearly heard again this morning, the wind blowing from the south-east...

29th October: By order of the authorities no bells are to be rung after six o'clock in the evening for the present, it having been shown that the sound is clearly heard for some distance upward, and might serve to indicate his whereabouts to some wandering hostile Airship. It is strange on Sunday evenings, at the accustomed hour for the Church Service, to hear no bell giving tongue; when, in the usual way, bells would be answering each other from all the neighbouring towers and steeples.

1917

8th January: The absence of sportsmen from their estates and the consequent diminution of shooting parties has had the effect of largely increasing the number of pheasants & partridges which for two years have been left largely unmolested. Complaints are appearing in the daily papers of the ravages of the birds in the fields and gardens in many parts of England, and it is even suggested that there must be, for the period of the War, some limitation of the Game Laws.

We have been sufferers in this neighbourhood from the over-stock of Game. The Rectory Garden has been constantly visited by pheasants from the adjoining woods, and early and late they have battened upon our green-stuff. Nearly every form of green vegetable has been stripped to the stalk, and this when we are being urged to make every yard of ground profitable!

23rd April: Police-officers were making domiciliary visits yesterday (Sunday) to enquire into the number of animals (domestic & farm) kept at each house, the object being, in these days of scarcity, to prevent unnecessary consumption by animals of grain & stores in any way suitable for human food.

5th May: During the last few days, with a prevailing light easterly wind, the roar of the Guns from the "Western" or French front has been well-nigh continuous... The windows of the Rectory chattered in response sometimes more loudly than others, as though at intervals guns of larger calibre still, or possibly mines, were being exploded...

6th May: A Proclamation was read in Church this morning, and is to be read on the three succeeding Sundays from the King to His people, calling on his loyal subjects to abstain from any avoidable consumption of Flour, and to reserve oats in like manner for human food.

4th July: Our gardener, William Penson, writes that he has been ordered to France. He has long been in khaki in England. May he win a name, & be safely restored to us at Stondon!

19th December: Supplies of Horse-Chestnuts have been collected this autumn & sent to London, it being discovered that certain chemicals may be extracted from them for the manufacture of munitions which have hitherto been obtained from flour. Thus food-supply may be saved. A ton of chestnuts is found to equal half a ton of grain. We have lately sent some 5 bushels to the 'Director of Propellant Supplies' at Westminster! ...

23rd December: The Scotch "seed" potatoes supplied by Government last year to small cultivators for gardens & allotments proved very successful... A similar offer has again been made, and after a small representative meeting in the School Room we have put in application for a further supply in the ensuing spring.

1918

5th January: Some German prisoners are engaged with a steam-plough on land at the Hall; and come to partake of luncheon in the old kitchen!

Meat is becoming scarce, especially beef. The Gov^{nt.} have named a maximum price for live weight, and the farmers are with-holding the animals. Possibly they may be "commandeered".

Sugar-rations became compulsorily enforced ($\frac{1}{2}$ lb. per week, per head) from Jan. 1st, — and meat seems likely to follow.

14th March: I spoke with Wm. Maryon, an Ongar baker, who has lately on several occasions been stopped on his rounds with his baker's cart by little batches of German prisoners, asking for bread. He told me that they were ready to pay for the bread, but would not be gainsaid, one taking the horse's bridle and others surrounding himself & the Cart.

It seems strange that they should be without their guard, and that they should have this "bread hunger," as they are generally believed to be well cared for.

16th April: William Maryon, the baker... has been fined £1 for supplying German prisoners with bread, though confessedly against his will.

The prisoners' plan, it appears, was to get possession of food with which they might at a fitting opportunity make their escape; the difficulty being to obtain provisions without discovery.

25th April: Our fellow-parishioner, Harry Ellis, so lately home on leave was reported early in the month wounded, & we now hear from the War Office he is seriously injured...

More Potatoes than ever are to be grown this year, & the Government are perfecting plant for the production of Potato flour.

Coals are shortly to be "rationed", on account of the difficulty of raising and circulating the coal.

The allowance to each householder will probably be in strict proportion to the size of his tenement...

21st July: A letter has been received from H. Ellis now working in the Labour Company in France. He has suffered much from rheumatism, and would be glad to be transferred to England for farm work.

27th September: School Children are everywhere employed

gathering the blackberries in School Hours under the control of their Teachers. The fruit is packed in baskets provided of regulation size, and sent by rail to the Army jam factories, while cheques are sent to the Teachers and payment authorized to the children of threepence per pound, a strict account having to be returned to the Authorities of money expended and weight received and despatched.

11th November: The Armistice was signed at 5 o'clock this morning, to take effect from 11 o'clock. The news was known early in London, and was made known by the hooting of sirens and the noise of maroons. Some in Stondon heard the distant bells at Brentwood. But it was not till the afternoon that definite tidings reached the villages and then it filtered through chiefly in the form of private messages... As soon as I had... official intelligence the Stondon Church bells were chimed... Distant rockets and other tokens of joy were heard around us as the evening advanced.

1919
24th January: Men are returning in every direction. The tradesmen at Ongar are becoming hopeful of receiving their workmen back, and of being once more able to deal with the claims of business.... Our gardener, William Penson, has been liberated from his duties at Scarborough, & has returned on a furlough of 28 days during which he receives military pay & rations, & is not to engage upon any civilian employment. By the end of February he will have resumed his occupation at the Rectory, much to his & our satisfaction.

24th February: William Penson returns to his work in the Rectory Garden today after over four years of "soldiering"...

Harry Ellis has returned to Stondon from France. He finds his brother Robert James has died from the effects of gas poisoning... [Harry] was badly wounded on April 9th last... A large number of his Regt. were "casualties", and out of 197 who joined the 13th Yorks. with himself only 12 now remain.... Ellis joined up in Class A1, he is discharged as B2, and believes that he will shortly hear that he has received a pension. He now feels little of his wound, and is getting the better of the gas-poisoning from which he once suffered. His trench rheumatism asserts itself at times, but after his 28 days "furlough", he will again commence work with Mr. J.T. Gann.... [Mr. Gann was a builder, whose own son had died at the front. In all, six Stondon men were to die as a result of the War.]

7th June: A large number of estates continue to be put on the market in all parts of the country... Stondon Manor and farms will come under the hammer, I understand, early in July.

[N.B. In a note made in 1922, Mr Reeve also wrote: 'Pte. William Langston... is still suffering from the effects of his campaigning... He has been under treatment, ever since his return, for his nerves & for deafness consequent on their shattered state. Also for injury to his right leg... Langston never complains, though suffering from frequent headaches & from physical debility, but accepts his limitations'.]

Notes

(Parliamentary Paper(s) = P.P.)

Chapter 1 (pages 1-23)

1. *Board of Agriculture and Fisheries: The Agricultural Output of Great Britain*, P.P.1912-13, Vol. X, 25.
2. A.G. Street, *Farmer's Glory*, London 1963 edn, 35-6. The book was first published in 1932.
3. See Minute Book of the Executive Committee of the National Farmers' Union, 1909-1916 at the Museum of English Rural Life, Reading, meetings 23 June 1909, 6 January and 10 November 1910.
4. Quoted in Pamela Horn, *The Rise and Fall of the Victorian Servant*, Dublin 1975, 21.
5. Noel Streatfeild ed., *The Day Before Yesterday*, London 1956, 111.
6. Christabel S. Orwin and Edith H. Whetham, *History of British Agriculture 1846-1914*, London 1964, 302.
7. F.M.L. Thompson, *English Landed Society in the Nineteenth Century*, London 1963, 322.
8. *The Land: The Report of the Land Enquiry Committee, Vol. 1, Rural*, London 1913, 361.
9. The Duke of Bedford, *A Great Agricultural Estate*, London 1897, 2.
10. Thompson, *English Landed Society*, 306-7. Avner Offer, *Property and Politics 1870-1914*, Cambridge 1981, 112, 363-83.
11. *The Observer*, 30 November, 1980.
12. *The Land*, 261.
13. Memorandum from the Duke of Bedford to his steward, C.P. Hall, 10 May, 1904 in R.4/25 at Bedfordshire Record Office.
14. Bedford Estate Correspondence, W.P. Hile to the Steward, C.P. Hall, at Bedfordshire Record Office, R.4/26. Decisions were delayed, for example, to see whether crops would recover from early attacks by game and rabbits.
15. B. Seebohm Rowntree and May Kendall, *How the Labourer Lives*, London 1918 edn, 26.
16. *Second Report by Mr. Wilson Fox on the Wages, Earnings and Conditions of Employment of Agricultural Labourers in the United Kingdom*, P.P.1905, Vol. XCVII, 22, 31, 81.
17. *The Land*, 21-2.
18. *The Land*, 140.

19. E.H. Hunt, *Regional Wage Variations in Britain 1850-1914*, Oxford 1973, 356.
20. B.S. Rowntree, *The Labourer and the Land*, London 1914, Introduction by David Lloyd George, 3.
21. Rowntree and Kendall, *How the Labourer Lives*, 28-31, 298-9.
22. Maud F. Davies, *Life in an English Village*, London 1909, 112-4.
23. *The Land*, 134.
24. *Board of Agriculture and Fisheries: Report on the Decline in the Agricultural Population of Great Britain 1881-1906*, P.P.1906, Vol. XCVI, 16.
25. Orwin and Whetham, *History of British Agriculture*, 343.
26. *Board of Agriculture and Fisheries: General Report on Wages and Conditions of Employment of Agricultural Labourers*, P.P.1919, Vol. IX, Report on Wales, 183, 186.
27. George Edwards, *From Crow-Scaring to Westminster*, London 1957 edn, 98. The book was first published in 1922.
28. Reg Groves, *Sharpen the Sickle!* London 1949, 140-2. L. Marion Springall, *Labouring Life in Norfolk Villages 1834-1914*, London 1936, 127-9.
29. Groves, *Sharpen the Sickle!* 144. Howard Newby, *The Deferential Worker*, London 1977, 228, produces a much lower membership figure of 4,734 for 1914. This is based on subscription income and Newby stresses the large turnover in membership. The union itself has no firm membership figures, but it seems likely that those owing residual loyalty to it were more numerous than Newby suggests.
30. Richard Hyman, *The Workers' Union*, Oxford 1971, 47. Groves, *Sharpen the Sickle!* 245.
31. A.D. Hall, *A Pilgrimage of British Farming 1910-1912*, London 1913, 443, notes of the farm worker at this date: 'he has no trade union to protect him from the occasional tyranny of his employer'. Even Rowntree, *The Labourer and the Land*, 25, notes pessimistically: 'Half the essential requirements of a successful trade union are absent', when discussing the position of the agricultural labourer.
32. Letter from Lord Carrington to his wife, 14th February, 1908, MSS Film 114, Bodleian Library.
33. Arthur W. Ashby, *Allotments and Small Holdings in Oxfordshire*, Oxford 1917, 184, 188.
34. Springall, *Labouring Life in Norfolk Villages*, 124-6.
35. *General Report on Wages and Conditions of Employment of Agricultural Labourers*, Report on England, 24.
36. John Saville, *Rural Depopulation in England and Wales 1851-1951*, London 1957, 26.

37. George Sturt, *The Wheelwright's Shop*, Cambridge 1963 edn, 197-8. First published in 1923.
38. *General Report on Wages and Conditions of Employment of Agricultural Labourers*, Report on England, 24.
39. G.E. Mingay ed., *The Victorian Countryside*, Vol. 1, London 1981, 115.
40. Thompson, *English Landed Society*, 317.
41. Hall, *A Pilgrimage of British Farming*, 438.
42. Lord Ernle, *English Farming Past and Present*, 6th edn, London 1961, 390, 391.
43. Springall, *Labouring Life in Norfolk Villages*, 122.
44. Edwin A. Pratt, *The Transition in Agriculture*, London 1906, 136-9.
45. Hall, *A Pilgrimage of British Farming*, 47.
46. Edith H. Whetham, *The Agrarian History of England and Wales, Vol. VIII, 1914-1939*, Cambridge 1978, 9.
47. Dairy Agreement between William Walker of Windle Farm, Thurvaston, Derbyshire and the Egginton Dairy Company, Reading University Library, DER.3/1/1.
48. Orwin and Whetham, *History of British Agriculture*, 365.
49. P.J. Perry, *British Agriculture 1875-1914*, London 1973, xxxii.
50. Alistair Mutch, 'The Mechanization of the Harvest in South-West Lancashire, 1850-1914' in *Agricultural History Review*, Vol. 29, Pt II (1981), 131.
51. Whetham, *The Agrarian History of England and Wales*, 8.
52. Marie Hartley and Joan Ingilby, *Life in the Moorlands of North-East Yorkshire*, London 1972, 39.
53. *Board of Agriculture and Fisheries: Agricultural Statistics for 1914*, P.P.1914-16, Vol. LXXIX.
54. Hall, *A Pilgrimage of British Farming*, 335-7.
55. *General Report on Wages and Conditions of Employment of Agricultural Labourers*, Report on Wales, 189.
56. Reminiscences of Mr F.W. Brocklehurst of Sheldon, Derbyshire, at the Museum of English Rural Life, Reading, D.72/1/1-6. Mr Brocklehurst was born in the 1890s.
57. Calculated from Saville, *Rural Depopulation in England and Wales*, 67.
58. Newby, *The Deferential Worker*, 329, quoting from R.E. Pahl.
59. 'George Bourne' [George Sturt], *Change in the Village*, London 1966 edn, 11. First published in 1912.
60. 'Bourne', *Change in the Village*, 117.
61. *Norfolk News*, 1 August, 1914.
62. M.K. Ashby, *Joseph Ashby of Tysoe*, Cambridge 1961, 290.
63. Vera Brittain, *Testament of Friendship*, London 1980 edn, 51. First published 1940.

Chapter 2 (pages 24-46)

1. Letter from Robert Saunders of Fletching to his son, William, in Canada, dated 15 August 1914, at the Imperial War Museum, 79/15/1.

2. Nicholas Mosley, *Julian Grenfell: His Life and The Times of His Death 1888-1915*, London 1976, 230.

3. Quoted in J.M. Winter, 'Britain's "Lost Generation" of the First World War' in *Population Studies*, Vol. 31 (1977), 452.

4. Neville Lytton, *The English Country Gentleman*, London n.d. [1925], 185.

5. *Norfolk News*, 8 August 1914.

6. Reminiscences of Old People at Essex Record Office, T/Z.25/789, Mr A. Green.

7. *Mark Lane Express*, 19 October 1914.

8. *Wiltshire Gazette*, 20 August 1914.

9. E.D. Mackerness ed., *The Journals of George Sturt*, Vol. 2, *1905-1927*, Cambridge 1967, 699.

10. Reminiscences of Old People, Mrs R. Tansley, at Essex Record Office, T/Z.25/803.

11. J.W. Rowson, *Bridport and the Great War*, London 1923, 20.

12. *Westmorland Mercury*, 14 August 1914.

13. *Mark Lane Express*, 24 August 1914.

14. *Hexham Weekly News*, 21 August 1914, and *Norfolk News*, 15 August 1914.

15. 'The Wounded at Woburn', reprinted from the *National Review*, September 1916, and preserved at the Bedford Estate Office, London.

16. *Sussex Express*, 13 August 1914.

17. *Wiltshire Gazette*, 6 August 1914. Guy Slater ed., *My Warrior Sons: The Borton Family Diary, 1914-1918*, London 1973, 11-2.

18. Bedfore Estate Correspondence: W.P. Hile to the steward, C.P. Hall, at Bedfordshire Record Office, R.4/26, entries on p. 281 concerning Privates B.S. Walker and H.W. Wright, dated 16 February 1918. Private Walker's mother had been receiving 7s. 6d. a week and Private Wright's wife, 8s. 6d. per week.

19. *Wiltshire Gazette*, 3 September 1914.

20. *Wiltshire Gazette*, 3 September 1914.

21. This happened, for example, at Lower Heyford in Oxfordshire. Reminiscences of Miss D.B. Dew of Lower Heyford.

22. *Country Life*, 23 January 1915.

23. *Stamford Mercury*, 4 and 11 September 1914.

24. *Westmorland Mercury*, 4 September 1914.

25. *Westmorland Mercury*, 4 September 1914.

26. *Bucks Herald*, 5 September 1914.

27. Reg Groves, *Sharpen the Sickle*! London 1949, 245, and Howard Newby, *The Deferential Worker*, London 1977, 216, 228.
28. Richard Hillyer, *Country Boy*, London 1966, 166, 169.
29. Lyn Macdonald, *Somme*, London 1983, 5.
30. Reminiscences of Old People at Essex Record Office, T/Z.25/789.
31. Siegfried Sassoon, *The Complete Memoirs of George Sherston*, London 1949 edn, 219-23.
32. Robert Saunders to William Saunders, 11 October 1914.
33. Robert Saunders to William Saunders, 14 February 1915.
34. Ivinghoe School Log Book at Buckinghamshire Record Office, E/LB/116/2 and *Bucks Herald*, 19 September, 1914. The men billeted at Tring and environs were mainly from the north of England, and included coalminers from the Barnsley area.
35. Oxford Diocese: Clergy Visitation Returns for 1918 at the Bodleian Library, Oxford, MS Oxf.Dioc.Pp.c.379. To be transferred to Oxfordshire County Record Office in 1984.
36. Christopher Holdenby, 'The Home Dwellers' in *Country Life*, 5 February 1916, 167-8.
37. Journal of the Rector of Stondon Massey, Essex, at Essex Record Office, Vol. 3, T/P.188/3, 101, entry for 10 February 1915.
38. Reminiscences of Old People at Essex Record Office, T/Z.25/630, Mrs I. Warren.
39. Milner diaries at the Bodleian Library, Oxford, MS Milner dep.85, for 1914.
40. The Defence of the Realm: Brentwood District Emergency Committee General Instructions in Case of Hostile Invasion, 1 February 1915, in War Records I at Essex Record Office. See similar instructions for Orsett Petty Sessional Division in the same county.
41. County of Hertford: Local Emergency instructions, at Essex Record Office, D/Z.77/1, n.d. [1915]. Hertfordshire was to provide the route through which the Essex migrants would pass, and it was estimated that the population would be on the move for about six days.
42. Circular letter from Major F.G. Danielson to Local Emergency Committees, 1 February 1915, at Essex Record Office, D/Z.77/1.
43. Rowson, *Bridport and the Great War*, 18.
44. Richard Holmes, *The Little Field-Marshal*, London 1981, 315.
45. Journal of the Rector of Stondon Massey, entry for 15 April 1916.
46. Journal of the Rector of Stondon Massey, entry for 3 April 1916.

47. *Westmorland Mercury*, 28 August 1914.
48. The War: Suspects, entry in leather-bound volume at Essex Record Office, J/P.12/6, reference no. 3/433. In all, 294 persons are listed as coming under suspicion in Essex alone.
49. Michael and Eleanor Brock ed., *H.H. Asquith Letters to Venetia Stanley*, Oxford 1982, 400. This was written by Asquith to Venetia on 27 January 1915.
50. *Norfolk News*, 14 November 1914.
51. Journal of the Rector of Stondon Massey, entry for 26 June 1915.
52. Journal of the Rector of Stondon Massey, entries for 8 and 30 October 1914, 10 November 1914, and 10 February 1915, for example.
53. *Hansard*, 5th Series, Vol. CXV (1919), cols 1419-20.
54. Vera Brittain, *Testament of Friendship*, London 1980 edn, 50-51.
55. J.M. Winter, 'Britain's "Lost Generation" of the First World War', 451.
56. Robert Graves, *Goodbye to All That*, London 1960 edn, 54.
57. C.F.G. Masterman, *England After War*, London n.d. [1923], 31.
58. Robert Wohl, *The Generation of 1914*, London 1980, 115. Denis Winter, *Death's Men*, London 1978 edn, 31.
59. J.M. Winter, 'Britain's "Lost Generation" of the First World War', 464. See also H.A. Doubleday and Lord Howard de Walden, *The Complete Peerage*, London 1932, Vol. 8, Appendix F.
60. See *Death Duties (Killed in War) Act, 1914*, which received the Royal Assent on 31 August 1914. On properties valued below £5,000 no death duties were payable.
61. F.M.L. Thompson, *English Landed Society in the Nineteenth Century*, London 1963, 328.
62. Slater ed., *My Warrior Sons*, 14.
63. Brigadier-General C.D. Bruce, *The Essex Foxhounds 1895-1926*, London 1926, 117.
64. Raymond Carr, *English Fox Hunting*. London 1976, 231. *Wiltshire Gazette*, 17 December 1914. *Kenilworth Advertiser*, 22 August and 10 October 1914.
65. *Country Life*, 16 January, 1915, 69.
66. Mackerness ed., *The Journals of George Sturt*, Vol. 2, 713.
67. F.E. Green, *A History of the English Agricultural Labourer*, London 1920, 234.
68. Oxford Diocese: Clergy Visitation Returns for 1918, MS Oxf.Dioc.Pp.c.379 — return for Emberton.
69. *Mark Lane Express*, 7 September, 1914.
70. *Stamford Mercury*, 25 September, 1914. The writer came from the village of Rushden and had been wounded by being knocked down by a waggon during a stampede at the front.

71. Winter, *Death's Men*, 26.
72. Oxford Diocese, Clergy Visitation Returns, 1918, MS Oxf.Dioc.Pp.c.379.
73. Oxford Diocese, Clergy Visitation Returns, 1918, MS Oxf.Dioc.Pp.c.378, 379.
74. Oxford Diocese, Clergy Visitation Returns, 1918, MS Oxf.Dioc.Pp.c.379, comment by the incumbent of Middle Claydon, Buckinghamshire.
75. Mackerness ed., *The Journals of George Sturt*, Vol. 2, 756.
76. Comment by the incumbent of Ellesborough, Buckinghamshire, in MS Oxf.Dioc.Pp.c.379.
77. Diary of R.T. Bull of Burnham-on-Crouch at Essex Record Office, T/B.245, for 1914.

Chapter 3 (pages 47-71)

1. Executive Committee Minute Book of the National Farmers' Union, Vol. 1 at the Museum of English Rural Life, University of Reading, entry for 24 February 1915.
2. *Board of Agriculture and Fisheries: Agricultural Statistics for 1916*, P.P.1917-18, Vol. XXXVI, 5, and *Agricultural Statistics for 1915*, P.P.1916, Vol. XXXII, 7.
3. N.B. Dearle, *An Economic Chronicle of the Great War for Great Britain and Ireland 1914-1919*, London 1929, 44. *Interim Report of the Departmental Committee Appointed to consider the Production of Food in England and Wales, 1915*, P.P.1914-16, Vol. V, 6. Hereafter referred to as *Interim Report of the Milner Committee*.
4. *Interim Report of the Milner Committee*, 4.
5. In July 1915, Selborne had written to the Cabinet, recommending acceptance of a guarantee system and point out it was unlikely to lead to any government expenditure: 'My opinion, for what it is worth, is that there is little chance of the price of wheat in this country falling below 45s. in the cereal years 1916-17 and 1917-18, even if the war were ended in the year 1916. . . . Many ships will have been destroyed . . . and very little extra tonnage created'. CAB.37/131/30 at the Public Record Office. Asquith's letter to the King, dated 4 August 1915 in CAB.37/132/3.
6. *Final Report of the Milner Committee*, P.P.1914-16, Vol. V, 15 October 1915, 3-6.
7. *Agricultural Statistics for 1916*, 13.
8. Dearle, *An Economic Chronicle of the Great War*, 89, 101.
9. Dearle, *An Economic Chronicle of the Great War*, 107, 157, 158, 160.
10. Lord Ernle, *The Land and Its People*, London n.d. [1925], 114-5.

11. Ernle, *The Land and Its People*, 108. Thomas H. Middleton, *Food Production in War*, Oxford 1923, 241. By 1918 the tillage area in England and Wales had risen by 1.7m. acres compared to 1914; in Scotland it was 0.22m. acres higher. *A Century of Agricultural Statistics: Great Britain 1866-1966*, HMSO 1968, 95.

12. In 1917, the fine was established as being up to £20 and the maximum period of imprisonment for non-co-operation was fixed at three months. *Corn Production Act, 1917*, Pt IV.

13. Ernle, *The Land and Its People*, 135-6. Middleton, *Food Production in War*, 8.

14. *Agricultural Statistics for 1914* in P.P.1914-16, Vol. LXXIX, see relevant county totals, and for *1918*, P.P.1919, Vol. LI.

15. Minutes of the Bedfordshire War Agricultural Executive Committee, meeting on 17 May 1917, at Bedfordshire Record Office, WAM.1.

16. Minutes of the Bedfordshire War Agricultural Executive Committee, meetings on 26 July, 20 September, 20 December, 1917 and 3 January 1918, for example. On the last occasion the rabbit catcher announced he had shot 124 animals at Everton. WAM.1 and 2 at Bedfordshire Record Office.

17 Essex War Agricultural Executive Committee Minutes, Vol. 2, at Essex Record Office.

18. Letter from Alfred Hills to Mrs Irving of Old Windsor, Berkshire, dated 10 April 1917 in D/DHn.E.19 at Essex Record Office. For examples of the orders issued by the Essex Committee see cultivation orders for the Hassobury estate, D/DG1/E21.

19. Middleton, *Food Production in War*, 220, 289-90.

20. Edith H. Whetham, *The Agrarian History of England and Wales*, Vol. VIII, *1914-1939*, Cambridge 1978, 122.

21. Essex War Agricultural Executive Committee Minutes, entry for late September n.d. [1917] and Report of a Conference between the War Executive Committee and principal land agents in Essex managing estates, D/DU.746/12, 21 September 1917, at Essex Record Office. Circular letter from the Chairman of Essex War Agricultural Executive Committee, 30 July 1917, in D/DU/746/10.

22. Whetham, *The Agrarian History of England and Wales*, 93.

23. Ernle, *The Land and Its People*, 146-7.

24. Ernle, *The Land and Its People*, 147.

25. M. Tracy, *Agriculture in Western Europe (after 1880)*, London 1964, 151. Ernle, *The Land and Its People*, 150.

26. *Mark Lane Express*, 29 April 1918, 417 and 6 May 1918, 431.

27. P.E. Dewey, 'Government Policy and Farm Profits in Britain in 1st World War', a paper presented to the Conference of the British Agricultural History Society, 5 December 1981.

28. *Ministry of Reconstruction: Report of the Agricultural Policy Sub-Committee*, P.P.1918, Vol. V,15-6. Hereafter cited as *Selborne Sub-Committee Report*. Pt I of the Report was issued on 30 January 1917 and Pt II was dated January 1918.
29. *Selborne Sub-Committee Report*, Pt I, 15. Edith H. Whetham, 'The Agriculture Act, 1920 and its Repeal — the "Great Betrayal" ' in *Agricultural History Review*, Vol. 22, Pt I (1974), 38-9.
30. Calculated from Reg Groves, *Sharpen the Sickle!*, London 1949, 163.
31. *Corn Production Act, 1917*, Pt II, §4.(1).
32. Groves, *Sharpen the Sickle!*, 165.
33. Howard Newby, *The Deferential Worker*, London 1977, 228.
34. A. Harris, 'Agricultural Change on a Yorkshire Estate: Birdsall 1920-1940' in *Journal of Regional and Local Studies*, Vol. 3, No. 1 (Summer 1983), 36.
35. *Hansard*, 5th Series, Vol. 108 (23 July 1918), cols. 1760-1, speech by Rowland Prothero.
36. *Hansard*, 5th Series, Vol. 108 (23 July 1918), col. 1771, comment by Sir F. Banbury.
37. *Hansard*, 5th Series, Vol. 108 (25 July 1918), col. 2080, comment by Sir John Spear.
38. Survey of S.E. Derbyshire by the War Agricultural Committee, 1917 at Derbyshire Record Office, D.331.
39. Ernle, *The Land and Its People*, 148-9.
40. *Selborne Sub-Committee*, Pt II, 39, 88.
41. Whetham, 'The Agriculture Act, 1920', 42.
42. Whetham, 'The Agriculture Act, 1920', 41.
43. *National Food Journal*, 10 October 1917.
44. Minutes of Sawbridgeworth Urban District Food Control Committee, 1917-20 at the Public Record Office, MAF.60/433, entries for 30 October and 4 November 1918.
45. Whetham, *The Agrarian History of England*, 114.
46. *Mark Lane Express*, 7 October 1918.
47. *National Food Journal*, 8 January 1919. See the same journal for 9 January 1918 and 8 May 1918, for the other cases mentioned.
48. Minutes of Bedfordshire War Agricultural Executive Committee, WAM. 1, 26 June 1917.
49. *Interim Majority Report of the Royal Commission on Agriculture, 1919*, Cmd. 473, 6.
50. *Interim Majority Report of the Royal Commission on Agriculture*, 7.
51. *Interim Minority Report of the Royal Commission on Agriculture*, 10, 12, 13.
52. Whetham, 'The Agriculture Act, 1920', 44.
53. Whetham, 'The Agriculture Act, 1920', 46.

54. Minutes of Evidence Taken Before the Royal Commission on Tithe Rentcharge, evidence of Mr S. Kidner of Beccles, 11 January 1935, in IR.101/9 at the Public Record Office.
55. Whetham. 'The Agriculture Act, 1920', 48.

Chapter 4 (pages 72-92)

1. Letter from Sir Sydney Olivier, Secretary to the Board of Agriculture, to the Secretary of the Man-Power Distribution Board, 25 September 1916 in NATS.1/329 at the Public Record Office.
2. Thomas H. Middleton, *Food Production in War*, Oxford 1923, 109.
3. Notes by the Secretary of State for War, CAB.37/128/30, Appendix 2.
4. *East Anglian Daily Times*, 17 and 27 March 1916.
5. *Farmer and Stockbreeder*, 8 February 1915.
6. *Report on the State of Employment in Agriculture in Great Britain at the end of January 1918, prepared by the Industrial (War Inquiries) Branch, Board of Trade*, 2, at the Public Record Office, NATS.1/241. Hereafter cited as *Board of Trade Report, January 1918*.
7. P.E. Dewey, 'Farm Labour in Wartime: The Relationship between Agricultural Labour Supply and Food Production in Great Britain during 1914-1918, with International Comparisons' (Reading University Ph.D. thesis, 1978), 170-1. Hereafter cited as Dewey *thesis*.
8. P.E. Dewey, 'Agricultural Labour Supply in England and Wales during the First World War' in *Economic History Review*, 2nd Series, Vol. XXVIII, No. 1 (Feb. 1975), 101.
9. Letter from Sir Sydney Olivier to the Secretary of the Man-Power Distribution Board, 25 September 1916, NATS.1/329.
10. Lord Ernle, *The Land and Its People*, London n.d. [1925], 103.
11. Middleton, *Food Production in War*, 266.
12. Dewey *thesis*, 158.
13. *Report of the War Cabinet for 1918*, P.P.1919, Vol. XXX, 237.
14. Letter from East Anglian Region, Ministry of National Service, dated 17 September 1917, in NATS.1/242 at the Public Record Office, and *Board of Trade Report, January 1918*, 6.
15. Letter from Castell Wray, agent, to Robert Jeffrey, bailiff on the home farm, 1 January 1918, in the Apethorpe correspondence, Box 3, at Northamptonshire Record Office, and *Hansard*, 5th Series, Vol. 101 (21 January 1918), cols 669, 756-7.
16. *Hansard*, 5th Series, Vol. 101, col. 670.
17. A.G. Street, *Farmer's Glory*, London 1963 edn, 186-7.

18. A.G. Street, *Wessex Wins*, London 1941, 58. A.G. Street, *Ditchampton Farm*, London 1946, 12.
19. *Mark Lane Express*, Supplement, 29 January 1917, 1.
20. Middleton, *Food Production in War*, 138-9.
21. E.H. Whetham, *The Agrarian History of England and Wales*, Vol. VIII, *1914-1939*, Cambridge 1978, 79.
22. Selborne papers, at the Bodleian Library, MS Selborne 81, f.103. See also a similar letter from a Sussex farmer, dated 12 October 1915, in MS Selborne 81, f.104.
23. *Hansard*, 5th Series, Vol. 75 (16 November 1915), col. 1745.
24. Letter from Walter Runciman to Selborne, 25 November 1915, quoting a speech by Selborne in the House of Lords in which the phrase was used. Runciman objected to it, but Selborne confirmed that his use of 'criminal carelessness' had been intentional. MS Selborne 82, f.52-3, f.55. See also a letter from Bernard Mallet to Lord Selborne, 25 November 1915 in MS Selborne 82, f.56.
25. See a letter from Alfred Hills, solicitor, of Braintree, Essex, to a farmer client, Mrs Irving, 3 July 1916, at Essex Record Office, D/DHn.E.19.
26. Walter Long to Lord Selborne, letter dated 3 April 1916, in MS Selborne 82, f.186-7, marked confidential.
27. Whetham, *The Agrarian History of England and Wales*, 100.
28. *Mark Lane Express*, Supplement, 29 January 1917, 2.
29. *The Times*, 1 March 1917, 12.
30. *Oxford Chronicle*, 9 February and 27 April 1917.
31. *Oxford Chronicle*, 12 January 1917.
32. Information provided by Clive Hughes of the Imperial War Museum, in correspondence with the author, July 1983.
33. Letter from Major Breese to Colonel E.W. Greg, Chester, dated 19 June 1916, in the National Library of Wales, NLW.9472 E.
34. Cardiganshire Appeals for Exemptions: Tribunal Papers at the National Library of Wales, applications dated 18 February 1916 and 25 April 1917. On 2 November 1917, the tribunal noted: 'Exemption: conditional on his continuing his present occupation'.
35. *Report of the Board of Agriculture and Fisheries on Wages and Conditions of Employment in Agriculture, P.P.1919*, Vol. IX, Report on Cardiganshire, 420.
36. Minute Book of East Denbighshire Recruiting Committee at the National Library of Wales, MS 5448C, Report of August 1915.
37. Information provided by Clive Hughes of the Imperial War Museum in correspondence with the author, July 1983.
38. *Mark Lane Express*, 7 and 21 May 1917 and 4 June 1917, 452, 497, 526, 540.

39. *The Times*, 9 July 1918.
40. See, for example, Lieut.Col. C. a'Court Repington, *The First World War 1914-1918*, London 1920, 336-7. Entries in the diaries of H.A.L. Fisher, 22 April, 26 April, and 10 October 1918 in MS Fisher 10 and 11, at the Bodleian Library, Oxford.
41. Reports of Women's County Agricultural Committees, 1916, MAF.59/1 at the Public Record Office.
42. Copy of a letter from P. Rogers, Bridge Farm, Comberton, to the Rt Hon. E.S. Montagu, dated 23 February 1916, in Selborne papers, MS Selborne 82, f.67-8.
43. Memorandum from Rowland Prothero, dated 22 April 1918, and Order under new Military Service Act, 1918, issued on 28 May 1918, by Sir Auckland Geddes, Director-General of National Service, NATS.1/282 at the Public Record Office.
44. Letter from Deputy-Director of Recruiting, South Western Region, Ministry of National Service to the Secretary, Ministry of National Service, dated 4 September 1918, in NATS.1/242.
45. *The Times*, 12 June 1918, 3.
46. *Wiltshire Gazette*, 24 December 1914.
47. *Wiltshire Gazette*, 31 December 1914.
48. Minute Book of the National Farmers' Union Executive Committee, meeting on 24 February 1915.
49. Letter from West Midland Region of the Ministry of National Service to the Secretary, Ministry of National Service, 4 September 1918, NATS.1/242. War Cabinet meeting on 26 June 1918, CAP.23/6/436 (14), comment by Sir Auckland Geddes.
50. *Hansard*, 5th Series, Vol. 107 (1 July 1918), col. 1509, speech by Rowland Prothero. War Cabinet meeting on 1 July 1918, CAB.23/7/438(11), comment by the Director-General of National Service, Sir Auckland Geddes, at the Public Record Office.
51. *Hansard*, 5th Series, Vol. 107 (1 July 1918), col. 1506.
52. Middleton, *Food Production in War,* 267. Minute from J. Seymour Lloyd, dated 11 October 1918, in NATS.1/242 at the Public Record Office.
53. Letter from the Regional Secretary to the Secretary, Ministry of National Service, 4 September 1918, NATS.1/242.
54. Table showing returns from Wales in response to the quota of 5,000 men imposed and sent by the Secretary of the Welsh Region of the Ministry of National Service, on 7 September 1918, NATS.1/242.
55. Letter from the Secretary of the Welsh Region of the Ministry of National Service to the Secretary of the Ministry of National Service, 7 September 1918, in NATS.1/242.

56. Calculated from P.E. Dewey, 'Agricultural Labour Supply in England and Wales during the First World War', 110-11. The statistics are based on man-units.

57. Minute Book of the National Farmers' Union, Executive Committee meeting 19 January 1915.

58. For accounts of the bad state of the roads on the Salisbury Plain, etc. see *Wiltshire Gazette* 5 and 12 November and 3 December 1914. On 5 November roads near the army camps were described as 'veritable quagmires'. A.G. Street, *The Gentleman of the Party*, London 1944 edn, 148-9.

59. Duplicate letter book for Manor Farm, Codford St. Peter, Wiltshire, on microfilm at University of Reading Library, P.388, letter dated 8 February 1916.

60. *Mark Lane Express*, 21 October 1918, 365.

61. Duplicate letter book for Manor Farm, Codford St. Peter, letter dated 25 October 1917. See also a similar letter of 16 May 1917, when the bailiff demanded compensation 'for Troops Drilling on Down & making... Trenches. The last three days the 4th Brigade New Zealanders have more or less occupied Two Enclosures.... Gates are left open. Crops damaged through not keeping to the roads.... Horses are turned loose & damage Crops or Land in front of House. Some this morning were on Vetch with a mounted man galloping after them.'

62. Minutes of Bedfordshire Agricultural Executive Committee, meeting on 16 August 1917, at Bedfordshire Record Office, WAM.1, for example.

63. *Mark Lane Express*, 5 February 1917, 129.

64. *Mark Lane Express*, 29 January 1917, Supplement, 2. Report of a meeting of the Executive of the National Farmers' Union.

65. Farm Ledger for Launceston Farm, Tarrant Launceston, Dorset, at the University of Reading Library, DOR.5/1/6. Already by October 1915, 2,098 gallons were being supplied to the camp. Throughout the period the amount supplied ranged between 1,414 gallons a month — in February, 1919, to the peak figure for July 1917 of 2,790 gallons.

66. Whetham, *The Agrarian History of England and Wales*, 72-3.

67. M.K. Ashby, *Joseph Ashby of Tysoe 1859-1919*, Cambridge 1961, 290.

68. Reminiscences of F.W. Brocklehurst of Sheldon, Derbyshire, at the Museum of English Rural Life, Reading, D.72/1/1-6.

69. *Hansard*, 5th Series, Vol. 65 (8 August 1914), col. 2204. See also debates on 5 August (col. 1965); 6 August (col. 2065); 10 August (col. 2263), where similar points were raised.

70. Whetham, *The Agrarian History of England and Wales*, 73.

71. *Hansard*, 5th Series, Vol. 68 (16 November, 1914), col. 176. *Board of Agriculture and Fisheries: Agricultural Statistics for 1915*, P.P.1916, Vol. XXXII, 11.

72. *Board of Agriculture and Fisheries: Agricultural Statistics for 1918*, P.P.1919, Vol. LI, 4, and *Report of the War Cabinet for 1918*, 238. F.M.L. Thompson ed., *Horses in European Economic History*, Reading 1983, 73.

73. M. and E. Brock, ed., *H.H. Asquith: Letters to Venetia Stanley*, Oxford 1982, 503.

74. Minute Book of the Executive Committee of the National Farmers' Union, entry for 28 April 1915.

75. *Daily News*, 17 November 1916 and reminiscences of Ernest E. Austin of Great Bromley, Essex, at Essex Record Office, T/Z.25/670.

76. *Sussex Express*, 4 December 1914.

77. Whetham, *The Agrarian History of England and Wales*, 74.

78. N.B. Dearle, *An Economic Chronicle of the Great War for Great Britain and Ireland*, London 1929, 165.

Chapter 5 (pages 93-111)

1. Minute Book of the National Farmers' Union at the Museum of English Rural Life, Reading, Executive Committee meeting on 28 April 1915.

2. *Hansard*, 5th Series, Vol. 72 (10 June 1915), col. 375 and Vol. 73 (19 July 1915), col. 1178.

3. Cabinet meeting, 1 August 1916, CAB.42/17/1. Memorandum by Board of Agriculture on Release of Soldiers for Agricultural Work.

4. J.K. Montgomery, *The Maintenance of the Agricultural Labour Supply in England and Wales during the War*, Rome: International Institute of Agriculture, 1922, 30. Thomas H. Middleton, *Food Production in War*, Oxford, 1923, 139.

5. Letter from Lord Selborne to Lord Kitchener at the War Office, 30 September 1915, in MS Selborne 81, ff.175-6.

6. Montgomery, *Maintenance of the Agricultural Labour Supply*, 30.

7. Information provided by Clive Hughes at the Imperial War Museum.

8. P.E. Dewey, 'Farm Labour in Wartime: The Relationship between Agricultural Labour Supply and Food Production in Great Britain during 1914-1918, with International Comparisons', Reading University Ph.D. thesis, 1978, 229. Hereafter cited as Dewey *thesis*.

9. Cabinet meeting, 1 August 1916, CAB.42/17/1, Memorandum by Board of Agriculture. *Hansard*, 5th Series, Vol. 90 (1 March 1917), col. 2187, statement by the Financial Secretary to the War Office.

10. Letter from Sir Sydney Olivier, secretary to the Board of Agriculture, to E.A.S. Fawcett, Man Power Distribution Board, 29 September 1916, in NATS.1/329 at the Public Record Office. Dewey *thesis*, 233.

11. Memorandum on the Supply of Military Labour for Agricultural Purposes, 16 August 1916, in CAB.42/17/7.

12. Montgomery, *Maintenance of the Agricultural Labour Supply*, 24. Dewey *thesis*, 229. *Hansard*, 5th Series, Vol. 90 (1 March 1917), col. 2188, statement by Financial Secretary to the War Office.

13. Griffith Jones, Anglesey War Agricultural Committee to Major C.E. Breese, 26 August 1916, in Breese MSS at the National Library of Wales, NLW 9472 E. Breese was the Military Representative for the War Agricultural Committees for Carnarvon, Anglesey and Merioneth.

14. Griffith Jones to Major C.E. Breese, letter dated 10 August 1916, in Breese MSS at the National Library of Wales, NLW 9472 E.

15. Montgomery, *Maintenance of the Agricultural Labour Supply*, 30.

16. *General Report of the Board of Agriculture and Fisheries on Wages and Conditions of Employment in Agriculture*, P.P.1919, Vol. IX, 50.

17. Lord Ernle, *The Land and Its People: Chapters in Rural Life and History*, London n.d. [1925], 69.

18. *General Report of the Board of Agriculture and Fisheries on Wages &c.*, 50, quoting the example of Herefordshire farmers.

19. Montgomery, *Maintenance of the Agricultural Labour Supply*, 32-3.

20. *Report of the Board of Agriculture and Fisheries on Wages &c.*, Report on Monmouthshire, 468.

21. *Hansard*, 5th Series, Vol. 107 (3 July 1918), col. 1704 and Vol. 105, cols 196-7. *Regulations for the Issue of Army Separation Allowance, Allotment of Pay, and Family Allowance*, HMSO 1918, Appendix VI.

22. *Hampshire Chronicle*, 31 August 1918.

23. Letter from Sub-Commissioner at Falkirk to General Commissioner, Edinburgh, relating to the use of military labour by farmers in Scotland, 5 June 1917, in NATS.1/669 at the Public Record Office.

24. *Mark Lane Express*, 14 May 1917, 485.

25. Minute Book of the Essex Agricultural Executive Committee at Essex Record Office, entry for 20 October 1917.

26. Minute Book of the Essex Agricultural Executive Committee, entry for 7 August and 29 August 1917.

27. *Hansard*, 5th Series, Vol. 90 (8 February 1917), col. 113.

28. 'Soldier Labour on Farms during the War' in *Journal of the Board of Agriculture*, Vol. 25, December 1918, 1110.
29. Ernle, *The Land and Its People*, 125.
30. Circular letter sent from Major Skelton at General Headquarters, Home Forces, to all Commands, Officers Commanding Agricultural Companies, &c., 11 July 1917, at Public Record Office, NATS.1/474.
31. Meeting of the War Cabinet, 19 January 1917, Appendix I, CAB.23/1/39(1).
32. Meeting of the War Cabinet, 29 November 1917, CAB.23/4/287(3).
33. Quoted in *Report of the Board of Agriculture and Fisheries on Wages &c.*, Report on Worcestershire, 371.
34. Ernle, *The Land and Its People*, 126. See also *Hansard*, 5th Series, Vol. 90 (1 March 1917), col. 2188, announcement by Mr Forster, Financial Secretary to the War Office. The comment by Norfolk union delegates is in Minutes of a Meeting of Delegates of the National Agricultural Labourers and Rural Workers' Union on 3 February 1917, at the Museum of English Rural Life, Reading, B.VI.2.
35. *Hansard*, 5th Series, Vol. 91 (22 March 1917), col. 2068.
36. *Annual Report of the War Cabinet for 1917*, P.P.1918, Vol. XIV, 160. Ernle, *The Land and Its People*, 143.
37. Minute Book of the Essex Agricultural Executive Committee, entry for 9 October 1917.
38. 'Soldier Labour on Farms during the War', 1111-2.
39. Montgomery, *Maintenance of the Agricultural Labour Supply*, 39.
40. *General Report of the Board of Agriculture and Fisheries on Wages &c.*, 49. Montgomery, *Maintenance of the Agricultural Labour Supply*, 41.
41. *General Report of the Board of Agriculture and Fisheries on Wages, &c.*, 48, 49.
42. See, for example, *Punch*, 6 June 1917, 364, and 10 July 1918, 28.
43. Clergy Visitation Returns for the Oxford Diocese, Berks Archdeaconry, for 1918 at the Bodleian Library, MS Oxf.Dioc.Pp.*c*.378, entry for Longworth.
44. Clergy Visitation Returns for the Oxford Diocese, Oxford Archdeaconry, for 1918 at the Bodleian Library, MS Oxf.Dioc.Pp.*c*.380, entry for Drayton St Leonard.
45. *Report of the Board of Agriculture and Fisheries on Wages, &c.*, Reports on the Holland Division of Lincolnshire, 159, and Carnarvonshire, 435.
46. *Report on the State of Employment in Agriculture in Great Britain at the end of January, 1918* in NATS.1/241 at the Public Record Office, 8. *Hansard*, 5th Series, Vol. 90 (1917), col.2188.

47. Minutes of a meeting of the Machinery Sub-Committee of the Pembrokeshire War Agricultural Executive Committee, 22 May 1918, PCC/SE/71/1 at Pembrokeshire Record Office.

48. Letter from Major-General H.A. Tagart, General Headquarters, Home Forces, to J. Harling Turner, Director, National Service Department, Agricultural Section, 24 July 1917, in NATS.1/474 at the Public Record Office.

49. See correspondence between Castell Wrey, the Apethorpe agent, and the Food Production Department, 20 February and 23 February 1918, for example, in Box 3 of the Apethorpe estate correspondence at Northamptonshire Record Office.

50. Apethorpe estate correspondence, letters dated 30 January and 31 January 1918, in Box 3.

51. *General Report of the Board of Agriculture and Fisheries on Wages &c.*, 48.

52. *Hansard*, 5th Series, Vol. 108 (18 July 1918), col. 1280, speech by Rowland Prothero, and Montgomery, *Maintenance of the Agricultural Labour Supply*, 41.

53. *Annual Report of the War Cabinet for 1918*, P.P.1919, Vol. XXX, 237, and 'Soldier Labour on Farms during the War', 1111.

54. Lists of Farmers applying for Soldier Labour for 1916 in Breese MSS at the National Library of Wales.

55. Solider Labour Book at Pembrokeshire Record Office, PCC/SE/71/31.

56. Pembrokeshire War Agricultural Executive Committee Letter Book at Pembrokeshire Record Office, PCC/SE/71/2, letter dated 10 August 1918.

57. Pembrokeshire Soldier Labour Book, PCC/SE/71/31.

58. Montgomery, *Maintenance of the Agricultural Labour Supply*, 29.

59. Ibid. 21.

60. War Cabinet meeting on 31 March 1919, statement by the President of the Board of Agriculture, CAB.23/9/552(4).

61. *Hansard*, 5th Series, Vol. 114 (16 April 1919), cols 2902-3; Vol 115 (6 May 1919), cols 738-9; Vol. 116 (21 May 1919), col. 373.

62. Reminiscences of W. Cox at the Imperial War Museum, 80/35/1, 23-24.

63. Notes for a History of Stondon Massey, Essex, by the Rector, T/P.188/3, at Essex Record Office, 258. Eight soldiers arrived at Stondon Massey on 14 July 1917, and stayed for about ten days to a fortnight.

64. Reminiscences of W. Cox, 49-50.

Chapter 6 (pages 112-139)

1. *Board of Agriculture and Fisheries: Report of Sub-Committee Appointed to Consider the Employment of Women in Agriculture in England and Wales* (HMSO, 1919), 26, 117. Hereafter cited as *1919 Report on Women in Agriculture.*

2. *1919 Report on Women in Agriculture*, 37. Mrs M. Silyn Roberts, 'The Women of Wales and Agriculture' in *Journal of the Board of Agriculture*, Vol. 25 (October 1918), 817. *Board of Agriculture and Fisheries: Report on Wages and Conditions of Employment of Agricultural Labourers*, Report on Cardiganshire, P.P.1919, Vol. IX, 412.

3. *1919 Report on Women in Agriculture*, 28.

4. Lord Ernle, *The Land and Its People: Chapters in Rural Life and History*, London n.d. [1925], 171.

5. *Board of Agriculture and Fisheries: General Report on Wages &c.*, 52.

6. Arthur Randell, *Sixty Years a Fenman*, ed. Enid Porter, London 1966, 17.

7. *1919 Report on Women in Agriculture*, 29.

8. *Board of Agriculture and Fisheries: General Report on Wages &c.*, 52.

9. Ibid.

10. P.E. Dewey, 'Farm Labour in Wartime: The Relationship Between Agricultural Labour Supply and Food Production in Great Britain during 1914-1918', University of Reading Ph.D. thesis, 1978, 287. Hereafter cited as Dewey *thesis. The Earnings of Agricultural Labourers in Each County of England and Wales for the Year 1912-1913*, Central Landowners' Association, London, 1913, 20. *Regulations for the Issue of Army Separation Allowance, Allotment of Pay and Family Allowance*, London HMSO 1918, Appendix II.

11. Reminiscences of Mrs M.M. Goodwin of Great Bromley at Essex Record Office, T/Z.25/668.

12. *Board of Agriculture and Fisheries: Report on Wages &c.*, Report on Northamptonshire, 236. *Report of a Conference Between Representatives of County Committees and the Rt. Hon. the Earl of Selborne on 'Women's Labour on the Land'*, 31 December 1915, HMSO 1916, 10.

13. Dewey *thesis*, 286-7. *Regulations for the Issue of Army Separation Allowance &c., 1918.*

14. *The Observer*, 14 November 1982. It was estimated in October 1914 that childless widows 'amount to no less than one-third of the whole'.

15. Women's Work Collection at the Imperial War Museum, LAND.2/3/2.

16. Letter from T.M. Taylor at the Ministry of Munitions of War to Major Lloyd Graeme, Ministry of National Service, 1 January 1918, in NATS.1/215.

17. Quoted in Arthur Marwick, *Women at War, 1914-1918*, London 1977, 74.
18. Minutes on the Further Employment of Women in Agriculture by Sir Sydney Olivier, at the Public Record Office, MAF.59/1, n.d. [early October 1916].
19. Minutes of the Annual General Council Meeting of the National Agricultural Labourers and Rural Workers' Union on 12 February 1916, at the Museum of English Rural Life, B.VI.1.
20. George Edwards, *From Crow-Scaring to Westminster*, London 1957 edn, 190-192. Copy for the union journal, *The Labourer*, issue no. 6, B.IX.5 at the Museum of English Rural Life, 'Report of Annual General Council Meeting'.
21. 'Organisation of the Supply of Women for Agricultural Work from the Outbreak of the War to the Present Date', December 1915, typescript at the Imperial War Museum, LAND.1/11.
22. J.K. Montgomery, *The Maintenance of the Agricultural Labour Supply in England and Wales during the War*, Rome 1922, 53 and General Reports on Women's County Committees, Summary of Work for the Year Ending 1916, MAF.59/1 at the Public Record Office. Report from Cornwall.
23. 'How to Enrol Country Women for War Service in their Spare Time', leaflet at the Imperial War Museum, LAND.1/24. Montgomery, *The Maintenance of the Agricultural Labour Supply*, 53.
24. Report of the Women's Defence Relief Corps for 1914-16, 1-2 at Imperial War Museum, LAND.4/6. Pamphlet on The Women's Farm and Garden Union at the Imperial War Museum, LAND.5/1/8. Material on the National Political League at the Imperial War Museum, LAND.3/1.
25. Minutes on the Further Employment of Women in Agriculture, n.d. [early October 1916], at the Public Record Office, MAF.59/1.
26. Reports of the Women's Defence Relief Corps for 1914-16, 4 and for 1917 1-2 and 6, at the Imperial War Museum.
27. Reports of the Women's Defence Relief Corps for 1914-16, 7, 8; for 1917, 7.
28. Report of the Women's Defence Relief Corps for 1914-16, 1.
29. Quoted in Marwick, *Women at War 1914-1918*, 81.
30. Letter from Mrs Hobbs to Miss Talbot, 6 October 1917, in MAF.42/8, file on Women's Legion at the Public Record Office. P.E. Dewey, 'Government Provision of Farm Labour in England and Wales, 1914-18' in *Agricultural History Review*, Vol. 27, Pt. II (1979), 114.
31. Minute, dated 13.12.1917 by A.D.H. [Hall], rejecting the idea of supporting the Women's Legion training centre at Cottesmore, MAF.42/8, file on Women's Legion.

32. Irene O. Andrews and Margarett A. Hobbs, *Economic Effects of the War upon Women and Children in Great Britain*, New York 1918, 64.

33. Report by the Women's National Land Service Corps on a Scheme for the Organisation of Women's Service on the Land, proposed at the end of 1916. Typescript at the Imperial War Museum, LAND.5/1/1.

34. Report from Cheshire County Agricultural Committee for the year ending August 1916 at the Public Record Office, MAF.59/1. *Essex Weekly News*, 16 April, 1916.

35. Montgomery, *The Maintenance of the Agricultural Labour Supply*, 56.

36. Ibid. See also Imperial War Museum, LAND.2/4/21: *Lincolnshire Standard*, 20 May 1916.

37. *Report of a Conference Between Representatives of County Committees*, 31 December 1915, 9.

38. Leaflet on 'Costume for Women Workers on the Land' issued by the Board of Agriculture in July 1916, Imperial War Museum, LAND.1/29.

39. Ernle, *The Land and Its People*, 177. *Hansard*, 5th Series, Vol. 108 (18 July 1918), col. 1282.

40. *Hampshire Chronicle*, 2 March 1918.

41. Report of the Women's National Service Corps for the period 1 October 1916 to 30 September 1917, 3, at the Imperial War Museum, LAND.5/1.

42. Andrews & Hobbs, *Economic Effects of the War*, 66.

43. Report of the Women's National Service Corps, 1 October 1916 to 30 September 1917, 7.

44. Report of the Women's National Land Service Corps, Interim Report from February 1916 to 30 September 1916, 17.

45. Report of the Women's National Land Service Corps from 1 October 1916 to 30 September 1917, 23-4.

46. Report of the Women's National Land Service Corps from 1 October 1916 to 30 September 1917, 20.

47. 'Scheme for the Organisation of Women's Service on the Land put forward at the end of 1916' by the Women's National Land Service Corps, 1, at the Imperial War Museum, LAND.5/1/1.

48. Annual Report of the Women's National Land Service Corps from 1 October 1916 to 30 September 1917.

49. Ernle, *The Land and Its People*, 181-5. Montgomery, *The Maintenance of the Agricultural Labour Supply*, 58-60. *The Times*, 19 July 1917, 8.

50. *Hansard*, 5th Series, Vol. 108 (1918), 1282.

51. Montgomery, *The Maintenance of the Agricultural Labour Supply*, 59-60.

52. Women's Land Army: Terms and Conditions of Service for Motor-Tractor Drivers, at Imperial War Museum, LAND.6/2/20. *The Times*, 31 October 1917 and 1 November 1917, 2.

53. Final Report of the Women's National Land Service Corps, 1919, 3.

54. Montgomery, *The Maintenance of the Agricultural Labour Supply*, 55. Leaflet on 'Gangs for Seasonal Work' issued by the Food Production Department of the Board of Agriculture, at Imperial War Museum, LAND.6/2/9. Annual Report of the Women's National Land Service Corps for the period 1 October 1916 to 30 September 1917, 10-11.

55. Ernle, *The Land and Its People*, 182.

56. See, for example, correspondence between Castell Wrey, agent for the Apethorpe estate, Northamptonshire, concerning the employment of a traineee molecatcher, March 1918, in Box 3, Northamptonshire Record Office.

57. *The Times*, 28 March 1917.

58. Ernle, *The Land and Its People*, 183. The Timber Supplies Department, Board of Trade: Terms of Service of Employment of Women on Timber Work, at Imperial War Museum, LAND.7/22 and Land.7/16: 'Women Foresters'.

59. Ernle, *The Land and Its People*, 183.

60. Reminiscences of Annie S. Edwards, Transcript in the Oral History Recordings sections of the Imperial War Museum, Accession No. 000740/15, 8.

61. *Board of Agriculture and Fisheries: General Report on Wages &c.*, 40. *Hansard*, 5th series, Vol. 90 (8 February 1917), col. 111.

62. 'Leaves from Organising Secretary's Diary', typescript at the Imperial War Museum, LAND.6/20, 1.

63. Olive Hockin, *Two Girls on the Land: War-time on a Dartmoor Farm*, London 1918, 21.

64. Diary of Miss C. Prunell at the Imperial War Museum, Box No. 79/23/1.

65. Reminiscences of Mary Lees, Transcript in the Oral History Recordings section of the Imperial War Museum, Accession No. 000506/07, 4 and 5.

66. *Board of Agriculture and Fisheries: General Report on Wages &c.*, 53.

67. 'The Women's Forestry Corps' by a Forewoman in *The Ladies' Field*, 2 February 1918, at the Imperial War Museum, LAND.7/15-16.

68. *The Times*, 2 October 1917, 9.

69. Letter from Rose Everard of Leicester, 3 July 1918, to Miss Meriel Talbot, MAF.42/8 at the Public Record Office.

70. Letter from Lady Mather Jackson, 4 July 1918, to Miss Meriel Talbot, MAF.42/8.

71. Letter and draft rules from Dorothy M. Ward of Tring to Miss Meriel Talbot, 20 August 1918, MAF.42/8.

72. 'Women's Land Army: Need for More Effective Control', Report by Miss Meriel L. Talbot, June 1918, MAF.42/8.

73. Marwick, *Women at War, 1914-1918*, 105.

74. Report on Welfare for guidance of the new Welfare Officers, 3 July 1918, in MAF.42/8. The Welfare Officers were to be paid £3 a week.

75. Ernle, *The Land and Its People*, 186-7. Copies of *The Landswoman* for 1918-1920 are available at the Imperial War Museum.

76. Summary of the Work of the Women's War Agricultural Committees for the Year ending August 1916, 'Report on Demonstrations in Cornwall' in MAF.59/1 at the Public Record Office.

77. *The Times*, 26 July 1917, 9.

78. *Report on the State of Employment in Agriculture in Great Britain at the end of January 1918* in NATS.1/241 at the Public Record Office, 6.

79. *Board of Agriculture and Fisheries: General Report on Wages &c.*, 101, and Report on Northamptonshire, 236.

80. Reminiscences of Mrs May G. Morris of Oxford, interviewed on 11 May 1982.

81. Montgomery, *The Maintenance of the Agricultural Labour Supply*, 60. Case Studies of Distinguished Service in the Land Army, typescript at the Imperial War Museum, LAND.6/21, 1 and 2.

82. Ernle, *The Land and Its People*, 182-183. *Journal of the Board of Agriculture*, Vol. 26 (March 1920), 754. Numbers in training fluctuated as demand for workers varied. In the spring of 1918 the number of women in training was between 300 and 400, yet by July it had reached 2,775.

83. Ernle, *The Land and Its People*, 128. Dewey *thesis*, 267.

84. Ernle, *The Land and Its People*, 179.

85. Letter from Major Lloyd Graeme, Ministry of National Service to T.M. Taylor, Ministry of Munitions, Labour Supply Department, 2 January 1918, in NATS.1/215.

86. Women's Work Collection at the Imperial War Museum, LAND.6/27.

87. Montgomery, *The Maintenance of the Agricultural Labour Supply*, 61. Ernle, *The Land and Its People*, 192.

88. *Hansard*, 5th Series, Vol. 120 (1919), col. 933 and Ernle, *The Land and Its People*, 192.

89. *1919 Report on Women in Agriculture*, 29.

90. *Census of Population, 1921: Occupations* (HMSO, 1924), 2, 54-5.
91. *Census of Population, 1921: County Surveys.*
92. Report of the Biennial Conference of the National Union of Agricultural Workers, 16 June 1922, B.VI.3, at the Museum of English Rural Life, Reading. The Union changed its name to National Union of Agricultural Workers in 1920.
93. Report from Cornwall Women's War Service Committee for year ending August, 1916, MAF.59/1.
94. Montgomery, *The Maintenance of the Agricultural Labour Supply*, 68.
95. Leaflet on 'War Service for Country Women', section 'For Workers', at Imperial War Museum, LAND.1/25.
96. *Essex Times*, 25 March 1916.
97. Inez Jenkins, *The History of the Women's Institute Movement of England and Wales*, Oxford 1953, 15-8. Gervas Huxley, *Lady Denman*, London 1961, 65-71. *Journal of the Board of Agriculture*, Vol. 26, (December 1919), 939-40.
98. *The Times*, 11 March 1918.
99. Letter from Lady Denman to the Ministry of Reconstruction, 2 August 1918, on Ministry of Reconstruction Committee file at National Federation of Women's Institutes headquarters.
100. Report of the National Federation of Women's Institutes (England and Wales), January 1918, at the Imperial War Museum, 12.
101. Memorandum on Women's Institutes [January 1917], Reconstruction Committee's Sub Committee on Adult Education, on Ministry of Reconstruction Committee file at NFWI headquarters.
102. Report of the National Federation of Women's Institutes for the period ending December 1918, 64, at the Imperial War Museum.
103. *Home and Country*, June 1919, 9. This was established as the journal of the Women's Institute movement in March 1919.
104. Simon Goodenough, *Jam and Jerusalem*, London 1977, 21.
105. *Journal of the Board of Agriculture*, (December 1919), 940. *Home and Country*, November 1919, 1.
106. *1919 Report on Women in Agriculture*, 99-100. Ernle, *The Land and Its People*, 170. Report of a meeting of a Deputation from the National Federation of Women's Institutes to the President of the Board of Agriculture on 27 June 1919, in MAF.42/8 at the Public Record Office.

Chapter 7 (pages 140-161)

1. *Report of the War Cabinet for 1918,* P.P.1919, Vol. XXX, 237.
2. *Journal of the Board of Agriculture,* Vol. 26 (Dec. 1919), 866-7, 945. *Hansard,* 5th Series, Vol. 120 (1919), col. 935.
3. *Mark Lane Express,* 19 October 1914, 464.
4. *Within Living Memory* (Norfolk Federation of Women's Institutes, 1971), 90-1.
5. J.K. Montgomery, *The Maintenance of the Agricultural Labour Supply in England and Wales during the War,* Rome 1922, 69.
6. *Mark Lane Express,* 8th February, 1915, 177. See also *Mark Lane Express,* 11 January 1915, 45.
7. His Grace the Duke of Bedford's Current Account, Abstract of Monthly Receipts and Payments, &c. for 1915, at the Bedford Estate Record Office, London.
8. See correspondence received by the rector of Llanfair, Merioneth, during the War at the National Library of Wales, NLW MS 9982 E.
9. His Grace the Duke of Bedford's Current Account, Abstract of Monthly Receipts and Payments, &c. for 1917. £4 14s. 6d. was, however, expended on unspecified 'allowances' to them in this year.
10. Report by Major Wrottesley, Ministry of National Service, 13 December 1917, on the Importation of Labour from Denmark for Agricultural Work, NATS.1/412 at the Public Record Office.
11. Montgomery, *The Maintenance of the Agricultural Labour Supply,* 69 and War Cabinet Minutes, CAB.23/4/297(8), 13 December 1917.
12. Report by Major Wrottesley on the Importation of Labour from Denmark and extract from War Cabinet Minutes No. 296, Minute 16 in NATS.1/412.
13. War Cabinet Minutes, CAB.23/4/296(8), 12 December 1917.
14. See letter from T.W. Phillips at the Ministry of Labour to C.F. Rey at the Ministry of National Service, 29 April 1918, NATS.1/412.
15. *Journal of the Board of Agriculture,* Vol. 25 (June 1918), 342.
16. P.E. Dewey, 'Farm Labour in Wartime: The Relationship Between Agricultural Labour Supply and Food Production in Great Britain during 1914-1918, with International Comparisons', (Reading University Ph.D. thesis, 1978), 242. Hereafter cited as Dewey *thesis.*
17. Cabinet minutes, meeting on 11 April 1916, CAB.37/145/28.
18. Report on The Employment of Prisoners of War, dated 23 September 1916, in CAB.42/20/7. Memorandum by the Adjutant General on the Employment of Prisoners of War, September 1916, in CAB.42/21/1. (Cabinet meeting on 3 October 1916).

19. *Hansard,* Vol. 87 (21 Nov 1916), col. 1173.
20. *Hansard,* Vol. 87 (21 Nov 1916), col. 1175.
21. Ministry of National Service: Instructions to Agricultural Commissioners, NATS.1/474, circular letter, dated 16 January 1917, from Sir Sydney Olivier, Permanent Secretary at the Board of Agriculture and Fisheries.
22. *Interim Report of the Prisoners of War Employment Committee,* NATS.1/1332,1. n.d. [February 1918]. This is a printed report. A manuscript version is also preserved with Ministry of National Service records.
23. Farm Ledger of Launceston Farm, Tarrant Launceston, Dorset, DOR.5/1/6, at Reading University Library.
24. Dewey *thesis,* 244.
25. Reports on Prisoner of War Camps: Blandford Camp and Dorchester Camp, August 1918, in NATS.1/1330.
26. Dewey *thesis,* 242.
27. *Hansard,* 5th Series, Vol. 108 (18 July 1918), col. 1280, speech by Rowland Prothero.
28. *Mark Lane Express,* 29 January 1917, 102.
29. Minutes of War Cabinet, 13 December 1917, CAB.23/4/297(9).
30. Jim Priest, *Parndon Recollections,* Harlow 1981, 66-7.
31. *The Times,* 19 November 1917.
32. *Report of the Board of Agriculture and Fisheries on Wages and Conditions of Employment in Agriculture,* P.P.1919, Vol. IX, Report on Cheshire, 38. *The Times,* 23 March 1918.
33. *Report of the Board of Agriculture and Fisheries on Wages &c.,* Report on Leicestershire, 147.
34. Minutes of a Conference of Norfolk Delegates, 3 February 1917, at the Museum of English Rural Life, Reading, B.VI.2.
35. *General Report of the Board of Agriculture and Fisheries on Wages & c.,* 52.
36. *The Times,* 2 July 1917, 9.
37. *Mark Lane Express,* 18 February 1918, 167.
38. Minutes of War Cabinet meeting, 12 December 1917, CAB.23/4/296(16).
39. *General Report of the Board of Agriculture and Fisheries on Wages & c.,* 51.
40. *Journal of the Board of Agriculture,* Vol. 24 (February 1918), 1294-5, and Vol. 26 (December 1919), 867.
41. See records of Prisoner of War Camps at Bedfordshire Record Office, WAV.13, involving men sent out on 30 March 1918. Similarly, on 6 April a party of 8 men was sent out 'stubbing bushes', without a formal escort.
42. Minutes of War Cabinet meeting, 13 December 1917, CAB.23/4/297(8), and *Journal of the Board of Agriculture,* Vol. 24 (July 1917), 467, quoting a Board circular of 20 June 1917.

43. *Journal of the Board of Agriculture*, Vol. 24 (February 1918), 1291.
44. See, for example, bill submitted by Bedfordshire Agricultural Committee, relating to Leighton Buzzard Camp, in WAV.12, when these charges were made. Machinery and horses and carts were also hired separately from the camp at varying rates, e.g. 7s. 6d. per day for a horse and 1s. 6d. per day for a cart. (Bedfordshire Record Office).
45. *Journal of the Board of Agriculture*, Vol. 24 (February 1918), 1291.
46. Notes by the Food Production Department as to the Present System of Employing Prisoners of War in Agriculture (n.d. summer 1918), in NATS.1/1131, 1-2.
47. *Interim Report of the Prisoners of War Employment Committee*, 5. Meeting of the Prisoners of War Employment Committee, 16 May 1918, noted that 'there was still a number of camps in which the accommodation had been prepared but where the Prisoners could not be employed owing to the lack of guards', NATS.1/1332.
48. Table of Prisoners of War and Interned Aliens at work on 20 May 1918. A similar Table showing the distribution of Prisoners of War in Great Britain by Industry on 10 September 1918. Both in NATS.1/1332.
49. Dewey *thesis*, 246.
50. *Reports on the State of Employment in Agriculture at the end of July 1917*, 2, and *at the end of January 1918*, 2.
51. *Report of the Board of Agriculture and Fisheries on Wages & c.*, Reports on Warwickshire, 354, and Worcestershire, 371.
52. *Interim Report of the Prisoners of War Employment Committee*, 7.
53. Lord Ernle, *The Land and Its People*, London n.d. [1925], 127. *Interim Report of the Prisoners of War Employment Committee*, 5, and Details of Prisoners of War during the week ended 30 June 1918, in NATS.1/1332.
54. Table showing the Distribution of Prisoners of War in Great Britain by Industry as at 10 September 1918, in NATS.1/1332.
55. *General Report of the Board of Agriculture and Fisheries on Wages &c.*, 52. Prisoners of War Employment Committee: Evidence of John Steel, farmer of Rochford, Essex, 7 June 1918, in NATS.1/1131, 2.
56. Dewey, *thesis*, 249.
57. D.S. Higgins ed., *The Private Diaries of Sir Henry Rider Haggard*, London 1980, 142-3.
58. *Prisoners of War Employment Committee: Prisoner Labour Enquiry: Draft Interim Report* n.d. [summer 1918], Appendix A, Supervision, in NATS.1/1131.
59. Prisoners of War Employment Committee, Evidence of John Steel, 7 June 1918, 6, 13.

60. War Cabinet meeting, CAB.23/4/245(3), meeting on 4 October 1917.

61. Prisoners of War Employment Committee: Evidence of F.J. Price of Sutton Bridge, Lincolnshire, interviewed on 7 June 1918, 40. Minutes of War Cabinet meeting, 12 December 1917, CAB.23/4/296(16).

62. See time sheet for 24 August 1918, from Turvey Camp, Bedfordshire, WAV.13, at Bedfordshire Record Office. The men were working for a farmer in Turvey.

63. Notes by the Food Production Department as to the Present System of Employing Prisoners of War in Agriculture n.d. [summer 1918], 4.

64. Prisoners of War: Rations for Prisoners engaged in heavy manual work: Policy file, NATS.1/570, Minute by C.F. Rey at the Ministry of National Service, 21 June 1918.

65. *Hansard*, 5th Series, Vol. 105 (24 April 1918), col. 988.

66. Minutes of Sawbridgeworth Urban District Food Control Committee, 1917-20, at the Public Record Office, MAF.60/433, entry for 16 February 1918.

67. *Hansard*, 5th Series, Vol. 107 (27th June, 1918), cols. 1203-4 and Vol. 110 (24 October 1918), col. 940.

68. Letter from Captain Powis at the Ministry of Food to T. Simpson in office of the Director General of National Labour Supplies, 9 August 1918, and circular letter to Commandants of Prisoners of War Camps, etc. from the War Office, 16 August 1918, in NATS.1/570.

69. *Hansard*, 5th Series, Vol. 104 (1918), col. 1147. Circular letter to Commandants of Prisoners of War Camps, etc. from the War Office, 16 August 1918. The letter also noted: 'Where no canteen exists, Commandants may make the purchases from local sources'.

70. Report on Chepstow Prisoner of War Camp, 5 September 1918, in NATS.1/1330.

71. *The Times*, 4 July and 19 July 1918.

72. Prisoners of War Employment Committee: Evidence of Colonel Bulkeley, 21 June 1918, in NATS.1/1131, 5.

73. Prisoners of War Employment Committee: Evidence of W.P. Theakston of Huntingdon, 7 June 1918, 18. Mr Theakston was the Executive Officer to the Huntingdon Agricultural War Committee.

74. *Report of the Board of Agriculture and Fisheries on Wages &c.*, Report on Northamptonshire, 236, and Prisoners of War Employment Committee, Evidence of John Steel, 7.

75. *Within Living Memory*, 90.

76. Reminiscences of Mrs M.M. Byford of High Roding, near Dunmow, at Essex Record Office, T/Z.25/658.
77. Minutes of Prisoners of War Employment Committee, 12 August 1918.
78. *Oxford Chronicle*, 8 November 1918.
79. *Report of the War Cabinet for 1918*, P.P.1919, Vol. XXX, 237. *Journal of the Board of Agriculture*, Vol. 26 (December 1919), 944.
80. Horse ploughing account sent to Mr Harry Banks, Pertenhall, 23 April 1919 by Bedfordshire Agricultural Executive Committee, in WAV.11 at Bedfordshire Record Office.
81. *Hansard*, 5th Series, Vol. 119 (6 August 1919), col. 347.
82. *Hansard*, 5th Series, Vol. 116 (3 June 1919), col. 1831.
83. *Country Life*, 17 May 1919, 547-8.
84. *Journal of the Board of Agriculture*, Vol. 26 (December 1919), 866-7, 944-5. Montgomery, *The Maintenance of the Agricultural Labour Supply*, 49.
85. *The Times*, 24 January 1917.
86. *Report of the Board of Agriculture and Fisheries on Wages &c.*, Report on Monmouthshire, 468.
87. Ernle, *The Land and Its People*, 127-8.
88. *Journal of the Board of Agriculture*, Vol. 26 (December 1919), 945.

Chapter 8 (162-182)
1. *Correspondence on School Attendance*, P.P.1914-16, Vol. L, 10.
2. Quoted in Pamela Horn, 'The Employment of Elementary School-children in Agriculture, 1914-1918' in *History of Education*, Vol. 12, No. 3 (1983), 204.
3. *Report of the Board of Education for 1914-15*, P.P.1916, Vol. VIII, 3.
4. *Dorset County Chronicle*, 8 October 1914.
5. Ivinghoe School Log Book at Buckinghamshire Record Office, E/LB/116/2, entry for 22 September 1914.
6. Ivinghoe School Log Book, entry for 8 December 1914.
7. Letter written by Robert Saunders of Fletching to his son, William, 1 November 1914, at the Imperial War Museum, 79/15/1.
8. *Bucks Herald*, 24 October 1914.
9. Llanychllwydog School Log book at Pembrokeshire Record Office, SS/1/67, entry for 23 October 1916.
10. *General Report of the Board of Agriculture and Fisheries on Wages and Conditions of Employment of Agricultural Labourers*, P.P.1919, Vol. IX, 54.

11. Jim Priest, *Parndon Recollections*, Harlow 1981, 49-50.
12. *Farmer and Stockbreeder*, 8 February 1915.
13. *Mark Lane Express*, 19 October 1914.
14. *Mark Lane Express*, 22 February 1915.
15. *Return on School Attendance and Employment in Agriculture*, P.P.1914-16, Vol. L, 18-9.
16. *Hansard*, 5th Series, Vol. 66 (28 August 1914), col. 274.
17. *Hansard*, 5th Series, Vol. 69 (4 February 1915), cols 147-8.
18. File on School Attendance and Employment in Agriculture at the Public Record Office, ED.11/78.
19. *Hansard*, 5th Series, Vol. 69 (17 February 1915), col. 1163.
20. *Returns of School Attendance and Employment in Agriculture, 31 January 1916*, P.P.1916, Vol. XXII, 2. Hereafter cited as *31 January 1916 Returns*.
21. *Correspondence on School Attendance*, 17. *Returns of School Attendance and Employment in Agriculture, February to April, 1915* (hereafter cited as *February to April, 1915 Returns*), P.P.1914-16, Vol. L, 4.
22. *Mark Lane Express*, 8 March 1915.
23. A. Susan Lawrence, 'Child Labour on Farms. Shall We Allow It', in *The Labourer* (February 1915), 10.
24. Minute by W.R. Barker at the Board of Education, dated 23 September 1916, at the Public Record Office, ED.11/78.
25. Reports submitted by HMI Owen on Individual Counties, n.d. c. July 1915 in ED.11/78.
26. *Hansard*, 5th Series, Vol. 70 (25 February 1915), col. 439.
27. *Hansard*, 5th Series, Vol. 70 (25 February 1915), cols. 403-5.
28. *Hansard*, 5th Series, Vol. 70 (25 February 1915), col. 447.
29. Minutes of the First and Second County Conferences of the National Agricultural Labourers and Rural Workers' Union held on 13 February and 27 March 1915, respectively, at the Museum of English Rural Life, University of Reading, B.VI.2.
30. Board of Education Circular No. 898 on School Attendance and Employment in Agriculture, dated 12 March 1915, at the Public Record Office, NATS.1/672.
31. *Returns of School Attendance and Employment in Agriculture, for 1st September, 1914 - 31st January, 1915 and 1st February, 1915 to 30th April, 1915*, in P.P.1914-16, Vol. L; for *31st January, 1916, 31st May, 1916*, and *16th October, 1916*, in P.P.1916, Vol. XXII.
32. *Returns of School Attendance and Employment in Agriculture, 31st May, 1916*, hereafter cited as *31st May, 1916 Returns*.
33. Reports submitted by HMI Owen on Individual Counties, n.d. [July 1915]. *Times Educational Supplement*, 1 August 1916.
34. Quoted in Horn, 'Employment of Elementary Schoolchildren in Agriculture', 208.

35. *Times Educational Supplement*, 4 January 1916.
36. Minutes of a meeting of a sub-committee of the War Workers' Emergency Committee c.23 July 1915, submitted to the Board of Education, and Report by HMI Fear, 28 July 1915, in ED.11/78.
37. Report by HMI Purdie, dated 27 July, 1915, in ED.11/78.
38. Circular from the Board of Education, No. 943, dated 29 February 1916, in NATS.1/672 at the Public Record Office.
39. Reports submitted by HMI Owen on Individual Counties, c. July, 1915, on Somerset and Norfolk in ED.11/78.
40. Draft article on 'The Child and Agriculture' by Herbert H. Elvin in the Records of the National Agricultural Labourers and Rural Workers' Union at the Museum of English Rural Life, University of Reading, B.IX.9.
41. See Circular No. 943, dated 29 February 1916.
42. *Times Educational Supplement*, 3 May 1917.
43. Minute by W.R. Barker at the Board of Education, 23 September 1916, in ED.11/78.
44. Minute by W.R. Barker at the Board of Education, 23 September 1916, ED.11/78.
45. Minute by W.R. Barker, 23 September 1916.
46. Minute by the Marquis of Crewe, dated 26 November 1916, in ED.11/78.
47. *31st May, 1916 Returns* and *16th October, 1916 Returns*.
48. Minute by the Marquis of Crewe in ED.11/78.
49. Circular from the Board of Education to Local Education Authorities, dated 3 April 1917 the Public Record Office, NATS.1/672.
50. See entry for 16 December 1917 in the Fisher Diary, MS Fisher 11, at the Bodleian Library, Oxford.
51. *General Report of the Board of Agricultur and Fisheries on Wages & c.*, 54.
52. *General Report of the Board of Agriculture and Fisheries on Wages &c.*, 55.
53. *Annual Report for 1918* of the Chief Medical Officer of the Board of Education, P.P.1919, Vol. XXI, 189.
54. Caroline Baker, *Homedwellers and Foreigners: The Seasonal Labour Force in Kentish Agriculture* (University of Kent at Canterbury M.Phil. thesis, 1979), 304-5.
55. As late as 10 September 1917, Warwickshire had had 401 children exempted. *Times Educational Supplement*, 19 September 1918.
56. P.E. Dewey, *Farm Labour in Wartime* (University of Reading Ph.D. thesis, 1978), 295.
57. *Hansard*, 5th Series, Vol. 97 (10 August 1917), col. 798.

58. Irene O. Andrews and Margarett A. Hobbs, *Economic Effects of the War upon Women and Children in Great Britain*, New York 1918, 146. Dewey *thesis*, 290.
59. *Mark Lane Express*, 22 February 1915.
60. *The Schoolmaster*, 24 November 1917.
61. *Report of the Chief Medical Officer of Health of the Board of Education*, P.P.1917-18, Vol. XI, 169.
62. For examples of agricultural hostility to the provisions of the 1918 Act see, for example, *Hansard*, 5th Series (13 March 1918), col. 104, col. 348.
63. *Times Educational Supplement*, 25 January 1917.
64. *The Schoolmaster*, 18 March 1916 (leader).
65. Andrews and Hobbs, *Economic Effects of the War upon Women and Children*, 146-9.
66. Reminiscences of Mr W.J. Shepherd of Sandleigh, Wootton, Abingdon, interviewed on 21 April 1982.
67. See, for example, the comments of the incumbent of Mortimer, Berkshire, in Clergy Visitation Returns for 1918, MS Oxf.Dioc.Pp.c.378 at the Bodleian Library Oxford. Also for Leafield in Oxfordshire, MS Oxf.Dioc.Pp.c.380 and for Radclive *cum* Checkmore in Buckinghamshire, MS Oxf.Dioc. Pp.c.379. Many other incumbents made similar comments.
68. Circular to Local Education Authorities, dated 6 March 1919, in ED.11/78.
69. F.E. Green, *A History of the English Agricultural Labourer*, London 1920, 240. *The Herald*, 13 January 1916.
70. *The Times*, 16 August 1917. Report on Schoolboy Labour: Harvest Camps, dated 26th October, 1917 and sent by the Cavendish Association to the Ministry of National Service, at the Public Record Office NATS.1/653.
71. Report on Schoolboy Labour: Harvest Camps, 26 October 1917.
72. Ibid.
73. J.K. Montgomery, *The Maintenance of the Agricultural Labour Supply in England and Wales during the War*, Rome 1922, 74-5.
74. See *Country Life*, 10 November 1917, 439. In September, 1917, *Country Life* had also included a long account of the work of a group of Uppingham school boys at a harvest camp near Cockermouth, where they were engaged in drainage, harvesting and weeding operations.
75. Report on Flax Weeding by Boy Scouts, May 1918, at the Public Record Office, NATS.1/672.
76. See file on 'Draft Scheme for Schoolboy Labour: 1919 harvest' at the Public Record Office, NATS.1/676.
77. Lord Ernle, *The Land and Its People*, London n.d. (*c.* 1925), 129.

78. See entries in Lower Heyford School Log Book in the possession of Miss D.B. Dew of Lower Heyford.
79. *Times Educational Supplement*, 23 August 1917. *The Times*, 16 January 1918. *Annual Report of the Board of Education for 1917-18*, P.P.1919, Vol. XXI, 5.
80. *The Times*, 23 January 1917.
81. 'Public Elementary Schools and Food Supply in War Time: Memorandum for Teachers in Rural and Suburban Schools' issued by the Board of Education in April 1916 and preserved at the Imperial War Museum.
82. Pitstone School Log Book at Buckinghamshire Record Office, E/LB/166/1.
83. *Annual Report of the Board of Education for 1917-18*, 3. *Annual Report of the Board of Education for 1916-17*, P.P.1918, Vol. IX, 'Elementary Schools in Wales', 19.
84. *Mark Lane Express*, 3 September 1917. Green, *A History of the English Agricultural Labourer*, 235.
85. Robert Saunders to William Saunders, 16 November 1918, at the Imperial War Museum, 79/15/1.

Chapter 9 (pages 183-208)

1. Clergy Visitation Returns for the Oxford Diocese, 1918 at the Bodleian Library, Oxford, MS. Oxf.Dioc. Pp.c.378 for Berkshire Archdeaconry and MS Oxf.Dioc.Pp.c.379 for the Buckinghamshire Archdeaconry.
2. Reminiscences of Mr Shepherd of Sandleigh, Oxfordshire, interviewed 21 April 1982. During the First World War Mr Shepherd lived with his family at Standlake, Oxfordshire.
3. Clergy Visitation Returns for Berkshire Archdeaconry, MS Oxf.Dioc.Pp.c.378.
4. George A. Panichas ed., *Promise of Greatness: The War of 1914-1918*, London 1968, 460.
5. Lord Ernle, *The Land and Its People*, London n.d. [1925], 104.
6. D.S. Higgins ed., *The Private Diaries of Sir Henry Rider Haggard*, London 1980, 146.
7. Material for a History of Stondon Massey by the Rector, the Revd E.H.L. Reeve, Vol. III, at Essex Record Office, T/P.188/3, 305-7.
8. D.R. Grace and D.C. Phillips, *Ransomes of Ipswich*, University of Reading 1975, 7-8.
9. R.A. Whitehead, *Garrett 200: A Bicentenary History of Garretts of Leiston*, London 1978, 101-3.

10. Clergy Visitation Returns for the Berkshire Archdeaconry, 1918.
11. A.G. Street, *The Gentleman of the Party*, London 1944 edn, 158-62.
12. M.K. Ashby, *Joseph Ashby of Tysoe 1859-1919*, Cambridge 1961, 292, 294. *Report of the Board of Agriculture and Fisheries: Wages and Conditions of Employment in Agriculture*, Report of the County of Buckinghamshire, P.P.1919, Vol. IX, 21.
13. Aubrey Moore, *A Son of the Rectory*, Gloucester 1982, 124.
14. Panichas ed., *Promise of Greatness*, 146.
15. Memoirs of Ernest Kingsbury at the Imperial War Museum, P.P./MER/44.
16. George J. Zytaruk and James T. Boulton ed., *The Letters of D.H. Lawrence, 1913-16*, Vol. 2, Cambridge 1981, 649. The letter was written on 1 September 1916, to Lady Cynthia Asquith, but there are many others in a similar vein, for example, on pp. 524, 526, 597.
17. Siegfried Sassoon, *Siegfried's Journey*, London 1982 edn, 14.
18. See, for example, a letter written by Gunner J.B. Titterton, a farmer of Middleton by Youlgrave, Derbyshire, from France, on 22 October 1918, 8492/F.1-16 at Derbyshire Record Office.
19. J.M. Winter, 'Some Aspects of the Demographic Consequences of the First World War in Britain' in *Population Studies*, Vol. 30 (1976), 541.
20. Denis Winter, *Death's Men*, London 1979 edn, 248-53.
21. Clergy Visitation Returns for the Oxford Archdeaconry, MS Oxf.Dioc.Pp.c.380.
22. Robert Graves, *Goodbye to All That*, London 1960 edn, 259.
23. *Hansard*, 5th Series, Vol. 92 (25 April 1917), col. 2466, comment by Commander Wedgwood.
24. Ronald Blythe, *Akenfield: Portrait of an English Village*, London 1969, 130.
25. Reminiscences of Mr Shepherd of Sandleigh.
26. *The Economist*, 24 July 1920, 140. According to this index, by July 1917, the cost of living was 80 per cent above its July 1914 level, and in July 1918, 100-105 per cent above. By July 1920 it was 152 per cent higher.
27. Minutes of the Food Control Committee for the Rural District of Midhurst, Sussex, 1917-1920, at the Public Record Office, MAF.60/431, entry for 14 May 1918.
28. *Report of a Committee Appointed by the Agricultural Wages Board into the Cost of Living of Rural Workers*, P.P.1919, Vol. VIII, 33.
29. Minutes of a Conference of Norfolk delegates of the National Agricultural Labourers and Rural Workers' Union at the Museum of English Rural Life, University of Reading, B.VI.2, entry for 3 February 1917.

30. Reg Groves, *Sharpen the Sickle!* London 1949, 165. J.K. Montgomery, *The Maintenance of the Agricultural Labour Supply in England and Wales during the War*, Rome 1922, 92.
31. Elizabeth Crittall ed., *Victoria History of the County of Wiltshire*, Vol. 4, London 1959, 113.
32. Minutes of the Tenth General Council Meeting of the National Agricultural Labourers and Rural Workers' Union, 9 March 1918, at the Museum of English Rural Life, B.VI.3.
33. *The Economist*, 25 December 1920, 1124.
34. A.G. Street, *Farmer's Glory*, London 1959 edn, 264.
35. Edith H. Whetham, 'The Agriculture Act, 1920 and its Repeal — the "Great Betrayal" ' in *Agricultural History Review, Vol. 22*, Pt 1 (1974), 41.
36. *Board of Agriculture and Fisheries: Agricultural Statistics for 1918*, P.P.1919, Vol. LI.
37. *Co-operation and the Supply of Farm Implements*, Leaflet No. 44, August 1917, issued by the Food Production Department, at the British Library, 07078.ff.10 and 'Monograph on the History of Agriculture in Anglesey during the Great War', n.d. typescript, Bangor 3191 at the University College of North Wales Library.
38. *Interim Report of the Royal Commission on Agriculture, 1919*, Cmd. 473, evidence of Mr Castell Wrey, 20 August 1919, Q.4241 develops this theme. *Report of the Board of Agriculture and Fisheries on Wages, &c.*, General Report on Wales, 201.
39. Sir John Ward to A. Crosbie Hill, 26 August 1917, and note by Mr Crosbie Hill, 28 August 1917 in Chilton Estate In Correspondence at University of Reading Library, BER.36/1/2(1).
40. Higgins ed., *The Private Diaries of Sir Henry Rider Haggard*, 115. This entry was made on 14 September 1917.
41. *Interim Report of the Royal Commission on Agriculture*, Evidence of Mr Castell Wrey, Q.3880.
42. *Interim Report of the Royal Commission on Agriculture*, Q.4153.
43. See, for example, *Country Life*, 3 May 1919, 482 and 17 May 1919, 547-8.
44. *Board of Agriculture and Fisheries: Agricultural Statistics for 1918*, 39.
45. F.M.L. Thompson, *English Landed Society in the Nineteenth Century*, London 1963, 328.
46. Calculated from J.J. MacGregor, 'The Economic History of Two Rural Estates in Cambridgeshire, 1870-1934' in *Journal of the Royal Agricultural Society of England*, Vol. 98, (1937), 146-9.
47. Higgins ed., *The Private Diaries of Sir Henry Rider Haggard*, 133 and 172, entries for 17 April 1918 and 7 July 1919.
48. *Interim Report of the Royal Commission on Agriculture*, Q.7895.

49. Heather A. Clemenson, *English Country Houses and Landed Estates*, London 1982, 110.
50. See *Finance Act*, 1919, 9 & 10 Geo. 5, Ch. 32, Third Schedule. For estates of £1m.-£1¼m. the new duty was 30 per cent, and this increased progressively to 40 per cent at £2m. or more. For conditions in 1914, see *Finance Act*, 1914, First Schedule.
51. Thompson, *English Landed Society* 335 and *Hansard*, 5th Series, Vol. 116 (21 May 1919), col. 441.
52. *Country Life*, 7 June 1919, 638. See also the comment by Lord Northampton in 1919 that he was selling because 'landowning on a large scale is now generally felt to be a monopoly and is consequently unpopular'.
53. *Mark Lane Express*, 8 April 1918, 357.
54. *Farmer and Stockbreeder*, 7 January 1918. Similarly on 29 April 1918, it commented: 'There is a very grave feeling of insecurity in agricultural circles owing to the large number of estate sales, and consequently to the notice under which farmers are working'.
55. *Mark Lane Express*, 15 April 1918, 373. *Farmer and Stockbreeder*, 29 April 1918.
56. *Mark Lane Express*, 15 April 1918, 379.
57. *The Times*, 28 December 1918.
58. Thompson, *English Landed Society*, 336 and *Country Life*, 3 January 1920, 28.
59. Street, *Farmer's Glory*, 212.
60. S.G. Sturmey, 'Owner-Farming in England and Wales, 1900-1950' in *Essays in Agrarian History*, Vol. 2, Newton Abbot 1968, 287.
61. Mark Bence.Jones, 'The Trust of Landowning' in *Burke's Landed Gentry*, 18th edn, Vol. 1, London 1965, xviii.
62. Edith H. Whetham, *The Agrarian History of England and Wales*, Vol. 8, *1914-1939*, Cambridge 1978, 121-2.
63. Whetham, *The Agrarian History of England*, 123.
64. Mrs C.S. Peel, *How We Lived Then: 1914-1918*, London 1929, 173.
65. Sassoon, *Siegfried's Journey*, 97.
66. Robert Saunders of Fletching to his son, William, in Canada, at the Imperial War Museum, 79/15/1, letter dated 1 June 1918.
67. Robert Saunders to his son, William, letter dated 16 November 1918.
68. Simon Goodenough, *Jam and Jerusalem*, London 1977, 18.
69. *Home and Country*, October 1919, 8.
70. *Country Life*, 22 November 1919, lxxxviii.
71. Street, *Farmer's Glory*, 205-6.
72. Sale Catalogue of the Clowance Estate, West Cornwall, 1923 in G.A.Gen.Top.b.30 at the Bodleian Library, Oxford.

73. Sale Catalogue of the Whittington Hall, Kirkby Lonsdale, Estate at the Bodleian Library, Oxford, for July 1924, in G.A.Gen.Top.b.30.

Chapter 10 (pages 209-239)

1. Phyllis Deane and W.A. Cole, *British Economic Growth 1688-1959*, Cambridge 1962, 298-9.
2. *Hansard*, 5th Series, Vol. 144 (4 July 1921), col. 95.
3. *A Century of Agricultural Statistics: Great Britain 1866-1966*, HMSO 1968, 83.
4. *National Farmers' Union Yearbook for 1932*, NFU, January 1932, 375.
5. *Ministry of Agriculture and Fisheries: The Agricultural Output and the Food Supplies of Great Britain*, HMSO 1929, 19.
6. M. Tracy, *Agriculture in Western Europe (after 1880)*, London 1964, 154.
7. Lord Ernle, *The Land and Its People*, London, n.d. [1925], 222.
8. The *Local Government Act* of 1929 finally relieved both agricultural land and buildings from rates.
9. Edith H. Whetham, *The Agrarian History of England and Wales*: Vol. VIII, *1914-1939*, 166-7.
10. Whetham, *The Agrarian History of England and Wales*, 166-7. Peter Self and Herbert J. Storing, *The State and the Farmer*, London 1962, 19.
11. *A Century of Agricultural Statistics*, 121.
12. Tracy, *Agriculture in Western Europe*, 153, 160.
13. Viscount Astor and Keith A.H. Murray, *The Planning of Agriculture*, London 1933, 135. *The Economist*, 'Commercial History Review of 1931', published 1932.
14. Interview of an early supporter of the Milk Marketing Board on the radio programme 'On Your Farm', 29 October 1983. Whetham, *The Agrarian History of England*, 249-55; *The Agricultural Output of England and Wales*, P.P.1933-34, Vol. XXVI, 23-7.
15. W.H. Williams, *The Sociology of an English Village: Gosforth*, London 1956, 28.
16. Accounts of a farmer from Queniborough, Leicestershire, at University of Reading, LEI.5/1/2.
17. Viscount Astor and B. Seebohm Rowntree, *British Agriculture*, London 1939 edn, 93.
18. A.G. Street, *Wessex Wins*, London 1941, 58. J.A. Venn, *The Foundations of Agricultural Economics*, Cambridge 1933 edn, 521.
19. A.G. Street, *Farmer's Glory*, London 1963, edn, 202.

20. Whetham, *The Agrarian History of England*, 238.
21. Williams, *The Sociology of an English Village*, 3.
22. Street, *Farmer's Glory*, 226.
23. Alwyn D. Rees, *Life in a Welsh Countryside*, Cardiff 1950, 64.
24. *1931 Census Report*, entries under the individual counties.
25. John Saville, *Rural Depopulation in England and Wales 1851-1951*, London 1957, 47-8.
26. *A Century of Agricultural Statistics*, 95.
27. Calculated from Whetham, *The Agrarian History of England*, 176-7, 302-3.
28. Whetham, *The Agrarian History of England*, 185.
29. Ibid. 237.
30. Ibid. 236-7.
31. *Report of the Committee on Land Utilisation in Rural Areas*, P.P.1941-42, Vol. IV, 15.
32. *The Agricultural Output of England and Wales*, 51, 67. Whetham, *The Agrarian History of England*, 263-4. Heather A. Clemenson, *English Country Houses and Landed Estates*, London 1982, 112.
33. *Hampshire Chronicle*, 13 February 1932. Burke's *Landed Gentry*, 18th edn, Vol. 1, London 1965, xx.
34. A. Harris, 'Agricultural Change on a Yorkshire Estate: Birdsall 1920-1940' in *Journal of Regional and Local Studies*, Vol. 3, No. 1 (Summer 1983), 37.
35. Astor and Murray, *The Planning of Agriculture*, 12.
36. Astor and Rowntree, *British Agriculture*, 247-9.
37. *National Farm Survey of England and Wales*, HMSO 1946, 25, 197. The information was collected in 1941-43.
38. *A Century of Agricultural Statistics*, 25.
39. F.M.L. Thompson, *English Landed Society in the Nineteenth Century*, London 1963, 334.
40. *The Tithepayer*, October 1931 and January 1932, includes lists of various Tithepayers' Associations. This was a quarterly journal designed to publicise the tithe payers' grievances.
41. Evidence submitted by W.S. Hall of Wymondham, Norfolk, in *Minutes of Evidence Taken Before the Royal Commission on Tithe Rentcharge, 1934-35*, 314, at the Public Record Office, I.R.101/9.
42. Clergy Visitation Returns for 1933/34, Oxford Diocese: Berkshire Archdeaconry, MSS.Oxf.Dioc.Pp.c. 392. *The Times*, 3 May, 1932 and 27 September, 1933.
43. Eric J. Evans, *The Contentious Tithe*, London 1976, 166. *Facts and Incidents of an Unequal Struggle*, Ashford, Hert and Sussex Tithe-payers' Association, n.d. [1950], 27-8.
44. J.A. Venn, *The Foundation of Agricultural Economics*, Cambridge 1933 edn, 533-5.

45. Whetham, *The Agrarian History of England*, 304-5.
46. Whetham, *The Agrarian History of England*, 210. See also F.M.L. Thompson ed., *Horses in European Economic History*, British Agricultural History Society, 1983, 73-93 for a discussion on the use of tractors and horses inter-war.
47. Williams, *The Sociology of an English Village*, 147.
48. Rees, *Life in a Welsh Countryside*, 94. Adrian Bell, *Silver Ley*, Oxford 1983 edn, xvi-xviii. First published in 1931.
49. Williams, *The Sociology of an English Village*, 146.
50. Williams, *The Sociology of an English Village*, 28. Rees, *Life in a Welsh Countryside*, 30.
51. *National Farm Survey of England and Wales*, 8 and 11.
52. Diary of William John Penn of Maidwell, at Northamptonshire Record Office, X. 7188.
53. Williams, *The Sociology of an English Village*, 28.
54. Quoted in Thompson, *English Landed Society*, 331, 340. Clemenson, *English Country Houses*, 136.
55. Adrian Bell, *Corduroy*, Oxford 1982 edn, 193. The book was first published in 1930.
56. Williams, *The Sociology of an English Village*, 185.
57. George Ewart Evans, *Where Beards Wag All*, London 1970, 105.
58. *A Pattern of Hundreds*, Buckinghamshire Federation of Women's Institutes, 1975, 53.
59. *Report of the Committee on Land Utilisation in Rural Areas*, 16.
60. Bell, *Corduroy*, 64.
61. *Report of the Committee on Land Utilisation in Rural Areas*, 19.
62. John Graves, *Policy and Progress in Secondary Education 1902-1942*, London 1943, 132-3.
63. Howard Newby, *The Deferential Worker*, London 1977, 228.
64. See, for example, *Hansard*, 5th Series, Vol. 144 (1921), col. 101 and col. 153. On the latter occasion, Mr Cautley remarked: 'if the Government's action is persisted in and the Wages Board and the guaranteed prices are swept away, I can see no reason to doubt that . . . we shall go back to the bad old times, when wages will fall of necessity, farmers will disappear, and land will go out of cultivation'.
65. Whetham, *The Agrarian History of England*, 154.
66. Newby, *The Deferential Worker*, 223-225. Groves, *Sharpen the Sickle!* 199.
67. *Hansard*, 5th Series, Vol. 174 (2 June 1924), col. 915.
68. J.R. Bellerby, 'Distribution of Farm Income in the United Kingdom, 1867-1938' in *Essays in Agrarian History*, Vol. II, ed. W.E. Minchinton, Newton Abbot 1968, 271.

69. Astor and Rowntree, *British Agriculture*, 213. *The Economist*, 26 November 1932.
70. *Ministry of Labour Gazette*, January 1941, 7-9. See also February 1941 for a further survey on rural households.
71. *The Times*, 16 May 1936. Sir Kingsley Wood also noted that with the help of a one million-pound government grant and assistance from rural district and county councils, schemes were in hand to provide a water supply for over two thousand parishes, at a capital cost of more than £6m. H.W. Richardson and D.H. Aldcroft, *Building in the British Economy between the Wars*, London 1968, 170, 187.
72. *Within Living Memory*, Norfolk Federation of Women's Institutes, 1971, 11.
73. *National Farm Survey of England and Wales*, 60.
74. *A Pattern of Hundreds*, 102.
75. Vera Brittain, *Testament of Friendship*, London 1981 edn, 397-8.
76. Rees, *Life in a Welsh Countryside*, 26.
77. Whetham, *The Agrarian History of England*, 152.
78. Reminiscences of W. Alexander of Blisworth at Northamptonshire Record Office. The reminiscences were compiled in 1958.
79. E.D. Mackerness ed., *The Journals of George Sturt 1890-1927*, Cambridge 1967, 825.
80. Rees, *Life in a Welsh Countryside*, 27.
81. Ibid. 28.
82. Anna M. Jones, *The Rural Industries of England and Wales*, Vol. 4, East Ardsley 1978 edn, 103-104. The book was first published in 1927.
83. Street, *Farmer's Glory*, 266.
84. Clergy Visitation Returns for 1936, Oxford Diocese, MS Oxf.Dioc.Pp.c.396 — for North Crawley.
85. *Report of the Committee on Land Utilisation in Rural Areas*, 27.
86. Astor and Rowntree, *British Agriculture*, 218.
87. Saville, *Rural Depopulation*, 137.

Bibliography

MANUSCRIPT AND ORAL SOURCES

Abbreviations: PRO = Public Records Office
NLW = National Library of Wales

Agriculture, Board of, Correspondence at the PRO in MAF.42/8, MAF.59/1, NATS.1/329 and NATS.1/474.

Anglesey, Typescript on the History of Agriculture in, during the Great War, at University College of North Wales Library.

Apethorpe Estate Correspondence, 1918, at Northamptonshire Record Office.

His Grace the Duke of Bedford's Abstracts of Monthly Receipts and Payments, 1914-18, at Bedford Estate Record Office, London.

His Grace the Duke of Bedford's Estate Correspondence at Bedfordshire Record Office.

Bedfordshire Agricultural Executive Committee Minute Books at Bedfordshire Record Office.

Breese MSS at NLW.

F.W. Brocklehurst's Reminiscences at the Museum of English Rural Life, Reading.

R.T. Bull diary at Essex Record Office.

Cabinet and War Cabinet Minutes and Papers at the PRO, 1914-1918.

Cardiganshire Appeals for Exemptions, Tribunal Papers at NLW.

Lord Carrington's letters to his wife in MSS Film 114 at the Bodleian Library, Oxford.

W. Cox Reminiscences at the Imperial War Museum.

Dairy Agreements, DER.3/1/1 at Reading University Library.

East Denbighshire Recruiting Committee Minute Book at NLW.

Denmark, Import of Labourers from, for Agricultural Work, at PRO, NATS./412.

S.E. Derbyshire Survey by War Agricultural Committee, 1917, at Derbyshire Record Office.

Miss D.B. Dew, Reminiscences of, in interview with the author.

Annie Edwards, Transcript of Reminiscences of, at Imperial War Museum, Oral History Recordings.

Essex Agricultural Executive Committee Minute Books at Essex Record Office.

H.A.L. Fisher diaries at Bodleian Library, Oxford.

Alfred Hills Correspondence at Essex Record Office.

Clive Hughes of Imperial War Museum, in correspondence with author.

Invasion Instructions, &c., at Essex Office.

Ernest Kingsbury, Reminiscences of, at Imperial War Museum.

Launceston Farm, Tarrant Launceston, Dorset, Ledgers of, at University of Reading Library.

Mary Lees, Transcript of Reminiscences, at Imperial War Museum, Oral History Recordings.

Rector of Llanfair, Merioneth, Correspondence of, at NLW.

Manor Farm, Codford St. Peter, Wilts., letter book, microfilm at University of Reading Library

Midhurst Rural District Food Control Committee Minute Book, 1917-20 at PRO MAF.60/431.

May G. Morris, Reminiscences of, in interview with the author.

National Agricultural Labourers and Rural Workers' Union Minute Books at Museum of English Rural Life, Reading.

National Farmers' Union Minute and Year Books at the Museum of English Rural Life, Reading.

National Federation of Women's Institutes, Reports of, at Imperial War Museum.

National Political League MSS at Imperial War Museum.

National Service, Ministry of, Correspondence relating to Agricultural Employment, at PRO: NATS.1/215; NATS.1/242; NATS.1/282; NATS.1/474; NATS.1/669.

Old People, Reminiscences of, at Essex and Northamptonshire Record Offices.

Oxford Diocese: Clergy Visitation Returns, 1918-1936, at Bodleian Library, Oxford; Spring 1984 to be transferred to County Record Office in Oxford.

Pembrokeshire Agricultural Executive Committee Correspondence, Soldier Labour Book, and Reports at Pembrokeshire Record Office.

W.J. Penn of Maidwell, diary of, at Northamptonshire Record Office.

Miss C. Prunell, diary of, at Imperial War Museum.

Queniborough, Leicestershire, Accounts of a farmer for 1930's, at University of Reading Library.

Robert Saunders, letters to his son, at the Imperial War Museum.

Sawbridgeworth Urban District Food Control Committee Minute Book, 1917-20 at the PRO, MAF.60/433.

School Attendance and Employment in Agriculture at PRO, ED.11/78, and NATS.1/672.

Schoolboy Labour: Harvest Camps, Reports on, at PRO, NATS.1/653, NATS.1/672 and NATS.1/676.

School Log Books, at relevant County Record Offices.

Selborne Papers at the Bodleian Library, Oxford.

W.J. Shepherd, Reminiscences of, in interview with the author.

Stondon Massey, Essex, Journal of the Rector of, at Essex Record Office.

Tithe Rentcharge, Royal Commission on 1934/35, Minutes of Evidence, Correspondence, &c., at PRO, IR.101.

J.B. Titterton, Correspondence of, at Derbyshire Record Office.

Trade, Board of, Reports on the State of Employment in Agriculture at PRO, NATS.1/241.

The War: Suspects, volume at Essex Record Office.

War, Prisoners of, Camps, Reports on at PRO, NATS.1/1330.

War, Prisoners of, Camps, Records of, at Bedfordshire Record Office.

War, Prisoners of, Employment Committee, Interim Report of, and Reports on Employment of Prisoners, at PRO, NATS.1/1131 and NATS.1/1332.

War, Prisoners of, Rations, at PRO, NATS.1/570.

Women's County Agricultural Committees, Reports of, at PRO, MAF.59/1.

Women's Defence Relief Corps, Reports, &c. at Imperial War Museum.

Women's Land Army, Reports and Correspondence of, at Imperial War Museum, LAND.6, and PRO, MAF.42/8.

Women's National Land Service Corps, Reports, &c., at Imperial War Museum.

Women's Work Collections at the Imperial War Museum, LAND.1, 2, 6 and 7.

OFFICIAL PAPERS

Abbreviations: PP = Parliamentary Paper.

Agricultural Statistics, A Century of, 1866-1966, HMSO 1968.

Agriculture, Interim Report of Royal Commission on, 1919, Cmd.473.

Agriculture and Fisheries, Board of, Annual Agricultural Statistics.

Agriculture and Fisheries, Report of Board of, on the Decline in the Agricultural Population of Great Britain 1881-1906, PP 1906, Vol. XCVI.

Agriculture and Fisheries, Report of Board of, on the Agricultural Output of Great Britain, PP 1912-13, Vol. X.

Agriculture and Fisheries, Report of Sub-Committee of Board of, Appointed to Consider the Employment of Women in Agriculture in England and Wales, HMSO 1919.

Agriculture and Fisheries, Report of Board of, on Wages and Conditions of Employment of Agricultural Labourers, PP 1919, Vol. IX.

Agriculture and Fisheries, Report of Ministry of, on the Agricultural Output and the Food Supplies of Great Britain, HMSO 1929.

Conference, Report of, between Representatives of County Committees and the Rt. Hon. the Earl of Selborne on 'Women's Labour on the Land', HMSO 1916.

Education, Board of, Annual Reports.

Land Utilisation in Rural Areas, Report of Committee on, PP 1941-42, Vol. IV.

National Farm Survey of England and Wales, HMSO 1946.

Population Census, 1921: Occupations, HMSO 1924.

Production of Food in England and Wales, Reports of Departmental Committee on, PP 1914-16, Vol. V.

Reconstruction, Ministry of, Report of the Agricultural Policy Sub-Committee, PP 1918, Vol. V.

School Attendance, Correspondence on, PP 1914-16, Vol. L.

School Attendance and Employment in Agriculture, Returns on, PP 1914-16, Vol. L and PP 1916, Vol. XXII.

Tithe Rentcharge in England and Wales, Royal Commission on, PP 1935-36, Vol. XIV.

Wages, Earnings and Conditions of Employment of Agricultural Labourers in the United Kingdom, Second Report on, PP 1905, Vol. XCVII.

War Cabinet, Report of, for 1917, PP 1918, Vol. XIV; for 1918, PP 1919, Vol. XXX.

Hansard

NEWSPAPERS AND JOURNALS

Bucks Herald	*Ministry of Labour Gazette*
Country Life	*National Food Journal*
Daily News	*Norfolk News*
Dorset County Chronicle	*Observer*
East Anglian Daily Times	*Oxford Chronicle*
The Economist	*Punch*
Farmer and Stockbreeder	*Schoolmaster*
Hampshire Chronicle	*Stamford Mercury*
Hexham Weekly News	*Sussex Express*
Home and Country	*The Times*
Journal of the Board of Agriculture	*Times Educational Supplement*
Kenilworth Advertiser	*The Tithepayer*
The Labourer	*Westmorland Mercury*
The Landswoman	*Wiltshire Gazette*
Mark Lane Express	

ARTICLES

Abbreviations: Ag. Hist. Rev. = Agricultural History Review

J.R. Bellerby, 'Distribution of Farm Income in the United Kingdom, 1867-1938' in *Essays in Agrarian History*, Vol. 2, Newton Abbot 1968.

P.E. Dewey, 'Agricultural Labour Supply in England and Wales during the First World War' in *Economic History Review*, 2nd Series Vol. XXVIII, No. 1 (Feb. 1975).

P.E. Dewey, 'Government Provision of Farm Labour in England and Wales, 1914-18' in *Ag. Hist. Rev.*, Vol. 27, Pt II (1979).

A. Harris, 'Agricultural Change on a Yorkshire Estate: Birdsall 1920-1940' in *Journal of Regional and Local Studies*, Vol. 3, No. 1 (1983).

Pamela Horn, 'The Employment of Elementary Schoolchildren in Agriculture, 1914-1918' in *History of Education*, Vol. 12, No. 3 (1983).

Pamela Horn, 'Prisoners on the Farm' in *The Countryman*, Vol. 88, No. 4 (1983).

J.J. MacGregor, 'The Economic History of Two Rural Estates in Cambridgeshire, 1870-1934' in *Journal of the Royal Agricultural Society of England*, Vol. 98 (1937).

Alistair Mutch, 'The Mechanization of the Harvest in South-West Lancashire, 1850-1914' in *Ag. Hist. Rev.*, Vol. 29, Pt II (1981).

S.G. Sturmey, 'Owner-farming in England and Wales, 1900-1950' in *Essays in Agrarian History*, Vol. 2, Newton Abbot 1968.

Edith H. Whetham, 'The Agriculture Act, 1920 and its Repeal — the "Great Betrayal" ' in *Ag. Hist. Rev.*, Vol. 22, Pt I (1974).

J.M. Winter, 'Britain's "Lost Generation" of the First World War' in *Population Studies*, Vol. 31 (1977).

J.M. Winter, 'Some Aspects of the Demographic Consequences of the First World War in Britain' in *Population Studies*, Vol. 30 (1976).

'The Wounded at Woburn' in *National Review* (Sept. 1916).

BOOKS AND PAMPHLETS (EXCLUDING NOVELS)

Irene O. Andrews and Margarett A. Hobbs, *Economic Effects of the War upon Women and Children in Great Britain*, New York 1918.

Arthur W. Ashby, *Allotments and Small Holdings in Oxfordshire*, Oxford 1917.

M.K. Ashby, *Joseph Ashby of Tysoe*, Cambridge 1961.

Cynthia Asquith, *Haply I May Remember*, London 1950.

Viscount Astor and Keith A.H. Murray, *The Planning of Agriculture*, London 1933.

Viscount Astor and B. Seebohm Rowntree, *British Agriculture*, London 1939 edn.

Duke of Bedford, *A Great Agricultural Estate*, London 1897.

Adrian Bell, *Corduroy*, Oxford 1982 edn.

Adrian Bell, *Silver Ley*, Oxford 1983 edn.
Ronald Blythe, *Akenfield: Portrait of an English Village*, London 1969.
'George Bourne' [George Sturt], *Change in the Village*, London 1966 edn.
Vera Brittain, *Testament of Friendship*, London 1980 edn.
Michael and Eleanor Brock eds, *H.H. Asquith Letters to Venetia Stanley*, Oxford 1982.
Brigadier-General C.D. Bruce, *The Essex Foxhounds 1895-1926*, London 1926.
Burke's Landed Gentry, 18th edn, 3 Vols. London 1965-1972.
Raymond Carr, *English Fox Hunting*, London 1976.
Heather A. Clemenson, *English Country Houses and Landed Estates*, London 1982.
E.J.T. Collins, *Sickle to Combine*, University of Reading 1969.
Co-operation and the Supply of Farm Implements, Leaflet No. 44, Aug. 1917, issued by Food Production Department (at British Library 07078.ff.10).
Elizabeth Crittall ed., *Victoria History of the County of Wiltshire*, Vol. 4, London 1959.
Maud F. Davies, *Life in an English Village*, London 1909.
Phyllis Deane and W.A. Cole, *British Economic Growth 1688-1959*, Cambridge 1962.
N.B. Dearle, *An Economic Chronicle of the Great War*, London 1929.
H.A. Doubleday and Lord Howard de Walden, *The Complete Peerage*, Vol. 8, London 1932.
Earnings of Agricultural Labourers in Each County of England and Wales for the Year 1912-13, issued by the Central Landowners' Association, London 1913.
George Edwards, *From Crow-Scaring to Westminster*, London 1957 edn.
Lord Ernle, *English Farming Past and Present*, London 1961 edn.
Lord Ernle, *The Land and Its People*, London n.d. [1925].
Eric J. Evans, *The Contentious Tithe*, London 1976.
George Ewart Evans, *Where Beards Wag All*, London 1977.
Simon Goodenough, *Jam and Jerusalem*, London 1977.
D.R. Grace and D.C. Phillips, *Ransomes of Ipswich*, University of Reading 1975.
John Graves, *Policy and Progress in Secondary Education 1902-1942*, London 1943.
Robert Graves, *Goodbye to All That*, London 1960 edn.
F.E. Green, *A History of the English Agricultural Labourer*, London 1920.
Reg Groves, *Sharpen the Sickle!* London 1949.
A.D. Hall, *A Pilgrimage of British Farming 1910-1912*, London 1913.
Marie Hartley and Joan Ingilby, *Life in the Moorlands of North-East Yorkshire*, London 1972.

Benjamin H. Hibbard, *Effects of the Great War Upon Agriculture in the United States and Great Britain*, New York 1919.

D.S. Higgins ed., *The Private Diaries of Sir Henry Rider Haggard*, London 1980.

Richard Hillyer, *Country Boy*, London 1966.

Olive Hockin, *Two Girls on the Land: Wartime on a Dartmoor Farm*, London 1918.

Richard Holmes, *The Little Field-Marshal*, London 1981.

Pamela Horn, *The Rise and Fall of the Victorian Servant*, Dublin 1975.

E.H. Hunt, *Regional Wage Variations in Britain 1850-1914*, Oxford 1973.

Gervas Huxley,, *Lady Denman*, London 1961.

Richard Hyman, *The Workers' Union*, Oxford 1971.

Inez Jenkins, *The History of the Women's Institute Movement of Englanl and Wales*, Oxford 1953.

Anna M. Jones, *The Rural Industries of England and Wales*, Vol. 4, East Ardsley 1978 edn.

The Land: The Report of the Land Enquiry Committee, Vol. 1, *Rural*, London 1913.

Neville Lytton, *The English Country Gentleman*, London n.d. [1925].

Lyn Macdonald, *Somme*, London 1983.

E.D. Mackerness ed., *The Journals of George Sturt*, Cambridge 1967.

C.F.G. Masterman, *England after War*, London n.d. [1923].

Arthur Marwick, *Women at War 1914-1918*, London 1977.

G.E. Mingay ed., *The Victorian Countryside*, London 1981.

Thomas H. Middleton, *Food Production in War*, Oxford 1923.

J.K. Montgomery, *The Maintenance of the Agricultural Labour Supply in England and Wales during the War*, Rome 1922.

Aubrey Moore, *A Son of the Rectory*, Gloucester 1982.

Nicholas Mosley, *Julian Grenfell: His Life and the Times of His Death, 1888-1915*, London 1976.

Howard Newby, *The Deferential Worker*, London 1977.

Avner Offer, *Property and Politics 1870-1914*, Cambridge 1981.

Christabel Orwin and Edith H. Whetham, *History of British Agriculture 1846-1914*, London 1964.

C.S. Orwin, *A History of English Farming*, London 1949.

George A. Panichas, *Promise of Greatness: The War of 1914-1918*, London 1968.

A Pattern of Hundreds, Buckinghamshire Federation of Women's Institutes, 1975.

Mrs C.S. Peel, *How We Lived Then: 1914-1918*, London 1929.

P.J. Perry, *British Agriculture 1875-1914*, London 1973.

Edwin A. Pratt, *The Transition in Agriculture*, London 1906.

Jim Priest, *Parndon Recollections*, Harlow 1981.

Arthur Randell, *Sixty Years a Fenman*, ed. Enid Porter, London 1966.

Alwyn D. Rees, *Life in a Welsh Countryside*, Cardiff 1950.

B. Seebohm Rowntree and May Kendall, *How the Labourer Lives*, London 1918 edn.

B. Seebohm Rowntree, *The Labourer and the Land*, London 1914.

J.W. Rowson, *Bridport and the Great War*, London 1923.

Sale Catalogues of Estates for 1920s and 1930s at Bodleian Library, Oxford.

Siegfried Sassoon, *Siegfried's Journey*, London 1982 edn.

John Saville, *Rural Depopulation in England and Wales 1851-1951*, London 1957.

Peter Self and Herbert J. Storing, *The State and the Farmer*, London 1962.

Guy Slater ed., *My Warrior Sons*, London 1973.

L. Marion Springall, *Labouring Life in Norfolk Villages 1834-1914*, London 1936.

Noel Streatfeild ed., *The Day Before Yesterday*, London 1956.

A.G. Street, *Ditchampton Farm*, London 1946.

A.G. Street, *Farmer's Glory*, London 1963 edn.

A.G. Street, *Wessex Wins*, London 1941.

George Sturt, *The Wheelwright's Shop*, Cambridge 1963 edn.

F.M.L. Thompson, *English Landed Society in the Nineteenth Century*, London 1963.

F.M.L. Thompson ed., *Horses in European Economic History*, Reading 1983.

M. Tracy, *Agriculture in Western Europe (after 1880)*, London 1964.

J.A. Venn, *The Foundations of Agricultural Economics*, Cambridge 1933 edn.

Doreen Wallace, *The Tithe War*, London 1934.

Edith H. Whetham, *The Agrarian History of England and Wales*, Vol. VIII, Cambridge 1978.

R.A. Whitehead, *Garrett 200: A Bicentenary History of Garretts of Leiston*, London 1978.

W.H. Williams, *The Sociology of an English Village: Gosforth*, London 1956.

Denis Winter, *Death's Men*, London 1978 edn.

Within Living Memory, Norfolk Federation of Women's Institutes, 1971.

Robert Wohl, *The Generation of 1914*, London 1980.

George J. Zytaruk and James T. Boulton, *The Letters of D.H. Lawrence*, Vol. 2, Cambridge 1981.

NOVELS

Siegfried Sassoon, *The Complete Memoirs of George Sherston*, London 1949 edn.

A.G. Street, *The Gentleman of the Party*, London 1944 edn.

THESES

Caroline Baker, 'Homedwellers and Foreigners: The Seasonal Labour Force in Kentish Agriculture', University of Kent at Canterbury M.Phil. thesis, 1979.

P.E. Dewey, 'Farm Labour in Wartime: The Relationship between Agricultural Labour Supply and Food Production in Great Britain during 1914-1918, with International Comparisons', Reading University Ph.D. thesis, 1978.

Alistair Mutch, 'Rural Society in Lancashire 1840-1914', University of Manchester Ph.D. thesis, 1980.

Index